Frommer's™

Scotland

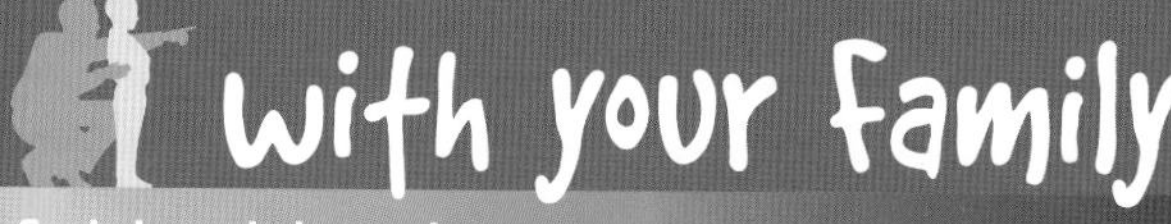

From peaceful highlands to cosmopolitan cities

by Ben Hatch & Dinah Hatch

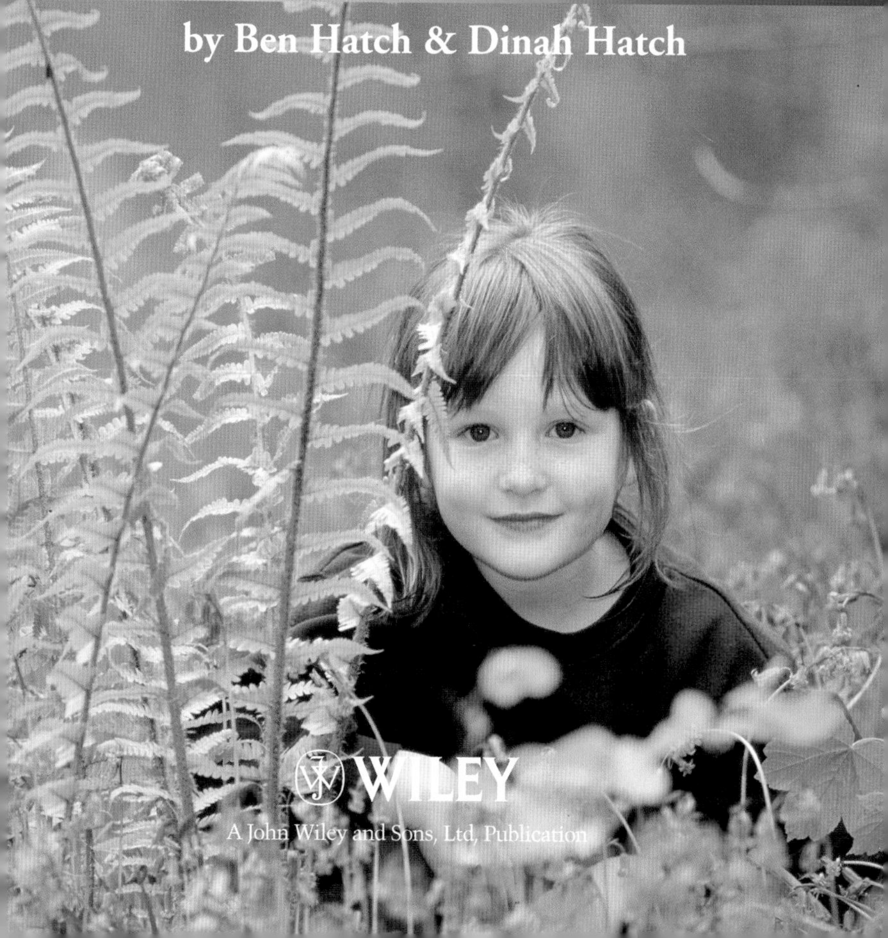

WILEY

A John Wiley and Sons, Ltd, Publication

Email (for orders and customer service enquiries): cs-books@wiley.co.uk. Visit our Home Page on www.wiley.com

UK Publisher: Sally Smith
Executive Project Editor: Daniel Mersey (Frommer's UK)
Commissioning Editor: Mark Henshall (Frommer's UK)
Development Editor: Donald Strachan
Project Editor: Hannah Clement (Frommer's UK)
Cartographer: Jeremy Norton
Photo Research: Jill Emeny (Frommer's UK)

Wiley also publishes its books in a variety of electronic formats. Some content that appears in print may not be available in electronic books.

British Library Cataloguing in Publication Data
A catalogue record for this book is available from the British Library

ISBN: 978-0-470-72302-9

Typeset by Wiley Indianapolis Composition Services
Printed and bound in China by RR Donnelley

5 4 3 2 1

Contents

About the Authors

Ben Hatch started out as a tea boy in the Royal Bank of Scotland. He became a recruitment consultant, sold advertising space then lawnmowers, worked in a video shop, as a postman and on the MacDonald chicken sandwich station before finally becoming a journalist on various local papers. He quit reporting to become a novelist in 1997. He has written two works of comedy fiction, *The Lawnmower Celebrity* and *The International Gooseberry.* Ben was tempted into travel writing by his wife Dinah who he lives with in Brighton.

Dinah Hatch went into travel journalism after deciding that crime reporting for regional papers involved just a few too many evenings talking to dodgy people in dark alleys. Since then she has worked for a wide variety of national newspapers, magazines, trade publications and websites and writes extensively on the travel industry.

Acknowledgements

Thanks to Charlie who, aged 6 weeks, we carted 4000 miles around Scotland and who only ever cried in his car seat when Paul Ross came on the radio. Also thanks to our daughter Phoebe, who cried a lot more than this every time we ran out of a) Chocolate Gems, b) clippety-clop stories, and c) saw a Victorian mannequin with whiskers. Thanks too to Chris and Pippa Banister for putting us up when we had nowhere else to go after Ben's dad got sick and also for making him a separate meal that night as he doesn't like casserole. We'd also like to thank Ben's step-mum Mary, his sister Penny and brother Dick, who were forced many times to look at our photos of Scotland and only occasionally told him to shut up about and put them away.

We'd also like to thank Dinah's mum Marian, who dropped everything to get on a plane and come and help out when Dinah had to go solo with the kids for a day or two in the Highlands after Ben flew home for his dad.

Dedication

For my dad – David Hatch

An Additional Note

Please be advised that travel information is subject to change at any time and this is especially true of prices. We therefore suggest that you write or call ahead for confirmation when making your travel plans. The authors, editors, and publisher cannot be held responsible for the experiences of readers while traveling. Your safety is important to us, however, so we encourage you to stay alert and be aware of your surroundings.

Star Ratings, Icons & Abbreviations

Hotels, restaurants and attraction listings in this guide have been ranked for quality, value, service, amenities and special features using a star-rating system. Hotels, restaurants, attractions, shopping and nightlife are rated on a scale of zero stars (recommended) to three (exceptional). In addition to the star rating system, we also use 5 feature icons that point you to the great deals, in-the-know advice and unique experiences. Throughout the book, look for:

FIND	Special finds – those places only insiders know about
MOMENT	Special moments – those experiences that memories are made of
VALUE	Great values – where to get the best deals
OVERRATED	Places or experiences not worth your time or money
GREEN	Attractions employing responsible tourism policies

The following **abbreviations** are used for credit cards:

AE	American Express
MC	Mastercard
V	Visa

A Note on Prices

In the Family-friendly Accommodation section of this book we have used a price category system.

An Invitation to the Reader

In researching this book, we discovered many wonderful places – hotels, restaurants, shops and more. We're sure you'll find others. Please tell us about them, so we can share the information with your fellow travellers in upcoming editions. If you were disappointed with a recommendation, we'd love to know that too. Please email: ***frommers@wiley.co.uk*** or write to:

> *Frommer's Scotland with Your Family*, 1st Edition
> John Wiley & Sons, Ltd
> The Atrium
> Southern Gate
> Chichester
> West Sussex, PO19 8SQ

Photo Credits

Cover Credits

Main Image: © Niall Benvie / Alamy
Small Images: © Ben Hatch
Back Cover: © Ben Hatch

Front Matter Credits

Pi: © Niall Benvie / Alamy; piii/piv: © Ben Hatch.

Inside Images

All images: © Ben Hatch with the following exceptions:

© John Glen Photography: p127.
© Robertson Wellen: p232.
© Roccofortecollection.com: p48, p53.
Courtesy of Alamy: p76 (© Robert Harding Picture Library Ltd); p175 (© David Robertson)

Courtesy of Axiom: p59 (© James Sparshatt).
Courtesy of FotoLibra: p1 (© Wayne Scott); p23 (© Bruce Sutherland); p135 (© Carolyn Wheeler); p237 (© Bob Falconer).
Courtesy of Hotel Du Vin, Glasgow: p8, p84.
Courtesy of Tigh na Croit Cottage, Balquhidder: p128.
Courtesy of TTL: p106, p109, p114 (© David Robertson).

Thanks to Culture and Sport Glasgow (Museums) for permission to take the image of Kelvingrove Art Gallery & Museum on p70.

1 Family Highlights of Scotland

Scotland has stood for different things at various stages of my life. As a boy it represented family holidays when my dad would stop the car beside yet another tree-lined loch and expect me to look up from my Donkey Kong games console. Then, as a teenager, my dad took me to the Edinburgh Festival for the first time. We'd see a dozen shows a day, sometimes staying only a few minutes as he whipped around the venues in his velvet green jacket, talent-spotting for the BBC. As we drank and discussed what we'd seen in pubs behind Princes Street, the country seemed the coolest place on earth – a giant *Charlie and the Chocolate Factory* for a boy into stand-up comedy. Then, as a young adult after university, Scotland changed again, becoming a racy place (easily accessible but far enough to feel remote) where I'd take brand-new girlfriends, hoping that the heady mix of mist-covered hills, narrow roll-mats and the cliff top castles we camped near might somehow goad our romance along to a hastier conclusion. After I married and we had children of our own, the circle completed itself. Now I'm leaping out of the car every few seconds with the camera, after yet another ecstatic exclamation about the beauty of a loch or hill or passing stream, to take pictures that my own children couldn't care less about.

Researching this book has been a joy. The concept of tourism started in Scotland in the 19th century, and it's not hard to understand why. On a sunny day gazing across a tree-lined loch framed by a snow-capped mountain, the countryside is as beautiful as anywhere on earth. Whether it's a steamship ride on the crystal-clear lochs of the Trossachs that so enchanted Sir Walter Scott, a cable car soaring above a reindeer herd on the slopes of the Cairngorms or the sandy white beaches of the east coast that teem with dolphins, there's something for nature lovers young and old.

When I was a youngster, however, that was your lot – nature. Scotland equalled nature. If you didn't appreciate the gradient of a particular munro that your dad fancied climbing, or enjoy the sight of a swooping osprey as you stood in soaking bracken on another 'interesting walk', you were finished. But that's not the whole story anymore. You can do all this, of course, but nowadays there are heaps more things for families to do. Whether its archery, dog sledding or mountain biking in Aviemore, following child-friendly trails around spooky Scottish castles, Nessie spotting, a visit to the location of children's TV series *Balamory*, or learning about the human body in one of the science centres that have sprung up in Glasgow, Dundee, Aberdeen and elsewhere, there is now no way your children will be bored. Accommodation and restaurants, unfriendly in the past, are welcoming to families and despite the odd frustration – Edinburgh can see itself as above children's menus and the weather is famously unreliable – it's a great place for a family holiday. Do it on a budget or at full tilt, depending on your wallet. There's something for older children and youngsters, in cities or out in the countryside.

My wife and I drove around Scotland for three months, with a two-and-half-year-old daughter and a baby son of six weeks whilst researching this book. We thought it might be a nightmare. We actually had the time of our lives. 'Haste Ye Back', they'll write on your bill on checkout. We're already planning our return.

SCOTLAND'S FAMILY HIGHLIGHTS

Best Family Events At the Edinburgh Festival Fringe there are dozens of children's events including puppet theatres, magic and storytelling sessions, as well as jugglers, stilt walkers, buskers and tumblers that take over the city in August. At Christmas, switching on the lights is followed by a spectacular ice-show and fireworks. Edinburgh's second-favourite festival concludes with the Great Scottish Santa Run. See p. 29.

Best Day Trip A must if you have toddlers (or fancy Josie Jump, as my wife claims I do) is a day out to Tobermory, the setting for children's TV show *Balamory*. An organised tour takes in the homes of Miss Hoolie, Spencer and PC Plum, as well as Edie McCreadie's garage. It includes a lunch stop in town, a visit to a farm and a fun ride on the Balamory Express. See p. 165.

Best Freak of Nature Dads who feel the need to impress their families can prove they're the next David Blaine at the Electric Brae on the A719 between Dunure and Croy Bay. An optical illusion created by the surrounding land means that if you put your car in neutral, release the brake and mumble a magic word, your car appears to roll uphill. See p. 232.

Giraffes at the Blair Drummond Safari and Adventure Park

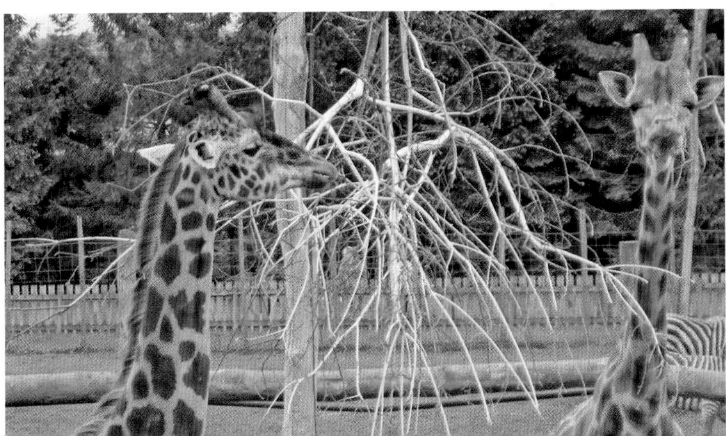

Best Distillery The Famous Grouse Experience is a surprisingly fun place for a two-year-old. Ours learned about Towser the Cat, the world mousing champion who used to live here, and had great fun chasing crazy moving jigsaw pieces in an interactive room. Before weakened by free drams of whisky I passed her a whole packet of toffees. Great fun. See p. 122.

Best Animal Park At the Blair Drummond Safari and Adventure Park near Callander, youngsters can boat around an island of chimps, drive through a big cat enclosure, feel the coat of a llama and then, if they're our daughter, lose their precious sleep-teddy while sunbathing with Vietnamese pot-bellied pigs in the petting zoo. Throw in a small fairground, sea lion and bird of prey shows, a giant slide, and the fact I accidentally lowered my wife's electric window in the tiger enclosure, and you've got yourselves a family day out. See p. 100.

Best Aquarium The Loch Lomond Aquarium at Balloch has an impressive ocean tunnel where children can see sharks and rays being fed, while in child-friendly touch-pools staff chip in with interesting sea creature facts as your little ones handle crabs and other marine life. The view from the café across Loch Lomond over the *Maid of the Loch* is worth a visit alone. See p. 110.

Best Beaches The sunniest sandy beach in Scotland is in the genteel town of Nairn. Near the unspoilt and always uncrowded white sand is a great outdoor pool and dunes, ideal for a game of hide-and-seek (see p. 154). For rock-pools the beach at St Andrews next to the stretch where they filmed *Chariots of Fire* is hard to beat (see p. 198).

Scone Palace

Best Swimming Pool The Stonehaven Open Air Pool is salt water, Art Deco in style and heated to an impressive 28°C with slides and chutes. It's ideal for making lame Hi-de-Hi! jokes to your wife ('Ted can't hear you') as she tries to tempt you in for a splash. On Wednesday nights in July and August, midnight under-the-stars romantic swims are also available (if you can get a babysitter). See p. 190.

Best Historic Attraction Scone Palace, north of Perth, has been capital of the Pictish kingdom, centre of the Celtic church, the seat of parliaments and the crowning place of kings. It has also been home to the Stone of Destiny, as well as being where Queen Victoria was taught curling on the polished floor of the longest room in Scotland. Here you can see needlework by Mary Queen of Scots, a desk belonging to Marie Antoinette, the largest orchid collection in the country, the only maze in Perthshire and one of the 50 most notable trees in Britain. See p. 121.

Craziest Story We Heard in Scotland At 9,000 years old the Fortingall Yew is believed to be the oldest living organism on Earth. According to legend, Pontius Pilate, the son of a local woman fathered by a visiting Roman ambassador, reportedly played under this very tree before rising through the Roman ranks and going on to crucify Jesus Christ. See p. 123.

Best Walk Hermitage Walk near Dunkeld is a fantastic mile's stroll along the rhododendron-clad banks of the River Braan to an idyllic waterfall overlooked by Britain's tallest tree – a 65m high Douglas Fir. Once part of the Scottish Grand Tour, nature lovers such as Wordsworth and Mendelssohn have been enjoying this walk for over 200 years. It's also ideal for buggy pushers. See p. 119.

Best Science Centre for Small Children The Satrosphere in Aberdeen gives youngsters the chance to put their hand inside a mini-tornado and work out what a pot of paint would weigh on Jupiter. The museum has around 50 interactive exhibits including fiendishly difficult puzzles and stuff suitable for tots. See p. 182.

Best Museums See how many children weigh as much as a baby elephant at the Kelvingrove Museum and Art Gallery. This children's mini-museum is packed full of interactive displays (see p. 70). At the Scottish Football Museum, Hampden Park in Glasgow, what self-respecting boy (or grown man) would shun the opportunity to have the speed of his kick electronically monitored? See p. 80.

Best Views So many to choose from, although our personal favourite was high above Loch Tummel at the back of the Queen's View Visitor Centre. From this vantage point you can see all the way up the spine of Scotland to the Glencoe mountains (see p. 120). Also worth a detour is Scott's View near Dryburgh Abbey, the favourite spot of novelist Sir Walter Scott. From the top of Bemersyde Hill above the River Tweed you can see the three peaks of the Eildon Hills and the Tweed Valley. See p. 228. Worthy mentions go to the views of Ailsa Craig from Turnberry (p. 230), Mersehead sands on the Solway Firth (p. 212) and the valley of Glencoe (p. 139).

Best Castle Urquhart Castle overlooking Loch Ness is the best location to spot Nessie. It's also a great place to annoy professional spotters by telling your toddler in a loud voice: 'Don't be silly, they proved it was a giant sturgeon years ago.' See p. 152.

Best Theme Park At the Landmark Forest Theme Park in Carrbridge, Inverness-shire, not only can you career over the equivalent of a 12m waterfall in a small pod and climb the tallest timber tower in the country, but also your children can ride go-karts or pat a massive Clydesdale horse called Lex. Alternatively, if you are my wife, you can climb a 10m wall in a pair of heels. See p. 160.

Best Dressing Up Children can pretend to be Mrs Tiggywinkle pegging out laundry on a miniature clothes line at the Beatrix Potter exhibition at the Birnam Institute (see p. 117). While at J.M. Barrie's cottage in Kirriemuir they can lie on a podium dressed as their favourite Peter Pan character and pretend they're flying to Neverland (see p. 196).

Best Wildlife It's a tough decision between bottle-nosed dolphin and insect spotting at Chanonry Point (see p. 159) and seeing a capercaillie, one of Britain's rarest birds, from the back of a jeep on a 16km safari on Deeside's Glen Tanar estate (see p. 186).

Best Up-Close Animal Experiences Youngsters can hand-feed reindeer at the Cairngorm Reindeer Centre in Aviemore (see p. 162), whereas at the Black Isle Wildlife and Country Park in North Kessock (see p. 156) they can hold ducks and rabbits. Also not to be missed is the chance to take football penalties against a goal-keeping dog at Bogbain Adventure and Heritage Farm, outside Inverness (see p. 149).

Black Isle Wildlife and Country Park

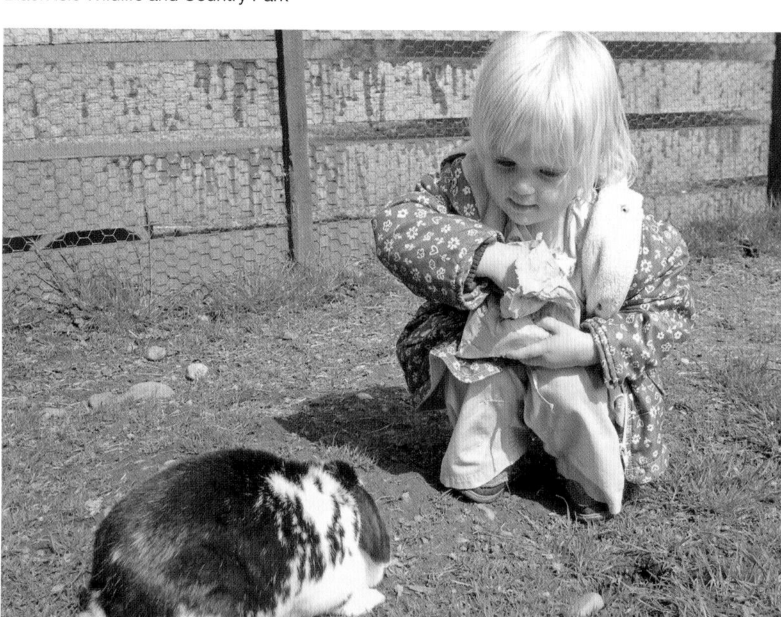

Most Terrifying Experiences Our daughter getting caught by the Countess Dowager of Cawdor weeing in her moat (see p. 155), closely followed by a swaying gondola ride to the upper slopes of Scotland's 8th highest mountain, Aonach Mor near Glencoe, on a windy day (see p. 146). And of course getting whipped by the small intestine from a dead corpse at the Edinburgh Dungeons (see p. 40).

Most Comical Attraction Doune Castle in the Trossachs has been a magnet for Monty Python fans since it was used in filming *Monty Python and the Holy Grail*. Comedy aficionados turn up in droves to shout from the ramparts, in their best John Cleese-voices: 'I fart in your general direction. Your mother was a hamster and your father smelled of elderberries.' The shop lends out coconut shells so you can mimic King Arthur approaching the castle on horseback in the movie's opening sequence. See p. 102.

Strangest Wildlife Spectacles The whistling guinea pigs (or did I have an ear infection that day) at the Heads of Ayr Farm Park are a sight not to be missed. Inside their own model village, so idyllic that my wife said she'd live there herself if it wasn't for the commute, these contented mammals seem to whistle the same eerie tune all at once (see p. 219). At Edinburgh Zoo's penguin parade, a posse of Emperors, including one (we kid you not) who is a full colonel-in-chief in the Norwegian Army, march *Happy Feet*-style behind their keeper (see p. 44).

Weirdest Things To Do If you are sick or just have a bad hand (maybe it was pecked very hard by a rhea at the Black Isle Wildlife Park; see p. 156), then leave an article of clothing at the creepy pre-Christian clootie well on the Black Isle. As the clothing decays, so the superstition goes, the sickness disappears. See page p. 158. The Sharmanka Gallery in Glasgow hosts a unique mechanical show featuring whirling lawn mower blades and scavenged scrap metal contraptions with eerie carved figures on top. It's a profound statement about the human condition, or something. See p. 78.

Spookiest Attraction Scotland's Secret Bunker in Troywood, Fife, was an emergency base for the government in the event of a Soviet nuclear strike. Here you can walk down the eerie 150m tunnel to the reinforced underground chambers with their own annexe for the Home Secretary and his wife. After any youngsters have had their thrills in the weapons room, return to the surface for the comforting sound of birdsong and the not-so-comforting din of small boys battling with plastic machine guns. See p. 200.

BEST FAMILY ACCOMMODATION

Most Child-friendly Hotel Our daughter's favourite hotel in Scotland was so good that when that conversation comes up about who'd look after your children if you both died in a freak accident, my answer has changed from my sister, who would take them in as her own, to Edinburgh's Balmoral Hotel. For weeks after our stay she felt emotionally traumatised by the absence of a teddy turndown service in her life. Then there was the box of toys, a gift (The Gruffalo) and children's bubble bath in the bathroom. If you have a baby expect soft toys, a bottle warmer, a steriliser, a changing mat and a stack of different sized nappies in your room. See p. 47.

Best Bargain The University Pollok Halls of Residence is a great way of avoiding sky-high Edinburgh rates. This student self-catering accommodation (available June–August) has 3–6-bed flats carefully prepared beforehand (so don't worry about finding rotting student food under your bed), all just a short walk from The Meadows, where circus acts practise for August's festival. See p. 51.

Best for Celebrity Spotting The Hotel Du Vin, once the favourite Glasgow haunt of Pavarotti and Elizabeth Taylor, is still pulling in the A-listers. It has its own 4-bed luxury mews suite, with a secret unmarked doorway at the back for celebs to slip out. See p. 84.

Best Hotel Children's Activity A day out pretending to be a Scottish farmer on a mini-quad at the Westin Turnberry Resort, where you get your very own collie, Merc, to whistle 'here, boy' to. This golf lover's favourite in Ayrshire, staging the 2009 Open Championship, also offers kite flying on the beach overlooking the Ailsa Craig,

Luxury suite at the Hotel Du Vin, Glasgow

East Haugh House, Pitlochry

pony-trekking and an owl-experience. See p. 230.

Best Campsite Drum Mohr Caravan and Camping Park near Edinburgh has views over the Firth of Forth and wooden 6- and 4-berth chalets with private hot-tubs. Inside the walled grounds of a former monastery, the site is family-run with a play-park, a shop selling home-baked bread and a shingle beach where seals sometimes bask. See p. 50.

Swankiest Self-Catering At Colt Cottage in Ballater you can stay within the security gate of Balmoral Castle, the Queen's summer residence (so, when friends ask for your holiday address just say 'Oh, send it to the castle'). Plus you can visit the castle free. See p. 203.

Friendliest Place to Stay At the East Haugh House by Pitlochry, it's a close run thing as to who's most friendly – owner Leslie McGown, who specially cooked porridge to the right temperature for our daughter, or her pet dog Lucy, the wire-haired Jack Russell who licked whatever was left of it off her face afterwards. This hotel (as well as saving you a fortune in wipes) is a haven for fishing fans, with the River Tummel just half an hour away: they have rods and children's waders and can arrange a trout fishing trip. See p. 129.

BEST FAMILY EATING

Most Child-friendly Restaurant At Est Est Est in Edinburgh, children get their own chef's hat and can 'make' their own pizzas. See p. 52.

Largest Portions At the Filling Station in Edinburgh I ate so much I went to sleep on my bloated stomach with arms and legs in the air like a penguin. There's a good children's menu and our daughter was presented with colouring packs and a helium balloon to play with/accidentally released to the ceiling, causing her to cry and another to be brought with the same result. See p. 55.

Best View On the terrace of the Kilted Skirlie in Balloch you can sip a razmopolitan (raspberry and vodka) as the sun sets against the backdrop of Loch Lomond and Ben Lomond. The only danger is that you might bump into fiery football manager Sir Alex Ferguson flinging a

The Filling Station, Edinburgh

shoe into the kitchen if his beef stroganoff is under-done; he and Rangers' Walter Smith are regulars. The restaurant is also handily placed for the aquarium. See p. 131.

Best Breakfast Stop At the adjoining Clantartan Centre of Callander's Kilmahog Woollen Mill we discovered that my wife is descended from the warlike Clan Gunn, famous for maintaining a 500-year feud with Clan Keith – a falling-out which helps explain why my wife is still arguing with me six years after we married about the correct way to load knives into the dishwasher. The 72-seater café has highchairs, baby-changing, children's snack boxes and serves all-day breakfasts including delicious filled rolls (bacon, sausage or egg) for a thrifty £2.30. See p. 134.

Best Service Eating at Hadrian's Brasserie in Edinburgh gave us an insight into what it must be like being Beyonce's mum and dad. At one point during our daughter's spaghetti bolognaise there were three members of staff around listening attentively as she extemporised on her perfect ice-cream ('With choccy. No, wafer. No, choccy. No, wafer. I want a choccy wafer...'). It left my wife and I to enjoy the excellent food served by Michelin-starred chef Jeff Bland. See p. 52.

Best Treat The Witchery By The Castle in Edinburgh gets its name from the spot right outside where witches were burnt until the 18th century. Inside, the atmosphere is theatrically gothic and entirely candle-lit, with Hogwarts-style oak panelling, tapestries and antiques. It's the setting that attracts the likes of actors Joanna Lumley, Steve Coogan and Michael Douglas, and Simpson's creator Matt Groening, although don't expect indulgent smiles if your toddler flips a soufflé to the floor in front of no-nonsense newsreader Jeremy Paxman. See p. 56.

2 Planning Your Trip

SCOTLAND

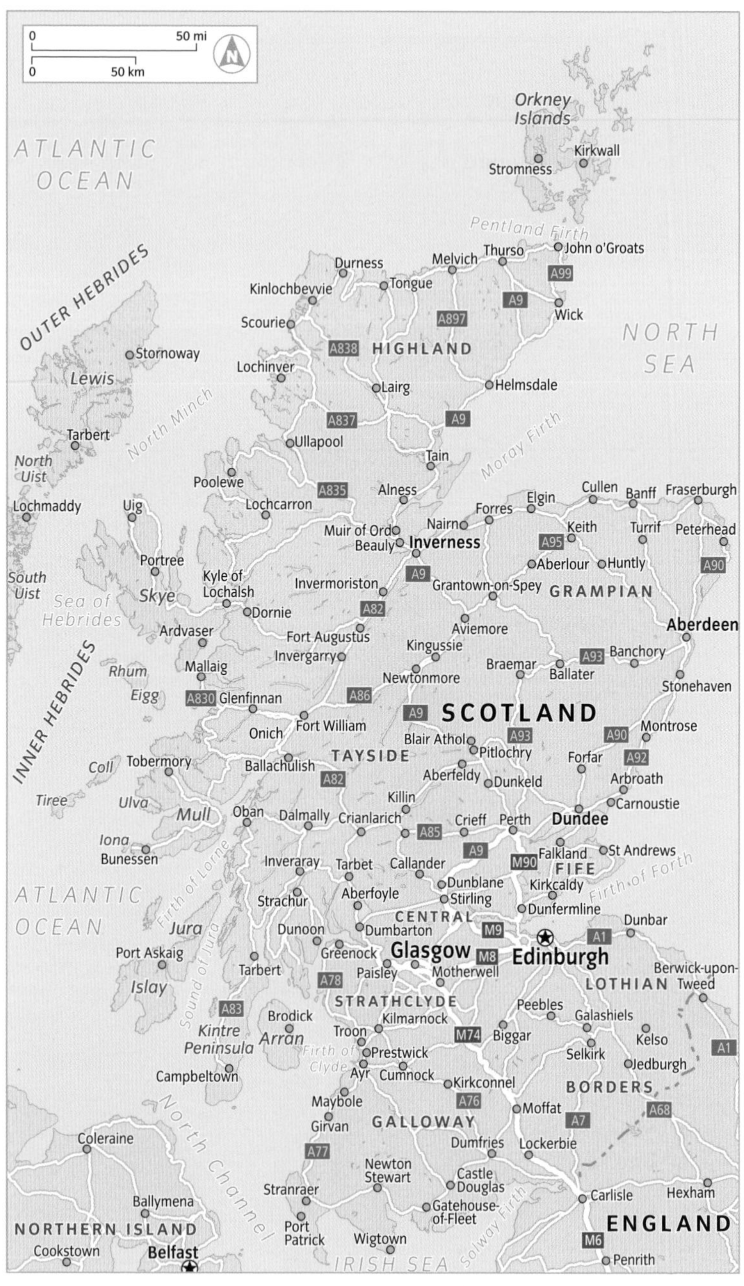
0
50 mi
0
50 km
Orkney Islands
Kirkwall
Stromness
ATLANTIC OCEAN
Pentland Firth
Thurso
John o'Groats
Durness
Melvich
Tongue
Kinlochbevvie
A99
A9
Wick
A897
OUTER HEBRIDES
Scourie
NORTH SEA
A838
HIGHLAND
Stornoway
Lochinver
Lewis
Lairg
Helmsdale
North Minch
A837
A9
Tarbert
Ullapool
Moray Firth
North Uist
Tain
Poolewe
A835
Alness
Cullen
Banff
Fraserburgh
Elgin
Lochmaddy
Uig
Lochcarron
Forres
Nairn
Keith
Turrif
Peterhead
Muir of Ord
Beauly
Inverness
A95
Portree
Aberlour
Huntly
A90
South Uist
Kyle of Lochalsh
A9
Invermoriston
Grantown-on-Spey
GRAMPIAN
Sea of Hebrides
Skye
Dornie
A82
Ardvaser
Fort Augustus
Aviemore
Aberdeen
Kingussie
INNER HEBRIDES
Invergarry
Braemar
A93
Banchory
Rhum
Mallaig
Ballater
Newtonmore
Stonehaven
Eigg
A830
Glenfinnan
A86
A9
SCOTLAND
Onich
Fort William
Montrose
Blair Athol
A93
A90
Coll
Tobermory
Ballachulish
TAYSIDE
Pitlochry
Forfar
A92
A82
Aberfeldy
Dunkeld
Arbroath
Tiree
Ulva
Killin
Carnoustie
Mull
Oban
Dalmally
Crianlarich
Crieff
Perth
Dundee
Iona
Bunessen
A85
A9
Falkland
St Andrews
Inveraray
Tarbet
Callander
M90
FIFE
Firth of Lorne
Dunblane
Kirkcaldy
ATLANTIC OCEAN
Aberfoyle
Stirling
Firth of Forth
Strachur
CENTRAL
Dunfermline
Jura
Dunoon
Dumbarton
M9
Dunbar
A1
Port Askaig
Greenock
Glasgow
M8
Edinburgh
Tarbert
Paisley
Motherwell
Berwick-upon-Tweed
Islay
Sound of Jura
A78
LOTHIAN
STRATHCLYDE
Peebles
A83
Brodick
Kilmarnock
Galashiels
Kintre Peninsula
Arran
Troon
M74
Biggar
Kelso
Firth of Clyde
Prestwick
Selkirk
A1
Campbeltown
Ayr
Cumnock
Jedburgh
Kirkconnel
BORDERS
North Channel
Maybole
A76
Moffat
A68
Girvan
GALLOWAY
A7
Coleraine
Dumfries
Lockerbie
A77
Newton Stewart
Castle Douglas
Stranraer
Carlisle
Hexham
Ballymena
Gatehouse-of-Fleet
Solway Firth
NORTHERN ISLAND
Port Patrick
ENGLAND
Wigtown
M6
Cookstown
Belfast
IRISH SEA
Penrith

Scotland is unfortunately just too big (almost 79,000 square kilometres) to road-test every single hotel, campsite, restaurant and attraction in the country – especially with two young children in a little Vauxhall Astra diesel car. So, to bring you the best on offer for families, we badgered locals and holidaymakers, pestered Visit Scotland and saw plenty for ourselves on the ground. This book reflects what we found.

I've divided the country up into six area chapters – Edinburgh, Glasgow, the Central Highlands, the Highlands and Islands, Aberdeenshire and the North East Coast, and Southern Scotland. Each chapter contains a mini-overview of the area, containing a few smart-alec comments where we could think of them, followed by a selection of attractions and our experiences at them. You'll also find accommodation and dining recommendations. Sometimes we'll self-indulgently inform you what our children ate, and occasionally said, about where we stayed, if we a) felt this was relevant, or b) thought it was funny, or c) had some space to fill and ran out of things to say about, for instance, baked neeps.

As a general rule we found most places in Scotland reasonably accommodating to children, particularly so in Glasgow, surely the most welcoming place in the UK (not counting my auntie's house where there's always fresh ginger biscuits even if you've just come to read the electricity meter). Most cafés, restaurants and pubs allow children (although check in Edinburgh, often the least welcoming place in Scotland). If they don't have a children's menu, restaurants usually at least provide scaled-down adult meals. Accommodation, as you can imagine, varies enormously, from simple static caravans to resort-style hotels, catering for every possible family need from crèches to sports activities. We had a great time researching the book and hope you will love Scotland as much as we do.

VISITOR INFORMATION

Researching a family holiday has never been easier thanks to the **Internet**. If you want a good general overview of Scotland try *www.visitscotland.com*. They have a special page, **Scotland for Families,** that contains attraction ideas for pre-schoolers, youngsters and teenagers. If you're worried about the weather (and do be, this is Scotland) *www.weatheronline.co.uk* provides one- to eight-day forecasts, historical data on average temperatures month-by-month and even weather poems (mostly about rain).

It's also well worth looking out for a **Visit Scotland 'Children Welcome'** logo at attractions you visit. It guarantees the following as a minimum:

family parking near the entrance;

storage space for buggies;

safety features in place;

highchairs, crockery and cutlery for youngsters, children's menu;

info at children's height;

baby-changing in public toilets;

play equipment well maintained.

Other useful websites include ***www.rampantscotland.com*** and ***www.undiscoveredscotland.com***, both with solid information on attractions, places to stay and so on. See the individual chapters for more recommended websites on each region of Scotland.

Holidays

The following **national holidays** are celebrated in Scotland: New Year's Day (1st and 2nd January), Good Friday (March or April), May Day Bank Holiday (first week in May), Spring Bank Holiday (last week in May), Summer Bank Holiday (August), St Andrew's Day Bank Holiday (November or December), Christmas Day, Boxing Day.

Hazards

If you are walking during the hunting season, make sure that there's no **deer stalking** or **grouse shooting** in progress, for obvious reasons. The season for deer stalking is 1st–20th September, running into October for stags. Hinds are culled from then until 15th February. Also take care in the grouse-shooting season (12th August–10th December) and in dimly-lit pubs in the Gorbals after midnight on a weekend.

If you're visiting anywhere north of Glasgow and Edinburgh, watch out for the **Scottish midge**. This relative of the mosquito is at its worst between July and August, and most inactive in May. For a daily check on midge levels in your area, get a report from ***www.midgeforecast.co.uk***: it gives a 1–5 midge rating ranging from negligible (go out in shorts) to nuisance levels (stay inside and stare at the nasty creatures through the window). The only **insect repellent** that works on them isn't even a repellent. It's a bottle of dry oil body spray from Avon's *Skin So Soft* range. Buy the green bottle, not the red one. If you don't believe us, ask the Royal Marines at Faslane – it's what they use. Made with shea butter and vitamins, as a side effect the spray will ensure your skin feels velvety soft, hour after hour. Other ways to avoid midges include sitting in the sun (they hate it) or moving around (they can't keep up). Midges also hate white clothing, being indoors with the lights on, and knockabout humour.

Getting There & Around

By Road The two main routes into Scotland from England are the **A1** and, from the M6, the **A74(M)** and **M74**. The A1 gives you the option of branching on to the A68, which takes the hour-longer, scenic route over the border; the M6 offers dual-carriageway driving the whole way. The journey to Edinburgh or Glasgow takes around eight hours from London, depending on traffic and 'I need a wee wee' stops (two hours less from Birmingham).

Scotland is well geared to the car, but with half its roads 'unclassified' prepare for two distinct sorts of motoring. Southern Scotland with Glasgow and Edinburgh has good roads, and routes reassuringly congested around main cities in rush hour. The Southern Uplands and the Highlands and Islands offer a less crowded experience, but with many single-track roads.

INSIDER TIP

As an average allow an hour for every 80km on the A1 or M74, and at least an hour for 64km in most of the rest of Scotland and 32km on single-track roads.

Something to watch out for on rural roads are locals driving Ford Transit vans: because they're working and you're not, they will expect you to do the reversing into passing bays while they growl at you and point aggressively towards where they are going with their plumbing/electrical tools. Also many roads in upland sheep-rearing areas are unfenced, and sheep with little road sense enjoy licking salt off road surfaces. The lambing season in spring needs particular care. If you come across a sheep on one side of the road and a lamb on the other, you can guarantee one will cross as you approach. It's not uncommon to come across cattle, goats and even deer on the road.

Useful driving websites include ***www.theaa.com*** and ***www.rac.co.uk***, both with free route planning tools; ***www.multimap.com*** provides area maps with address searches and traffic information.

Sat nav: Because we'd be doing a lot of driving and my wife's directions have caused arguments in the past (under pressure she doesn't know her right from left, up from down and also what the toll booth lane is for), we bought a Tom Tom GPS from eBay. Sounds like a good idea although I'm afraid the kit became a running family gag after about the 10th time we pitched up at some forlorn industrial estate in the middle of nowhere with 'Unnamed Road' flashing up on the screen, and the witless machine smugly declaring 'You have reached your destination.' Even our daughter, aged two, lost it in the end. By the time we reached Glasgow, whenever it tried to bully us off course onto a non-existent B-road ('Turn right now'), she was shouting 'No, we won't, will we Daddy?' Our machine was admittedly second-hand and maybe it was just bad luck but basically, if you know where you're going in Scotland sat nav's great, if not, it's like having a senile old man sat beside you who's been to where you're trying to get to, except ages ago, probably when he was incredibly drunk and possibly being sick into a bag.

TIP Driving with Children

1 Getting in and out of the car at destinations as fast as possible is wise, especially if you have toddlers or babies liable to wake up the moment you turn off the ignition. So try to pack only what you'll need – I'm thinking of the back-up baby steriliser we took, and that emergency travel cot weighing as much as a tree that I lugged uselessly in and out of the boot 100 times because 'we'll kick ourselves if we don't bring it'.

2 If you have a small car, consider buying a roof box. They are available from **Halfords** (☎ *0845 057 9000*, ***www.halfords.com***) in half, three-quarter and full car width sizes. Prices start from £115 and staff will fit them for free. It's like suddenly having an attic conversion on your car. Just be careful you don't lose the tiny sliver of a key that unlocks it, like we did in Skye.

3 On long journeys when I-Spy wanes, an in-car DVD player will stop those plaintive whines of 'Are we nearly there yet.' Check the socket that plugs into where the car's cigarette lighter normally sits is a good fit. If my wife so much as glanced at the lead from our one, the film required reloading.

4 When nothing else would quell our daughter, we told her stories. The stories that kept her most enthralled were ones where we substituted the names of normal characters like Little Red Riding Hood or Cinderella with her own name and those of family and friends. Although just be careful when you tell the one about the three little pigs if your wife is sensitive about her weight after a sticky toffee pudding at lunch. Perhaps best to make her the wolf.

5 If everything fails, and your children are so bored they are actually wailing, the best thing to do is a) put on Classic FM at maximum volume and kid yourself you're not muffling their protests with a louder din but actually educating them about Haydn or b) wail yourself.

That said, it was useful when we got totally lost. A woman called Jane (the character we chose as our navigational companion) had the vocal authority of a newsreader to tell us which direction to go when our map told us otherwise. Another warning, however. If using the sat nav, be careful when keying in postcodes for large attractions, especially zoos and safari parks. This postal address won't always (in fact will hardly ever) tally with the location of the entrance gate. I lost count of the times we turned up at some section of security fencing hoping to find a ticket office when the only sign of life was maybe an alpaca staring back at us. The best idea is ring ahead. Staff will normally be aware of the problem and give you a more accurate sat-nav-friendly postcode.

By Train There are two main lines into Scotland from England. **National Express East Coast** (formerly GNER) trains from London King's Cross run up the east coast via Peterborough, York and Newcastle, to Edinburgh; some continue to Glasgow,

Aberdeen or Inverness, including overnight sleeper services. **Virgin Trains** meanwhile run up the west coast from London Euston via Crewe, Preston and Carlisle, to Glasgow. Outside London, there are direct services with Virgin from Birmingham to Edinburgh or Glasgow. The **CrossCountry** service links Cardiff, Paignton, Penzance, Bournemouth and Brighton with Glasgow, Edinburgh and Aberdeen via Birmingham. Journey times from London can be around 4½ hours to Edinburgh, 5 to Glasgow; from Manchester knock off 2 hours, from Bristol add 2. (And add 2½ hours for Aberdeen, 3½ hours for Inverness).

Scotland has a modest rail network that fades to almost non-existent in the Islands. **First ScotRail** runs the majority of services serving all major towns, sometimes on lines that count among the great scenic routes of the world. The **West Highland Line** to Fort William and Mallaig and the journey from Inverness to Kyle of Lochalsh are amongst the most beautiful.

Useful contact details:

First ScotRail (✆ *0845 755 0033*, ***www.firstgroup.com/scotrail***)

National Express East Coast (✆ *0845 722 5225*, ***www.nationalexpresseastcoast.com***)

National Rail Enquiries (✆ *0845 748 4950*, ***www.nationalrail.co.uk***)

Virgin Trains (✆ *0845 722 2333*, ***www.virgintrains.co.uk***).

For detailed information on rail connections to/from **Glasgow**, see p. 62; for **Edinburgh**, see p. 26; for **Fort William**, see p. 142; for **Inverness**, see p. 148; for **Aberdeen**, see p. 180.

By Bus Buses are the cheapest way to get to Scotland, but probably the most arduous. The main operators are **National Express** (✆ *0870 580 8080*, ***www.gobycoach.com***) and its subsidiary *Scottish Citylink* (✆ *0870 550 5050*, ***www.citylink.co.uk***), with regular services from all major UK cities. A daily overnight service from London to Glasgow/Edinburgh is operated by **Silver Choice Travel** (✆ *01413 331400*, ***www.silverchoicetravel.co.uk***). **Megabus** (✆ *0900 160 0900*, ***www.megabus.com***) has very cheap one-way fares from London to Glasgow. Scottish Citylink runs a daily service from Belfast and Dublin to Edinburgh.

Within Scotland the national network is also run by Scottish Citylink, whose buses serve all major towns. For off-the-beaten-track journeys, consult **Traveline** (✆ *0870 608 2608*, ***www.travelinescotland.com***). Remote villages can often be reached only by **Royal Mail postbuses** (✆ *0845 774 0740*, ***www.postbus.royalmail.com***). These are usually mini-buses, sometimes four-seater cars, driven by postal workers on mail runs. As you can imagine, routes are often fairly long-winded.

Bus passes can be purchased from Citylink, saving money if you're travelling by bus a lot.

For detailed information on bus connections to/from **Glasgow**, see p. 63; for **Edinburgh**, see p. 27; for **Fort William**, see p. 143; for **Inverness**, see p. 148; for **Aberdeen**, see p. 180.

By Air Scotland's biggest airports are **Glasgow International, Glasgow Prestwick, Edinburgh, Aberdeen, Inverness** and **Dundee**. The cheapest fares from the UK are from the likes of **Ryanair** (☎ *0871 246 0000*, *www.ryanair.com*), which flies into Glasgow Prestwick, and **Easyjet**, which serves Aberdeen, Glasgow International, Edinburgh and Inverness from London and other regional airports. One-way fares can be as low as £15, but must be booked well in advance and are usually non-refundable. The highest fares are generally mid-June to mid-September, Christmas and New Year. For Edinburgh, Festival time is usually a nightmare.

Other airlines flying to Scotland include: **British Airways** (☎ *0870 850 9850*, *www.ba.com*), **KLM** (☎ *0870 507 4074*, *www.klm.com*), **bmi** (☎ *0870 607 0555*, *www.flybmi.com*), **bmibaby** (☎ *0871 224 0224*, *www.bmibaby.com*), **Eastern Airways** (☎ *0870 366 9100*, *www.easternairways.com*), **Flybe** (☎ *0870 889 0908*, *www.flybe.com*), **jet2** (☎ *0871 226 1737*, *www.jet2.com*) and **ScotAirways** (☎ *0870 142 4343*, *www.scotairways.com*).

For detailed information on air connections to/from **Glasgow**, see p. 62; for **Edinburgh**, see p. 26; for **Dundee**, see p. 192; for **Inverness**, see p. 148; for **Aberdeen**, see p. 179.

TIP When to Go?

The main holiday period, April–September, has its height in July–August during school holidays when accommodation (especially in Edinburgh) is at a premium. Public transport is cut back in the winter, and some attractions close between the end of October and March. As for the rain...I'm afraid that could happen any time, although the east coast is drier than the west. The area around Fort William is the wettest place in Britain. But as poet laureate Ted Hughes (who had clearly never been to Scotland) once said, 'There is no such thing as bad weather, only inadequate clothing.' Scotland's mountains are still snow-covered in April and May, June brings out the rhododendron blossom, and the famous purple **heather** shows in August. **Seabird colonies** are best in the nesting season between April and July. You can see **dolphins** and seals all year in the Solway Firth and **whale watching** peaks in August.

Value Accommodation

Staying on a university campus is even cheaper than normal self-catering. If you're lodging in a big city over the summer holiday, most big universities have rooms suitable for families. They're generally cleaner and more modern than the average hotel. You'll need to book well ahead, especially in Edinburgh, and doubly so in festival time. For more details contact **Venuemasters** (☎ *01142 493090*, ***www.venuemasters.co.uk***). You'll find our recommended campus accommodation in **Edinburgh** on p. 51 and in **St Andrews** on p. 205.

ACCOMMODATION

Camping

There are hundreds of camping and caravan parks, usually with a shop and often a restaurant on site. Most are principally aimed at those caravanning rather than in tents (something to do with the weather, we expect), and open only between April and October. Campsites are increasingly adding static homes and upmarket lodges to attract holidaymakers year-round. If you're planning a lot of camping, the **Camping and Caravanning Club** (☎ *02476 694995*, ***www.campingandcaravanningclub.co.uk***) offers discounts. ***www.Scottishcampingguide.com*** lists hundreds of sites in Scotland, detailing facilities and often featuring campers' reviews too.

Self-catering

A cottage or serviced city apartment is a good way to cut down costs. It also gives you more freedom and a home-from-home feel to your trip, useful if you have younger children on fixed routines. There are many places to choose from. Visit Scotland's self-catering guide (***www.visitscotland.com***, ☎ *0845 225 5121*) has more than 100 listings. Also worth a look are the following: **Country Holidays** (☎ *01282 846137*, ***www.countryholidays.co.uk***), **Scottish Holiday Cottages** (☎ *01463 224707*, ***www.scottish-holidays-cottages.co.uk***) and **MacKay's Agency** (☎ *0870 429 5350*, ***www.mackays-self-catering.co.uk***).

B&Bs

These work out pricey for families unless you're all sharing the same room, not always the ideal arrangement if you have a snuffling baby or a toddler who has arguments in her sleep about biscuits ('that's *my* bourbon'). Some B&Bs have interconnecting rooms, but most will not. Pubs-with-rooms are unlikely to have child-specific facilities. For more information, ***www.scotlandsbestbandbs.co.uk*** has listings of 4- and 5-star B&Bs in Scotland, with contact numbers and details on facilities. **Bed and Breakfast Nationwide** has yet more lists (***www.bedandbreakfastnationwide.com***, ☎ *01255 831235*).

FUN FACT Scotland: Did You Know...? 

1 Unsurprisingly, bearing in mind the weather, it was a Scot, Charles Macintosh (1766–1843), who invented the raincoat that bears his name.
2 Other less well known Scottish inventions include the decimal point, morphine, the grand piano and looking at you in a funny way if you're being too chirpy.
3 Scotch whisky accounts for 13% of Scotland's exports.
4 11% of Scottish people are ginger-haired.
5 *God Save The King* was originally a Jacobite rebel song.
6 Homer Simpson's catchphrase 'Doh!' was based on that of actor James Finlayson born, in Falkirk, who starred alongside Laurel and Hardy in many of their movies.
7 Kilts are not native to Scotland; they originated in France.
8 Christmas was not celebrated in Scotland until the 1950s, because it was considered by Protestants to be a Catholic holiday.

Hotels

A hotel is often the most expensive option. Most will offer a range of accommodation – half-board, full-board, B&B – and occasionally more private self-catering apartments or lodges, with use of the hotel's facilities. There are some wonderful family-friendly hotels in Scotland (many are hydros – located near to spas) catering for every possible need – crèche, children's club, swimming pool, sports and games – which are ideal for parents of older children who want a real break, too. Useful websites include ***www.tripadvisor.com***, with reviews of attractions and places to stay and eat (but be wary of places with hundreds of similar-sounding reviews as the chances are they've been written by the place themselves) and ***www.laterooms.com***, with daily-updated lists of discounted hotel rooms; expect to bag savings of up 70%.

EATING OUT

There's growing pride in **local food** in Scotland, as evidenced by a) the growth of farmers' markets and delis, many of which now have cafés too, and b) the look on the faces of staff if you accidentally ask for a 'full English' instead of a 'full Scottish' at breakfast. Overall standards of cuisine have improved enormously. Pubs, cafés and restaurants increasingly make a point of using local producers wherever possible, so in classier restaurants expect to know where your beef or lamb has come from, sometimes down to the nearest field.

Many restaurants also now begin their evening menu from **6pm** to cater for families with younger children, who are almost always welcome except in the snootier restaurants of Edinburgh. If they don't have children's menus (in the

Speciality Scottish Food

Arbroath Smokie – A wood-smoked haddock produced in small family smoke-houses in the east-coast fishing port of Arbroath.
Bannocks (or Oatcakes) – A barley- and oat-flour biscuit baked on a griddle, now often eaten with cheese.
Black Bun – Rich fruitcake, made with raisins, currants, finely-chopped peel, chopped almonds and brown sugar plus cinnamon and ginger.
Colcannon – Made from boiled cabbage, carrots, turnip and potatoes, this Western Isles dish is stewed with butter, and seasoned with salt and pepper and served hot.
Crowdie – A white cheese, made from the whey of slightly soured milk seasoned with salt and a touch of pepper, and rolled in oats.
Cullen skink – A thick, milky soup made with smoked Finnan haddock, potato and onion.
Forfar Bridies – A hot oval delicacy of plain pastry seasoned with a pinch of salt and brushed with milk containing minced beef, suet and a sprinkling of finely chopped onion.
Haggis – Made from sheep's offal (or pluck). The windpipe, lungs, heart and liver of the sheep are boiled and then minced. This is mixed with beef suet and lightly toasted oatmeal. This mixture is placed inside the sheep's stomach, which is sewn shut. The resulting haggis is traditionally cooked by further boiling.
Hot Toddy – A teaspoon-full of sugar and a teaspoon-full of Scottish heather honey added to a measure of Scotch whisky and topped up with boiling water.
Scotch Broth or Hotch-Potch – A rich, piping hot stock-soup traditionally made by boiling mutton, beef, marrow-bone or chicken then adding barley and diced vegetables such as carrots, cabbage, turnips and celery.
Stovied Tatties (or Stovies) – A potato-based dish, designed to use up leftover meat and vegetables.

Highlands and Islands the chances are they won't), most will serve half-portions of adult dishes where possible.

Family Dining Tips

❶ In big cities the pre-theatre (5–7pm) menu is often 10–20% cheaper than the equivalent evening sit-down.

❷ Some hotels offer free children's meals if you're a) staying there and b) eating *en famille*. Ask about this when you book, and on check-in be cheeky and ask for an upgrade. Some hotels will automatically upgrade if they can; others may take pity on your screaming brood and do so for their own karma.

❸ Ring ahead, explain you'll be bringing children and ask for a table away from the main action, so if your children kick up you won't feel so self conscious when you bellow: 'I said BE QUIET.'

❹ If you don't fancy reaching round your baby for each forkful of food, a good way to avoid the baby-in-the-lap dinner is to bring along the car seat; although keep it well away from clumsy waiters, especially if contemplating baked Alaska.

❺ Ask for crayons and colouring books. Lots of restaurants have these but may only get them out if you ask.

❻ Order food youngsters can play with. Our daughter spent several entire meals buttering slice after slice of bread as if she worked in a busy sandwich shop, enabling my wife and I to enjoy a pleasant dialogue over the table.

GETTING CHILDREN INTERESTED IN SCOTLAND

Before you go, watch famous movies made about Scotland to create mood. Here are a few for children, parents and *just* parents:

Braveheart (1995), starring Mel Gibson.

Shallow Grave (1995) starring Christopher Eccleston and Ewan McGregor.

Loch Ness (1996), with Ted Danson and Joely Richardson.

Trainspotting (1996) with Ewan McGregor and Robert Carlyle.

Highlander (1986) starring Christopher Lambert and Sean Connery.

Rob Roy, (1995) starring Liam Neeson and John Hurt.

Local Hero (1983) starring Burt Lancaster.

Gregory's Girl, (1981) with John Gordon Sinclair.

Brigadoon, (1954) directed by Vincente Minnelli.

Whisky Galore (1949) starring James Robertson Justice.

You can listen to music from famous Scottish bands including: Belle & Sebastian, Travis, Wet Wet Wet (actually don't), Simple Minds, Teenage Fanclub, Bay City Rollers, Primal Scream, The Proclaimers, Texas, Mull Historical Society, Big Country, Snow Patrol, Franz Ferdinand, Jesus and Mary Chain, Runrig, Del Amitri, Altered Images, Aztec Camera, Eurythmics, Cocteau twins, Dogs Die in Hot Cars, Lulu, Shamen and last and by all means least, Deacon Blue.

3 Edinburgh

EDINBURGH

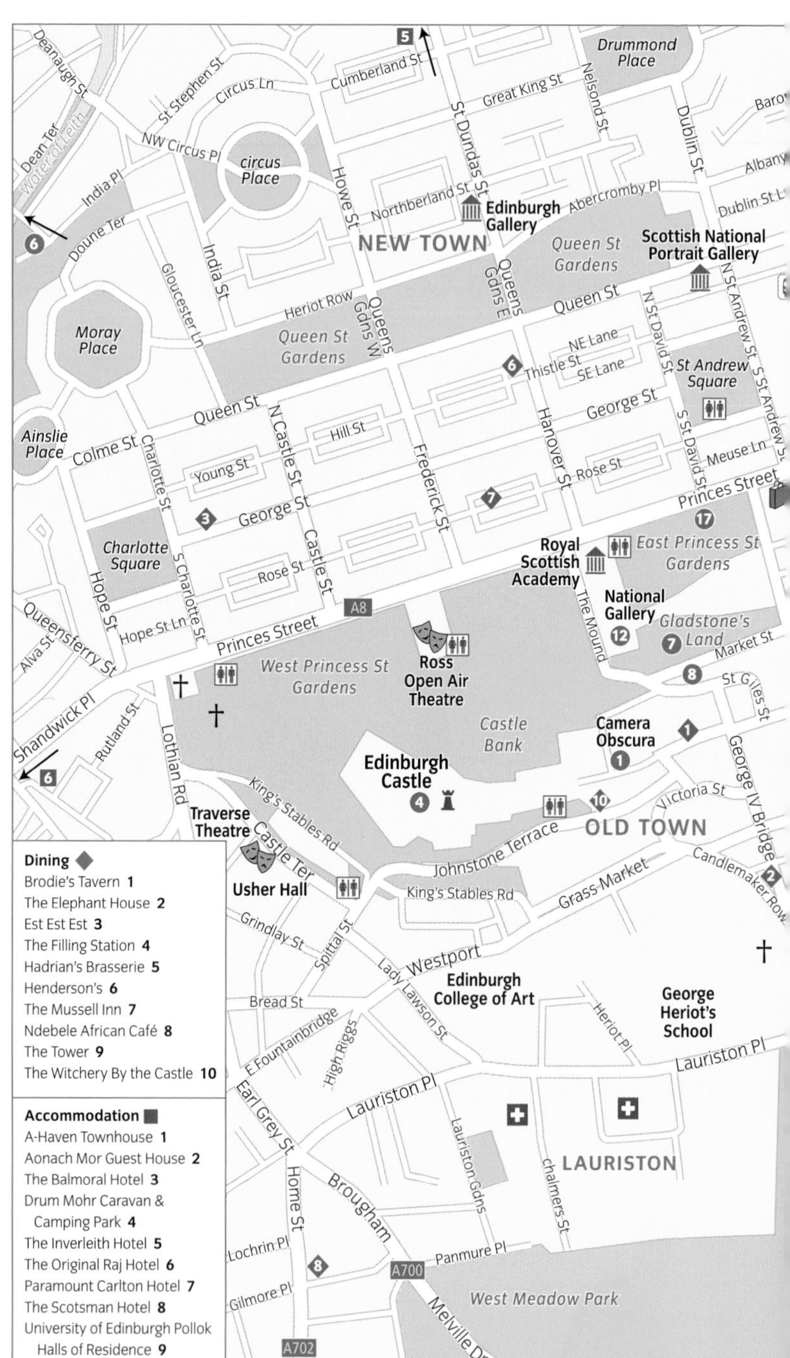

Drummond Place
Cumberland St
Great King St
Nelsond St
Dublin St
St Stephen St
Circus Ln
NW Circus Pl
circus Place
Deanaugh St
Dean Ter
Water of Leith
India Pl
Doune Ter
Howe St
St Dundas St
Northberland St
Abercromby Pl
Albany
Dublin St L
Edinburgh Gallery
NEW TOWN
Queen St Gardens
Scottish National Portrait Gallery
India St
Gloucester Ln
Heriot Row
Queens Gdns W
Queens Gdns E
Queen St
Moray Place
N St David St
N St Andrew St
NE Lane
Thistle St
SE Lane
St Andrew Square
S St Andrew St
George St
Ainslie Place
Colme St
Charlotte St
N Castle St
Hill St
Frederick St
Hanover St
S St David St
Meuse Ln
Young St
Rose St
Princes Street
Castle St
Charlotte Square
S Charlotte St
Hope St
Royal Scottish Academy
East Princess St Gardens
Hope St Ln
A8
The Mound
National Gallery
Gladstone's Land
Queensferry St
Alva St
Market St
West Princess St Gardens
Ross Open Air Theatre
St Giles St
Shandwick Pl
Rutland St
Lothian Rd
Castle Bank
Camera Obscura
George IV Bridge
Edinburgh Castle
King's Stables Rd
Victoria St
Traverse Theatre
Castle Ter
Johnstone Terrace
OLD TOWN
Candlemaker Row
Usher Hall
King's Stables Rd
Grass Market
Grindlay St
Spittal St
Lady Lawson St
Westport
Edinburgh College of Art
Bread St
E Fountainbridge
High Riggs
Heriot Pl
George Heriot's School
Lauriston Pl
Earl Grey St
Lauriston Gdns
LAURISTON
Chalmers St
Home St
Brougham
Lochrin Pl
Panmure Pl
A700
Gilmore Pl
West Meadow Park
Melville Dr
A702
Dining
Brodie's Tavern 1
The Elephant House 2
Est Est Est 3
The Filling Station 4
Hadrian's Brasserie 5
Henderson's 6
The Mussell Inn 7
Ndebele African Café 8
The Tower 9
The Witchery By the Castle 10
Accommodation
A-Haven Townhouse 1
Aonach Mor Guest House 2
The Balmoral Hotel 3
Drum Mohr Caravan & Camping Park 4
The Inverleith Hotel 5
The Original Raj Hotel 6
Paramount Carlton Hotel 7
The Scotsman Hotel 8
University of Edinburgh Pollok Halls of Residence 9

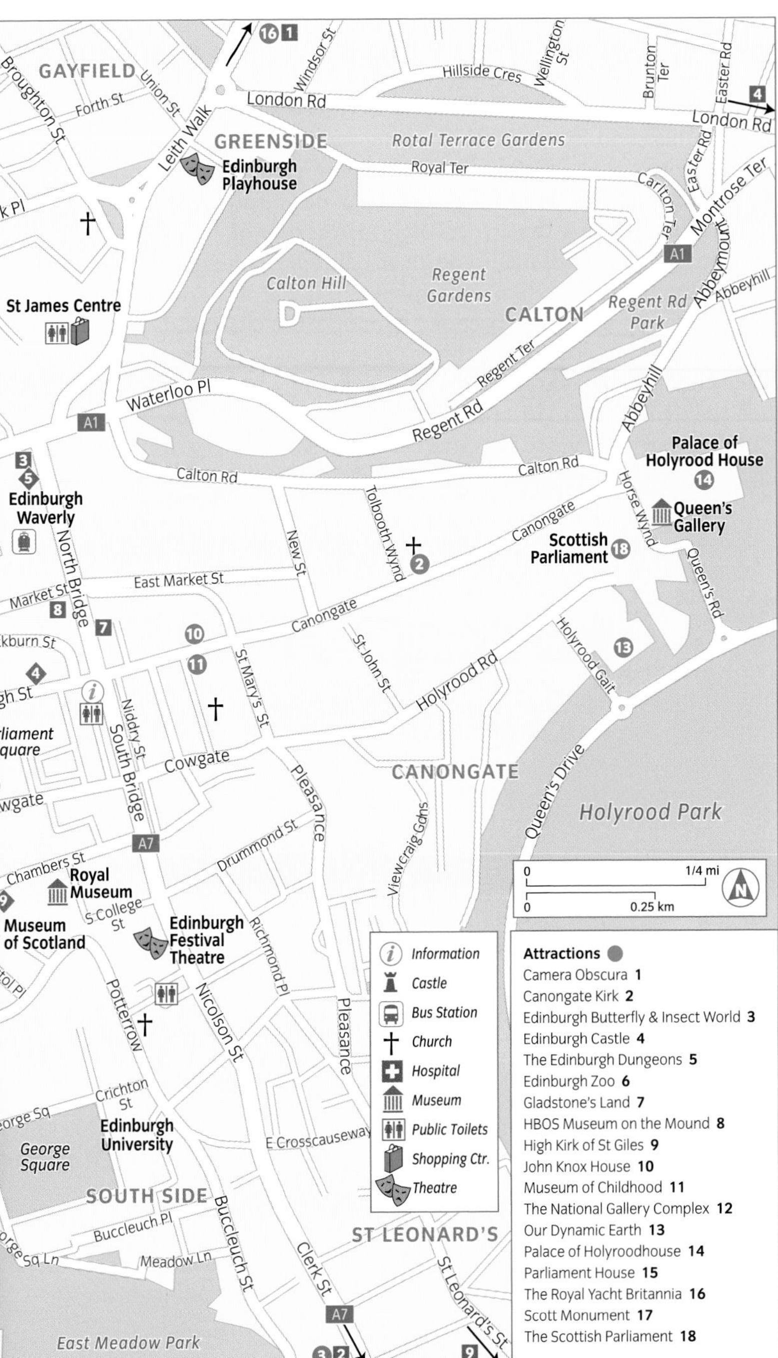
GAYFIELD
Broughton St
Forth St
Union St
Leith Walk
16 1
Windsor St
London Rd
Hillside Cres
Wellington St
Brunton Ter
Easter Rd
4
London Rd
GREENSIDE
Rotal Terrace Gardens
Royal Ter
Edinburgh Playhouse
Carlton Ter
Easter Rd
Montrose Ter
A1
Abbeymount
Abbeyhill
Calton Hill
Regent Gardens
CALTON
Regent Rd Park
St James Centre
Regent Ter
Waterloo Pl
Regent Rd
A1
Abbeyhill
Palace of Holyrood House
14
Queen's Gallery
Calton Rd
Calton Rd
3
5
Edinburgh Waverly
North Bridge
New St
Tolbooth Wynd
2
Canongate
Scottish Parliament
18
Horse Wynd
Queen's Rd
East Market St
Market St
8
7
Canongate
10
11
St Mary's St
St John St
Holyrood Rd
Holyrood Gait
13
4
Niddry St
South Bridge
Cowgate
Pleasance
CANONGATE
Queen's Drive
Holyrood Park
A7
Drummond St
Viewcraig Gdns
0 1/4 mi
0 0.25 km
N
Chambers St
Royal Museum
9
Museum of Scotland
S College St
Edinburgh Festival Theatre
Richmond Pl
Potterrow
Nicolson St
Pleasance
Information
Castle
Bus Station
Church
Hospital
Museum
Public Toilets
Shopping Ctr.
Theatre
Crichton St
George Sq
George Square
Edinburgh University
E Crosscauseway
SOUTH SIDE
Buccleuch Pl
Buccleuch St
ST LEONARD'S
George Sq Ln
Meadow Ln
Clerk St
St Leonard's St
A7
East Meadow Park
3 2
9
Attractions
Camera Obscura 1
Canongate Kirk 2
Edinburgh Butterfly & Insect World 3
Edinburgh Castle 4
The Edinburgh Dungeons 5
Edinburgh Zoo 6
Gladstone's Land 7
HBOS Museum on the Mound 8
High Kirk of St Giles 9
John Knox House 10
Museum of Childhood 11
The National Gallery Complex 12
Our Dynamic Earth 13
Palace of Holyroodhouse 14
Parliament House 15
The Royal Yacht Britannia 16
Scott Monument 17
The Scottish Parliament 18

With its Georgian and Victorian architecture and winding medieval streets, it's not hard to see why Edinburgh was made a Unesco World Heritage Site. The setting is breathtaking. Edinburgh Castle, perched on the crag of an ancient volcano bang in the centre of the city, dominates the skyline. Edinburgh also punches above its weight in the intellectual and literary worlds, with names such as Adam Smith and (maybe) J.K. Rowling forever associated with the city. The August arts festival is the biggest of its kind in the world, and whether it's watching the penguin parade at Edinburgh Zoo, visiting the world's first skyscrapers on a Mercat tour of The Royal Mile, or frightening yourself half to death at Edinburgh Dungeons, Scotland's capital is perfect for families.

In addition, as you'd expect of a cosmopolitan city of Edinburgh's stature, there are dozens of great places to eat and stay, many within the Neoclassical masterpiece of the New Town, where the rich once fled the stench of 'Auld Reekie' (the Old Town's nickname), but now gather to pay homage to the city's culinary revolution.

ESSENTIALS

By Air There are direct flights to Edinburgh from most UK airports. Edinburgh is just one hour from London by plane. Edinburgh Airport (*0870 040 0007* ***www.edinburghairport.com***) is 11km west of the city centre. Take Airlink bus 100 from Stand 19 outside arrivals to Waverley Bridge near Princes Street (£3 one way, £5 return). The journey takes 25 minutes. Services run every 10 minutes from 4.45am to midnight. The night bus (N22) from the same stand operates half-hourly through the night. Edinburgh Shuttle (*0845 500 5000*, ***www.edinburghshuttle.com***) runs a door-to-door minibus service leaving from collection point 5 at the coach park outside arrivals, running every 15–30 minutes. Fares are £8 but reduced for multiple passengers travelling to the same destination. There are also three taxi ranks managed by Executive Onward Travel (*0131 333 2255*). Private taxis operate from the eastern end of the terminal, black cabs adjacent to the coach park. The pre-booked taxi rank is on the ground floor of the short-stay multi-storey carpark. The fare to the city centre is £15, journey time 20 minutes.

By Train Two train companies operate services from London to Edinburgh. Virgin Trains (*0845 722 2333*, ***www.virgintrains.co.uk***) uses the west-coast mainline, National Express East Coast, formerly GNER (*0845 722 5225*, ***www.nationalexpresseastcoast.com***), the east-coast mainline. Virgin Trains depart from London's Euston Station and National Express services from King's Cross. Both arrive at Waverley Station and fares are roughly the same. Slightly better is National Express, if you can remember not to get off a stop early at Haymarket Station. The east-coast journey time is half an hour shorter (4½ hours) and if you're sitting on the righthand-side of the train (you can book this) there are spectacular coastal views approaching the Scottish Borders.

For the cheapest deals book well in advance (months) as discounted fares (starting at £15.70, rising to £42) go fast. A standard single £97 (£98 return), increases to £117 (£144 return) if travelling before 9am. National Express services run half hourly weekdays from 6.15am–11.30pm (Saturdays 6.15am–12.30pm and Sundays 9am–10.10pm). Virgin Trains run hourly weekdays 6.46am–11.40pm (weekends 6.19am–9.25pm). For detailed timetables, see **www.nationalrail.co.uk**.

Another option from London is the First Scotrail (*0845 755 0033*, **www.firstgroup.com/scotrail**) overnight Caledonian Sleeper departing London's Euston station at 11.45pm (Monday–Thursday) and 11pm on Fridays (weekend times vary) and arriving at Edinburgh roughly 7½ hours later. Book online well in advance (three months) for Advance tickets £66 (£99 return). Standard open singles cost £110 (£155 return). Interconnecting rooms are £172 (£301 return).

By Bus If you can stand nine-hours of 'Are we there yet?' National Express (**www.nationalexpress.com**) operates six daily services (two direct) from London Victoria coach station to Edinburgh's St Andrew's Square. Coaches go via Manchester or Birmingham. A single Apex Return (purchased seven days in advance with very little flexibility: no refunds or open returns) costs £30 (Fridays £38).

By Car Enter the city from the southeast via the A68 or A7, from the east on the A1, or the A702 from the north. The A71 or A8 comes in from the west, the A8 connecting with the M8 west of Edinburgh.

The journey from London lasts eight hours plus potty breaks and precious driving time wasted on a coin-operated Bob the Builder machine at Leicester Forest East services. From Glasgow, the trip should take you about an hour. See Getting Around, below, for parking advice.

VISITOR INFORMATION

The Edinburgh and Scotland Information Centre (*0131 473 3800* **www.edinburgh.org**) at Princes Mall, 3 Princes St, has info about what's on, and places to stay. It also sells bus tours, theatre tickets and gives advice on hotel offers. It's open May, June and September Monday–Saturday 9am–7pm, (Sunday 10am to 5pm); July and August, Monday–Saturday 9am–8pm (Sunday 10am–8pm); October and April, Monday–Saturday 9am–6pm (Sunday 10am–5pm); November–March, Monday–Wednesday 9am–5pm, Thursday–Saturday 9am–6pm (Sunday 10am–5pm).

Orientation

The Royal Mile is the main thoroughfare of the Old Town, running from Edinburgh Castle to the Palace of Holyroodhouse. It's made up of four adjoining streets: Castlehill, Lawnmarket, High Street and Canongate. The New Town, a network of classic squares, streets and townhouses, lies below across Princes Street Gardens. Edinburgh's Southside and West End are residential. North of the city lies the Port of Leith, which fans of Irvine Welsh (author of *Trainspotting*) will know for its rough reputation. Now gentrified luxury apartments are being built there these days.

Getting Around

On Foot Walking is the best way to see Edinburgh's main attractions, although the hill back up from the New Town is steep and with a laden buggy can make you feel like Magnus Ver Magnusson in the *World's Strongest Man* lorry pull.

By Bus Buses are useful for jaunts to Edinburgh Zoo (p. 44) and the Edinburgh Butterfly and Insect World (p. 44). The main operator is **Lothian Buses** (☎ *0131 555 6363* *www.lothianbuses.co.uk*). A single fare (any distance within the city) is £1 (60p for 5–15s). Up to two children aged under 5 go free with a fare-paying adult. Day tickets allow unlimited travel £2.50 (children £2). A RIDACARD offers unlimited travel for a week £13 (children £9). These are available from Travelshops at Waverley Bridge, Hanover Street and Shandwick Place, or at 200 PayPoint outlets throughout the city. Drivers cannot give change, so have the exact fare.

By Taxi There are ranks at Waverley Station, Haymarket Station, Hanover Street, North Street, St Andrews Street and Lauriston Place. It costs roughly £7 from the city centre to the Royal Yacht Britannia in Leith. Alternatively ring **Central Radio Taxis** (☎ *0131 229 2468*) or **City Cabs** (☎ *0131 228 1211*).

By Car Forget it – it's a nightmare. Parking is expensive, hard to locate and traffic wardens are aggressively active. Parking in permit bays or yellow lines risks a £60 fine. You may even be towed like we were. The retrieval cost is £135 (plus a strop from your partner). If you still want to go for it, there are car parks at Castle Terrace, Lothian Road at the west end of Princes Street and St John Hill, and at St James Centre (accessed via York Place).

Sightseeing Bus There are three main operators: **City Sightseeing** (☎ *0131 555 6363*, *www.city-sightseeing.com*), **Mac Tours** (☎ *0131 556 2244*, *www.mactours.co.uk*), and **Majestic Tours** (*0131 220 0770*). Each tour is open top, hop-on/hop off and covers roughly the same city centre route, although the Majestic takes you to the Royal Yacht Britannia in Leith. The fares are the same: £9 (children £3, under-5s free). Services start from Waverley Station at around 9.30am, and finish slightly later in the summer on the **City Sightseeing** bus at 7.15pm. We used Mac Tours because it has vintage buses and my wife wanted a photo of me on one doing my 'Blakey' face from the 1970s comedy show ***On the Buses***. All tickets are valid for 24 hours, include on-board audio commentary or a guide, and give up to 20 per cent discounts on various attractions.

Child-friendly Events & Entertainment

Bank of Scotland Children's International Theatre Festival

01312 258050, www.imaginate.org.uk.

Britain's biggest performing arts festival for children aged 3–12 takes place at theatres across the city at the end of May. The week-long festival of shows gathered from all over the world includes anything from adaptations of classic fairytales such as Hansel and Gretel to baby raves (salsa dancing) for 0–4 year-olds.

Edinburgh Christmas Festival

www.edinburghschristmas.com.

Christmas in Edinburgh starts at the end of November with the switching on of the lights. It's followed by an ice show and fireworks to launch the ice-rink and big wheel next to Princes Street. The highlight is the Great Scottish Santa Run, which sees thousands of people dressed up as Father Christmas skipping a mile around Princes Street Gardens for charity.

Edinburgh Festival Fringe

01312 260026, www.edfringe.com.

Dozens of children's events take place over the city in August, including puppet-theatres, magic and storytelling sessions, as well as street entertainers such as jugglers, stilt walkers, buskers and tumblers.

Edinburgh International Book Festival

01317 185666, www.edbookfest.co.uk.

Running alongside the adult festival programme is a host of activities for toddlers and children including music and story sessions plus other events about anything from outer space to creepy-crawlies. Children's authors here have included J.K. Rowling.

Edinburgh Science Festival

Assembly Rooms, George Street, 01315 587666, www.sciencefestival.co.uk.

This festival staged over the Easter holidays is great for budding scientists, aspiring surgeons or wannabe secret agents. Events include things such as walking into a human cell, digging for dinosaur bones and experimenting with electronics. Admission is £9, £5 for 3–6-year-olds, under-3s are free.

FAST FACTS: EDINBURGH

Business hours Most attractions open 9am–5pm daily.

Dentist For emergencies, the Edinburgh Dental Institute (*01315 364931*) is at 39 Lauriston Place, Monday–Friday 9am–3pm.

Doctor Edinburgh Royal Infirmary (*01315 361000*), 1 Lauriston Place; it's open 24/7.

Internet Costa Coffee (*01312 21932935*) at Shandwick Place; Monday–Saturday 8am–8pm (Sunday 10am–7pm); £4 per hour.

Pharmacy No 24-hour pharmacies, but Boots (*0131 225 6757*) at 46–48 Shandwick Place is open Monday–Friday 8am–9pm, Saturday 8am–7pm, Sunday 10am–5pm.

Post Office 8–10 St James Centre (*0845 722 3344*); open Monday–Friday 9am–5.30pm, Saturday 8.30am–midday.

WHAT TO SEE & DO

The best introduction to sightseeing is the **Edinburgh Pass** (*0131 473 3630*, *www.edinburghpass.com*). Available from tourist information centres, it provides free entry to 30 city attractions (not the Castle) and includes discounts at retailers and restaurants as well as free transport on Lothian buses and a return airport transfer with Airlink. Prices are as follows: adult £24 a day, £36 for two days and £48 for three days; children (ages 5–15) £16 a day, £24 for two days and £32 for three days. The pass will pay for itself over three days.

Children's Top 10 Attractions

1. **Journey back** to the Big Bang and crash into a volcano, then come face to face with a dinosaur, at Our Dynamic Earth. See p. 37.

2. **Get whipped** by the small intestine from a dead corpse and hide from a mad cannibal at the Edinburgh Dungeons. See p. 40.

3. **Watch** the penguin parade at Edinburgh Zoo. See p. 44.

4. **Stay the night** at Balmoral Hotel, where staff will make you feel like royalty. See p. 47.

5. **Take comfort** in how naughty children were treated in Victorian times at the Museum of Childhood. See p. 36.

6. **Make your own** pizza at Est Est Est. See p. 52.

7 **Shake hands** with yourself and swap noses with the person next to you at the Camera Obscura. See p. 31.

8 **Visit** Edinburgh Castle and put your head down a 15th century cannon. See p. 32.

9 **Listen to a tale** about fairies at the John Knox House Scottish storytelling centre. See p. 35.

10 **Take a tour** of the Royal Yacht Britannia in Leith. See p. 46.

The Old Town

The heart of the old Town is The Royal Mile – so called because it's a scots mile in length (1⅛ english miles) and connects two royal houses, Edinburgh Castle and the Palace of Holyroodhouse.

Camera Obscura

549 Castlehill Rd, ☏ 01312 263709, ***www.camera-obscura.co.uk.***

A rotating periscope-like lens at the top of the Outlook Tower next to Edinburgh Castle, this attraction has fascinated visitors with its live moving panorama of the city for more than 150 years. Here, as well as spying on tourists stocking up on tartan tea-towels on the esplanade, you'll be treated to some alternative Edinburgh history, such as the fact that Sean Connery used to pose naked at the City Art College and once had a milk round in the city. The projection room is dark so watch out if your toddler, like ours, is afraid of unexpected darkness and/or trivia about the early lives of former James Bonds; he/she might start shouting: 'Get my out of here. My want to get out. I don't like it. I don't like it. My don't like it.'

As well as the camera obscura, there are three floors packed with optical illusions, fibre optic gimmickry as well as holograms including one of a giant creeping tarantula I still try not to think about when I take the bins out at night. Children can shake hands with themselves, stare into the largest plasma dome in Europe or watch themselves distort in wacky mirrors. At the observation deck there are panoramic views and telescopes (you don't have to put money in) with helpful boards pointing out prominent buildings and landmarks.

I hate to flag up gift-shops but the one here is great for secret message pens, puzzles, magnifying glasses and a superb array of magic tricks including one that made my nephew a few

FUN FACT **Did You Know?**

Early visitors to the camera obscura, witnessing illuminated moving images for the first time, promptly fainted. They suspected the pictures projected onto a concave table in the darkened interior of the camera obscura were put there by dark magic.

FUN FACT Mistaken Identity

The name Ebenezer Scrooge has become shorthand for meanness, although the real Scrooge that the Dickensian character was based on could not have been more different. It was 1841 and Dickens was killing time after giving a talk in Edinburgh when he came across a headstone in the Canongate Kirk graveyard that he misread because of the failing light and his mild dyslexia. The headstone was for Ebenezer Lennox Scroggie, born in Kirkcaldy, a generous, rambuctious, although slightly licentious man who staged wild parties, impregnated several wenches, and once famously interrupted the General Assembly of the Church of Scotland by 'goosing' the Countess of Mansfied. The slab reads: 'Ebenezer Lennox Scroggie – meal man', referring to his trade as a corn merchant, although the author mistakenly saw this as 'mean man'. Shocked by the description, it gave him an idea and two years later, he published *A Christmas Carol*. Scroggie's final resting place was lost to redevelopment in 1932, and the name Ebenezer as a parental choice for a child's first name hasn't fared too well either.

weeks later think I might actually be a wizard named Galtaroi.

***Open** daily July and Aug 9.30am–7.30pm, Sep–Oct 9.30am–6pm, Nov–Mar 10am–5pm, Apr–June 9.30am–6pm. **Adm** £7.50, children (5–15) £5.00, under-5s free. **Amenities** shop.*

Canongate Kirk

*153 Canongate, ☎ 01315 563515, **www.canongatekirk.com**.*

This 17th century stone church is the official Kirk of Holyroodhouse Palace, and thus the place of worship for the Royal Family when in residence. Its graveyard is where such luminaries as economist Adam Smith (1723–1790) are buried. It is also where Charles Dickens had his inspiration for *A Christmas Carol* (see 'Mistaken Identity', above).

***Open** dependent on services. **Adm** free.*

Edinburgh Castle

*Castlehill, ☎ 01312 259846, **www.edinburghcastle.biz**.*

Scotland's most visited tourist attraction is every child's dream of what a castle should look like, right down to the actor dressed like Mel Gibson in *Braveheart* wandering around for you to take photographs of or follow around pointing at (our daughter). Perched on Castle Rock, this Edinburgh icon, visible from all over the city, makes a great day out if you can tolerate all the climbing and haven't got a sleeping Gina Ford baby on your hands when they fire the one o'clock gun. (The one o'clock gun was originally fired in the 16th century to help ships in Leith set their clocks and is still useful if you bought a dodgy diving watch at Glasgow's Barras market (p. 83) the week before.)

FUN FACT **Did You Know?**

In what might have made the ultimate 19th century *Cash in the Attic* episode, the Scottish Crown Jewels ('the Honours'), missing for over a 100 years, were discovered by novelist Sir Walter Scott. He was rooting about in an old linen cloth chest inside the castle.

The castle, besieged, retaken and burned on numerous occasions, is dripping in Scottish history. Amongst other milestones, Mary, Queen of Scots gave birth here to James VI, England's James I. If that doesn't appeal, you can always put your head down the end of the Mon Meg cannon and shout 'booooobie' – our daughter's idea. Other attractions include the oldest building in the city, 12th century St Margaret's Chapel, the Scottish Crown Jewels and views over Princes Street Gardens.

Open *1st Apr—31st Sep Mon–Sun 9.30am–6.00pm, 1st Oct—31st Mar Mon–Sun 9.30am–5.00pm.* ***Adm*** *£11.00 (children 5–15, £5.50).* ***Amenities*** *audioguide, children's trail, guided tours (£3, £1 children 5–15, under-5s free).*

Gladstone's Land

477b Lawnmarket, 01312 265856, ***www.nts.org.uk.***

This 17th century tenement home of merchant Thomas Gledstanes gives children an insight, should they want one, into everyday life 300 years ago. Amongst items on display in the first floor kitchen (a difficult spiral staircase, so no buggies), you'll find an ingenious old wooden toddler-walker similar to those today (only without Nemo hanging from it) along with ladies' platform shoes – not a fashion statement but a practical accessory to keep long skirts out of the mud. Downstairs is a reconstructed 17th century cloth shop, and there are guides on hand to answer questions and keep an eye on youngsters, like ours anxious

Find the Scottish Crown Jewels in Edinburgh Castle

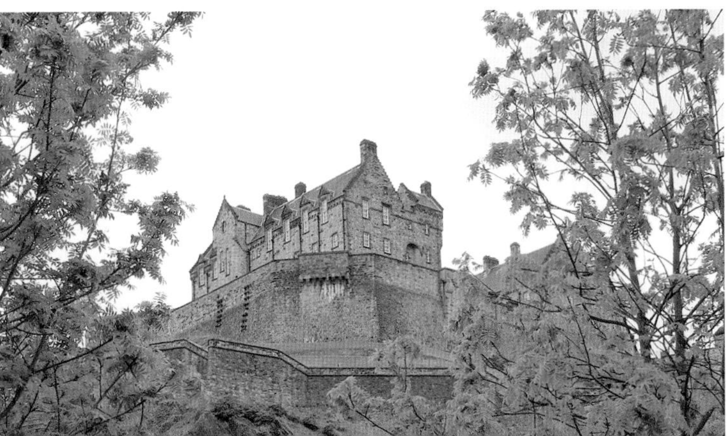

to touch/take/break willow-patterned vases. Our daughter's highlight was the sleeping, fibre-glass pigs. Pigs would have been kept at the property and ridden in races by boys (hence the term piggy-back ride) down the Royal Mile.

There are no baby-changing facilities or toilets and be careful of the low doorways. I banged my head so hard leaving the building that for five minutes I almost bought a hand-made eight yard kilt at James Pringle.

***Open** daily 31st Mar–30th June, and 1st Sep–31st Oct 10.00am–5.00pm (1st July–31st Aug 10.00am–7.00pm). **Adm** £5.00, family tickets (two adults, up to four children) £14.00.*

HBOS Museum on the Mound

The Mound, 01312 435464, www.museumonthemound.com.

Parents harbouring a suspicion they may have a budding banker on their hands might like to pass a rainy spell at this altar to cash, which tries admirably to make the subject of money, rates of interest and the history of the building society entertaining. Here you'll find Scotland's oldest bank note, the world's first mechanical calculator, cowrie shells once used as currency in Uganda and, more importantly, a display showing what a million pounds looks like in crisp new Scottish £20 notes (all unfortunately stamped cancelled).

After you've spent 20 minutes imagining how you'd remove this stamp and then break in and steal the cash and flee to Mexico, you can go and find your children, who hopefully aren't sitting on the 1806 nightwatchman's chair wiping bogies down the arms. There's also a safe containing chocolate money you can have a go at cracking/burst into tears at the mention of, demanding your own chocolate money. The tale of John Currie, who had his ear nailed to Tron Kirk after forging 20 shillings notes, will right your moral compass before you leave.

***Open** Tues–Fri 10am–5pm, Sat–Sun 1pm–5pm. **Adm** free.*

High Kirk of St Giles

High Street, 01312 259442, www.stgilescathedral.org.uk.

One of the most important architectural landmarks along the Royal Mile, this is where Scotland's Martin Luther, John Knox (see p. 36), preached his sermons on the Reformation. Lit by the sunlight filtering through

FUN FACT **Did You Know?**

Atheist and thinker David Hume (1711–1776), who was a key figure in the Scottish Enlightenment and famously denounced religion as 'vulgar superstition', was forced to convert to Christianity by brawny Edinburgh fishwives. They would only rescue him, after he fell into the mire of the recently drained Nor' Loch, once he'd recited the Lord's Prayer. Hume thereafter claimed Edinburgh fishwives were the 'most acute theologians' he'd ever met.

FUN FACT Jenny Geddes

Jenny Geddes, who like many Scots of the time was a post-Reformation presbyterian, threw her stool to protest at the creeping Roman Catholicism of Charles I's reign. He'd commissioned the *Book of Common Prayer* shortly after his coronation in 1633. Geddes' violent act was the start of a general tumult which saw many of the congregation shouting abuse and throwing bibles. The rioters were eventually ejected but, for the rest of the service, hammered at the doors and threw stones at the windows. More serious rioting in the streets (and in neighbouring cities) ensued and with Charles I unyielding, oppositon to his proposed religious changes was formalised into the Covenanter movement, which led indirectly to the English Civil War itself.

its stained glass, the 12th century church, often called St. Giles Cathedral, played host to one of the most important moments in British history. On 23rd July 1637, market trader Jenny Geddes threw a three-legged stool at the head of the Dean of Edinburgh in the middle of the first reading of the *Book of Common Prayer* in Scotland, shouting at him the words we've all wanted to use: 'Devil cause you severe pain and flatulent distention of your abdomen, false thief: dare you say the Mass in my ear?' (see above).

INSIDER TIP

If you're finding it hard to persuade your youngster to go along with another tour of a 'boring old church' or are worried once inside they might take vandalising inspiration from Jenny Geddes, there is an excellent café in the Lower Aisle serving Orkney ice-cream.

On your way out, outside the west door of the Kirk, is the Heart of Midlothian, a heart-shaped mosaic built into the pavement. Along with nearby brass markings it records the position of the 15th century Tolbooth, demolished in 1817, that was the administrative centre of the town prison and a site of public execution. You might notice locals spitting on the Heart, especially after the pubs close. This goes back to the tradition of criminals spitting on the door of the Tolbooth as they passed, for luck. Although more likely the spitting is done by Hibernian football fans, city rivals of Heart of Midlothian F.C.

***Open** excluding services May–Sep Mon–Fri 9am–7pm, Sat 9am–5pm, Sun 1pm–5pm, Oct–Apr Mon–Sat 9am–5pm, Sun 1pm–5pm. **Adm** free.*

John Knox House

*43–45 High Street, Royal Mile, 01315 569579, **www.scottishhistorytellingcentre.co.uk**.*

At what might or might not be Knox's 15th century former townhouse (no one knows if he really lived here) you can learn about his speeches and beliefs, and examine the historical importance of the Reformation, while your kids play with a medieval puzzle that involves beheading a stranger. Children can also try on period hats and capes and there's an audio enactment of a debate between Knox and his arch (Catholic) enemy Mary, Queen of Scots: our daughter seemed lost in theological argument, until we realised her glassy-eyes meant actually she was on the verge of an unplanned wee. While you're here don't miss the free storytelling room on the ground floor. Here, in a special bothy (hut), children will hear Scottish themed stories about anything from lost animals to lochside fairies. Professional storytellers walk dramatically about as they tell their tales. Ring ahead for times, although there is usually something on daily in school holidays and at weekends. There's also a storytelling wall, dotted with doors behind which lie mini-tableaux of stories for children, and a theatre where anything might be shown from a documentary about the rise of Italian nationalism to a puppet play about Little Red Riding Hood.

This is a listed building, so there are no lifts.

Open *Mon–Sat 10am–6pm, Sun July, Aug and Sep noon–6pm.* ***Adm*** *£3.00, Children £1 (under-6s free).* ***Amenities*** *café (children's goody bag £2.75), highchairs.*

INSIDER TIP

After you've visited John Knox's house look for spot Number 23 in the car park at the back of the High Kirk of St Giles. This is where Knox is supposedly buried. The brass plaque proclaiming this fact was covered up after repeated graffiti attacks. Likewise, the small stained glass window that bears his initials is shuttered at night.

Museum of Childhood

42 High Street, Royal Mile, 01315 294142, ***www.museumofchildhood.org.uk****.*

John Knox

John Knox, born in East Lothian around 1510, is the father of the Protestant Reformation in Scotland. He oversaw the replacement of the Roman Catholic Church by a disestablished, democratic, Presbyterian Church of Scotland. Although originally ordained as a Catholic priest, Knox became a protestant after meeting the rebel preacher George Wishart (1513–1546), whose death at the stake he avenged by assisting in the murder of Cardinal Beaton. That earned Knox two years as a galley slave. Bitterly opposed by Mary, Queen of Scots, Knox was nevertheless ordained as minister of St Giles Kirk in Edinburgh (in 1559), and renowned for his fiery preaching. He died in Edinburgh in 1572.

The good news for 19th century children was no Naughty Step. But there was bad news: poor behaviour was blamed on sluggish bowels, so they were force-fed Epsom Salts. Edinburgh's Museum of Childhood charts this and other changes in child-rearing since children were 'to be seen and not heard'. The museum was ironically set up by child-hater Joseph Patrick Murray, who once caused outrage with a proposed memorial window to 'Good King Herod' the famous child slaughterer.

It's now pleasingly child-friendly, apart from a few too many *Don't Touch* signs: buggies can be left at the entrance, there are steps to help smaller ones see higher-up exhibits and activities including teddy bear colouring-in. Children will love the potted history of Thomas (*The Tank Engine*), although there was disappointment (huge tantrum) when our daughter couldn't find Toby. Look out for a particularly creepy collection of waxen dolls with black glass eyes and real human hair on the 2nd floor. The real nightmare-causers are dolls 4, 8 (withered arm) and 12. Elsewhere the nostalgic sweets collection is a must for 30-somethings not quite over the absence of Mojos in their lives, as is the collection of Taliban-approved Victorian board games: anyone for a game of Virtue Rewarded, Vice Punished?

Open *Mon–Sat 10am–5pm, Sunday 12pm–5pm.* ***Adm*** *free.* ***Amenities*** *baby-changing.*

Our Dynamic Earth

*Holyrood Road, 01315 507800, **www.dynamicearth.co.uk**.*

Set beneath the volcanic rock formation known as Arthur's Seat, this museum is appropriately dedicated to the natural forces of the world. Resembling a mini-Millennium Dome, it gives visitors the opportunity to journey back to the Big Bang, crash into a volcano, wander through a rainforest, experience an earthquake, and come face-to-face with a dinosaur. That said, our daughter's favourite exhibit was a giant block of ice that we had to stop her from licking like a giant Mini Milk, and she was a little scared of the beetle the size of a mouse in the

FUN FACT

One Cuddly President

Ever wondered how the teddy bear became so popular? Thank former US president Teddy Roosevelt, whose refusal to shoot a bear cub presented to him on a Mississippi hunting trip made the papers. In 1902 the incident was immortalised in cartoons by Clifford K. Berryman in the *Washington Post*. It gave New York shopkeepers, Morris and Rose Michtom, a great idea. They made a replica of the bear to display in their shop, naming it Teddy after the president. It was such a hit that they changed their shop's name to Teddy and went on to found the Ideal Toy and Novelty Company.

Our Dynamic Earth

jungle thunderstorm room. There are loads of interactive exhibits and gizmos to keep children busy plus Vasco Energy Boost Children's Lunchboxes available in the café (which has great views of the Scottish Parliament and Salisbury Crags).

The only quibble is when you're outside 90 minutes later...it's a little hard to know where you go after you've looked through the Hubble telescope to the beginning of creation. Somehow it doesn't quite cut it to suggest, 'We'll go back to the hotel now, shall we? I think *The Treacle People* might be on.'

***Open** Apr–Oct 10am–5pm, July–Aug 10am–6pm, Nov–Mar 10–5pm (closed Mon and Tues). Last entry always an hour and a half before closing. **Adm** £8.95, children (5–15) £5.75, under-5s £1.95. **Amenities** café.*

Palace of Holyroodhouse

Canongate, The Royal Mile, 01315 565100, www.royalcollection.org.uk

Opposite the new Scottish Parliament, and set against the spectacular backdrop of Arthur's Seat, the Queen's official summer residence in Scotland is a good place to catch up on Royal history, and see if you spot any of her things lying about. (We saw an empty packet of Revels on a chair in the Great Gallery but they probably belonged to the security guard).

Founded in 1498 by James IV, the palace has witnessed many dramatic episodes, in Mary, Queen of Scots' life in particular. She was crowned and also witnessed the stabbing to death of her Italian secretary David Rizzio here. Her apartments, including the spot Rizzio was knived 57 times, are open to visitors although blood-thirsty buggy-pushers (me) will be disappointed. There are 25 steep, narrow steps to ascend and no lift. Perhaps the ghoulish lock of Mary, Queen of Scot's hair on display here that's mellowed from ginger to strawberry blonde with the passing of the years can make up for this. (No – I wanted to see the murder scene).

The Palace is as formal as you'd expect from a lived-in royal residence, so beware of officious security, who, when not scoffing

Mary, Queen of Scots

1 Mary, Queen of Scots was the first woman to practise golf in Scotland. She had a good short game, but caused a scandal when she was seen stepping out of a bunker at St Andrews within days of her husband Lord Darnley's murder.
2 It took three swings of the executioner's axe to sever Mary's head. To the horror of the crowd, her body then started to move, although it was just her pet terrier, Geddon, who had wisely hidden under her gown throughout the proceedings.
3 The crucifix she carried, and her bloodstained clothes, and even the block she lay her head on, were burned at Fotheringhay Castle because the authorities wanted no relics.
4 Mary was actually a babe. Very pretty, over 6ft tall and not at all as ugly as her portraits suggest, she had an active social life and liked to dress up as a stable boy and escape at night into the streets of Edinburgh incognito to party.

Revels, will be on your little ones before you can say 'Off With Their Heads' if they dart across the cropped lawns of the palace courtyard. We had a muddled Benny Hill scene here that went down so badly I thought we might end up in the tolbooth.

A simplified audio tour livens things up for youngsters, and make sure you ask for the family activity bag including questions for children to answer as they go round, to keep them occupied and thus guard against them, say, wiping jam on the Darnley Jewel. There are sometimes seasonal children's activities in the palace coach-house including plaster-casting and Christmas craft making. The ruins of the 12th century abbey where Mary, Queen of Scots was married make for a pleasant wander before lunch and recriminations at the Mews Courtyard.

Open *Nov–Mar 9.30am–4.30pm, Apr–Oct 9.30am–6pm.* ***Adm*** *£9.50, under-17s £5.50, under-5s free. Family (two adults, three under-17s) £24.50.* ***Amenities*** *audioguide.*

Parliament House

Parliament Square, 01312 252595, ***www.scotscourts.gov.uk****.*

The seat of Scottish Government until the 1707 Act of Union with England, Parliament House now accommodates Scotland's Criminal Court of Appeal and the Court of Session. It's open to the public and accessed via a metal detector in the lobby (our double-buggy was waved through after a quick check of a Petit Filou yoghurt).

The main draw is the magnificent hammerbeam roofed Parliament Hall, home to some fine Henry Raeburn portraits but more interesting as a hangout for lawyers, who can be seen in multiple tandems pacing up and down the long empty room with clients in tow like swimmers doing lengths at a municipal bath. They're discussing cases and keep on the move for privacy, although you can, if you sit on the benches at the sides, hear passing fragments. I was sure I heard the word 'poison' and also 'you killed her', whereas my wife who is slightly deaf in one ear maintains I've been watching too much of the Scottish TV crime series *Taggart* and that the words were actually 'person' and 'your kilt, sir'. Although children aren't encouraged to sprint towards the Great South Window shouting 'Eeeeeeee', while waving a yoghurty spoon there is no one to stop them.

Also based here is the National Library of Scotland, whose literary treasures include the letters of Mary, Queen of Scots, and the original manuscripts of both Sir Walter Scott's *Waverley* and Charles Darwin's *Origin of the Species*.

Open *10am–4pm Mon–Fri.* ***Adm*** *free.*

Parliament House

The Edinburgh Dungeons

*31 Market St, 01312 401000, **www.thedungeons.com**.*

Not for the faint-hearted, here you'll be exposed to torture, witchcraft, grave robbing and the plague, as well as possibly being whipped by a length of small intestine. The tongue-in-cheek attraction (definitely not for toddlers) tells the story of Edinburgh's gory past through live actors. Your journey begins in a 17th century court of law where a mad judge hauls visitors into the dock to accuse them of

Tour the Royal Mile

One of the best ways for an overview of the Royal Mile is on a Mercat Tour (*0131 2255445*, ***www.mercattours.com***). Their 'Secrets of the Royal Mile' tour includes the original Parliament Hall, the High Kirk of St Giles and some lesser-known attractions. The friendly guide was even patient when our hungry baby piped up at inopportune moments and our toddler decided to run away near the David Hume statue. Tickets can be bought online, at the Mercat Cross office, which closes at 6pm, or the Tourist Information Centre at Princes Mall. Princes St. Tours begin at the Mercat Cross next to St Giles Cathedral.

FUN FACT An Unusual Horse

In the centre of Parliament Square off the Royal Mile is a lead statue of King Charles II mounted on a horse. It was one of the earliest equestrian statues in Britain, but didn't agree with the Scottish weather. Soon after it was installed its joints began to crack. The statue filled up with rainwater and appeared to bulge. To drain it, workmen bored holes underneath but made the mistake of doing so at the rear of the animal and on a Sunday morning just as the High Kirk ladies were leaving St Giles. Affronted by the spectacle, the controversy raged for weeks. Hence the statue's nickname, 'The Peeing Horse'.

an array of crimes (when we were there a school child was accused of 'mincing' down Princes Street), the guilty verdict for which is nearly always death. Elsewhere you'll be accosted by cannibal Sawney Bean, stand in a burning croft during the Glencoe Massacre, get lost in a haunted labyrinth and witness the horrifically bloody dissection of a corpse at an anatomy theatre. Expect an alarming amount of audience participation with the impressively hideous actors not averse to shouting abuse. As well as being whipped with a piece of small intestine in the anatomy room, I was called a minger to the delight of my young nephew I took along who, like the rest of the school children here, threw himself wholeheartedly into the fun, booing and hissing and actually answering back on my behalf. 'He's been doing the 3am bottle feed, he's tired – leave him alone.' You actually used to be able to get in for free if you passed an Ugly Test on the door and although this no longer applies (perhaps a mixed blessing for me) there are often half-price deals on tickets (particularly at *www.lastminute.com*). The church not so long ago tried to ban this attraction for promoting Satanism, although in fact it is a great piece of pantomime.

***Open** Nov–9th Mar Mon–Fri 11am–4pm, weekends 10.30am–4pm, 10th Mar–29th June daily 10am–5pm, 30th June–2nd Sept daily 10am–7pm, 3rd Sept–26th Oct 10am–5pm, 27th Oct–31st Oct 10am–6pm. **Adm** £12.95, children (5–14) £8.95.*

The Scottish Parliament

*Horse Wynd, 01313 485000, **www.scottishparliament.uk**.*

This is worth a visit if only to have an opinion of Scotland's most controversial building. Popular with architects – it won the Stirling Prize in 2005 – its expense (£450 million) upset many. Designed by Catalan architect Enric Miralles, it is made almost entirely from Scotland's finest raw materials (not including shortbread). The design was based on Miralles dropping a leafy twig onto a white piece of paper.

Tours take in the debating chamber where you can see the ceremonial mace inscribed with the most admirable Scottish virtues – wisdom, compassion, justice and integrity, though strangely but appropriately in this case, not thrift. They also include the committee rooms and the futuristic garden lobby with its fabulous skylighting.

If your children aren't that interested in the difference between reserved and devolved powers, and if you are a bit hungry, there's a free 10-place crèche for children aged 6 weeks to 5 years old (maximum stay four hours) operating 8am–6pm (*01313 486192*). Now we are not suggesting that anybody do this, although there is nothing to stop them, but people (not us or necessarily you) could leave their child (who they love but might want a tiny bit of time away from) in the free crèche and, instead of listening to a debate on the local governance bill or going on the Parliament tour, they could, although as we say we're not suggesting it, go for lunch on the Royal Mile. Where we are not suggesting anybody go for lunch is Mai Tai, round the corner on Holyrood Road, for beef in coconut milk and cold Singha beer.

The Scottish Parliament, which we now think deserved the Stirling Prize and all that money, has guided tours (one hour) on non-business days: Monday, Friday, and weekends. Arrive 20 minutes early.

***Tours** 10.20am–2.40pm weekends all year, weekdays 1st Apr–31st Oct 10.20am–4.40pm, 1st Nov–30th Mar 10.20am–2.40pm. **Adm** free. Tours £5, children 5–16 £3, under-5s free. **Amenities** baby-changing, crèche (free), disabled access.*

New Town

Because the New Town was built during the 18th century reign of Hanoverian King George III, after the failed Jacobite Uprisings, many of the streets have a purposeful connection with the British monarch. Names were chosen to stamp his identity on the people of Edinburgh: George

The Scottish Parliament

Princes Street Gardens

Street, Hanover Street, Frederick Street, Charlotte Square, Queen Street (both named after the king's wife, Queen Charlotte), and Princes Street after King George's sons.

Scott Monument

*East Princes Street Gardens, 01315 294068, **www.cac.org.co.uk**.*

Ever felt you deserved a medal for your sightseeing efforts? Those with the stamina/pigheadedness to take on the 287 steps to the top of the Sir Walter Scott Monument don't quite get a medal to mark their achievement but a certificate to put on their wall, or maybe give to their orthopaedic surgeon to explain the fused knee joints. On your way up, pause and, while your breathful daughter scampers on ahead shouting 'Come ON daddy,' like you're some ailing pit pony, take a look at the 64 niches built into the monument and wonder if it's all worth it (the climb, life, having children). Each niche contains a statuette of a character from a Scott story.

***Open** Apr–Sep Mon–Sat 9am–6pm, Sun 10am–6pm, Oct–Mar Mon–Sat 9am–3pm, Sun 10am–3pm. **Adm** £3.*

The National Gallery Complex

*The Mound, 01316 246560, **www.nationalgalleries.org**.*

Conjoined below ground with the Royal Scottish Academy, the complex is home to masterpieces spanning the history of painting, by Raphael, Titian, Diego Velázquez, Rembrandt van Rijn, Peter Paul Rubens, Vincent Van Gogh, Claude Monet, Paul Cézanne, Edgar Degas and Paul Gauguin. All the major Scottish names, including portrait painters Allan Ramsay, Henry Raeburn and David Wilkie, and landscape artist William McTaggart, are also represented.

FUN FACT

Did You Know?

Princes Street Gardens used to be a lake – Nor' Loch – where in 1502 there was a device for ducking fornicators and testing for witchcraft. The witches were 'dooked', thrown in with their thumbs tied to their big toes. If they sank and drowned they were innocent, if they floated they were guilty and burnt at the stake. When the city authorities drained the loch around 1760, they removed mounds of skeletons.

On the first Sunday in the month the gallery hosts Art Cart, a hands-on activity programme between 2pm and 4pm for youngsters aged 3 to 12. On some Saturdays an Art Club taken by professional artists involves painting, printing and crafts aimed at 5–7-year-olds.

***Open** daily 10am–5pm (Thurs to 7pm). **Adm** free. **Amenities** baby-changing, café, disabled access.*

Further Out of Town

Edinburgh Butterfly and Insect World

*Dobbies Garden World, Melville Nursery, Lasswade, 01316 634932, **www.edinburgh-butterfly-world.co.uk**. City bypass at Gilmerton/Sheriffhall. Lothian Bus 3 or First Bus 28.*

Here you can handle tarantulas, pythons and stick insects, watch a colony of leafcutter ants and have multicoloured butterflies land on your head (a nice image until you learn it's to drink your sweat). Next to a garden centre 20 minutes by car from the city, the centre runs reptile and insect daily handling sessions at 12pm and 3pm, and Friday afternoons you can watch pythons being fed. Not to be missed is the leafcutter ant area, where the insects slice up and then transport an array of multicoloured leaves from one room to the next via a rope ladder above your head (it's a little like that clever squirrel advert for Carling Black Label). Other highlights include walking among hundreds of free-flying butterflies, the glow-in-the-dark scorpions and Milly the giant millipede. For arachnophobes (like my wife: also scared of tortoises, cats and a bug-eyed face I sometimes pull during horror films) there are free sessions with a Human Insect Liaison Officer on curing spider fear, something I failed to interest her in despite/because of creeping up behind her with a tarantula in a large bucket and going 'ahhhhhh-haaa'.

***Open** 31st Mar–31st Oct 9.30am–5pm, 1 Nov–30 Mar 10pm–5pm. Adm £5 (children £3.85).*

Edinburgh Zoo

*134 Corstorphine Rd, 01313 349171, **www.edinburghzoo.org.uk**. Bus: 12, 26, 31 from Princes Street.*

Many visitors come to this home to more than 1,000 animals simply for the Emperor penguins. They parade *Happy Feet*-style each afternoon over the zoo lawns

FUN FACT An Officer & a Penguin

On a visit to the annual Edinburgh Tattoo, Lieutenant Nils Egelien of the Norwegian King's Guard became so interested in the zoo's penguins that when the Guards returned in 1972, his unit adopted one. Named Nils Olav in honour of himself and King Olav V of Norway, it was given the rank of lance corporal. Nils was, of course, promoted each time the Guards returned to the Tattoo and made sergeant by 1987. When Nils Olav died he was replaced by Nils Olav II, his two-year-old double, who was promoted in 1993 to regimental sergeant major and in 2005 to Colonel-in-Chief.

following their keeper around for fishy rewards. The zoo opened in 1909 and was the first in the UK to show penguins. Among the 120 here is one who (and I'm not saying they'd be easy to beat in a war) is a Colonel-In Chief of the Norwegian Army (see 'An Officer & a Penguin', above).

As well as the usual suspects – giraffes, lions, tigers, chimps, crocodiles, gorillas, rhinos, hippos, camels, kangaroos, wallabies, pandas – they have blue frogs whose poison skin Columbian tribes use to make arrowheads.

The zoo has over 33 hectares of parkland and is built into a steep incline, so buggy pushing is exhausting. Instead, take the free hilltop safari train (first at 10am, last at 3.30pm, leaving from outside the sea-lion enclosure; with commentary). There are plenty of other activities, including play-parks. We spent about an hour in the one opposite the red ruffed lemur enclosure trying to persuade our daughter that maybe a rare Siberian tiger once on the precipice of extinction was more interesting than, say,

Emperor penguins at Edinburgh Zoo

crossing a rope bridge for the 18th time on your bum. 'Close Encounter' sessions allow visitors near to the friendlier small mammals, insects, snakes and lizards. You can also meet rangers to ask about their jobs, the feistier animals, and whether they like Smarties lollies (our daughter's question). The zoo is home to the UK's only polar bear, Mercedes, who's been alone since her original partner Barney choked to death on a plastic toy thrown into the enclosure by a young visitor. Now more than 20-years-old, Mercedes is the subject of a freedom campaign by animal rights groups angered at her enclosure – roughly, they say, one millionth the area polar bears roam in the wild.

Open *daily Apr–Sep 9am–6pm, Oct–Mar 9am–5pm, Nov–Feb 9am–4.30pm.* ***Adm*** *£10.50, children (3–14) £7.50, under-3s free. Family ticket (two adults, two children £34; two adults, three children £38.50).* ***Amenities*** *baby-changing, parking (£2), two restaurants (children's lunchboxes £3.50).*

The Royal Yacht Britannia

Ocean Terminal, Leith, ☎ 01315 555566, ***www.royalyachtbritannia.co.uk****. Bus: 11, 22, 34, 03, 35.*

The Royal Yacht *Britannia* served the British Royal Family for over 40 years, voyaging a million nautical miles to become the most famous ship in the world. As well as hosting hundreds of state visits, Prince Charles and Princess Diana spent their honeymoon on board in 1981.

Launched in 1953, the *Britannia* continued an unbroken Royal Yacht tradition going back 300 years to the reign of Charles II, and was last used to withdraw the final British governor from Hong Kong in 1997. That said, the yacht is more interesting for children (OK, me) because of the windbreak on the balcony deck designed to prevent a rogue breeze lifting royal skirts.

Buggy access is good and the audio tour, conducted at our pace (zigzagging back and forth depending on what our daughter wanted to see/lean dangerously over), gives a fascinating insight into the queen's private tastes. Her bedroom, with its simple 1950s-style décor, looks not unlike a Travelodge. The ship's company serving her Majesty – an admiral and 250 yachtsmen – were subject to exacting standards. The yacht's Burmese teak decks were scrubbed each day and all work near the royal rooms had to be carried out by 8am in total silence. A thermometer was kept in the Queen's bathroom to ensure the water was always the correct temperature.

Open *daily Apr–Oct 9.30am–4.30pm, Nov–Mar 10am–3.30pm (last entry).* ***Adm*** *£9.50, children £5.50 (under-5s free).* ***Amenities*** *baby-changing, guided tour.*

INSIDER TIP

To avoid queues, especially in August, pre-book on the telephone number above.

FAMILY-FRIENDLY ACCOMMODATION

EXPENSIVE

Paramount Carlton Hotel

*19 Northbridge, 01314 723000, **www.paramount-hotels.co.uk/carlton**.*

This hotel is handy for the Royal Mile, and has a great attitude to children, even when you ring down at 5.30am and request warm milk 'that's not too hot nor too cold, if you see what I mean'. There's a swimming pool with floats, and on check-in children are given a 'Bear Brigade' hamper including crayons, a balloon, colouring-in books and a passport book that's completed by finding bear logos around the hotel. Top marks, too, to the concierge who recommended child-friendly places to visit and eat, while kindly slipping us a free parking pass (usually £15.50) after taking pity on us, so loaded down it looked like we were fleeing a flash flood.

If you have energy left after a day's sightseeing with recently potty-trained youngsters, there are squash courts, a jacuzzi, and a gym I headed for once but never made because of an enticing sign for the Bridge Bar. Southern rooms have views of Edinburgh Castle, eastern ones Arthur's Seat, and at the Bridge restaurant children accompanied by two paying adults eat free from the children's menu.

***Rates** double/twin rooms £70–200 (an extra z-bed £40). Interconnecting rooms (one double and single) £105–210. **Credit** AmEx, MC, V. **Amenities** gym, restaurant, spa, sauna, bar, laundry, parking (£15.50/night), pool. **In room** TV, Internet, free paper, safe.*

The Balmoral Hotel

*1 Princes Street, 01315 576727, **www.the balmoralhotel.com**.*

If Howard Hughes had been a little girl aged three this is where he'd have chosen to go insane. The Balmoral was our daughter's favourite hotel in Edinburgh and maybe the whole of Scotland. It was so good, that when conversation comes up about who'd look after our children if we both died, my answer has changed from my sister, who'd welcome them as her own, to the Balmoral Hotel for their Junior Accessories. For weeks after our stay we felt emotionally traumatised by the absence of a teddy turndown service in our daughter's life and I admit, the whisky turndown service (a bedside glass of single malt 12-year-old Glenallarchie Speyside whisky) in mine.

In our room, waiting for us, there was a bag of baby toys, a bottle warmer, steriliser, a changing mat and a stack of different sized nappies that we felt like lying on the bed and flinging in the air like stolen money. For our daughter there was a huge box of toys, a book (*The Gruffalo*) and, in the bathroom, a Balmoral plastic duck, children's bubble bath, and a fluffy white dressing gown with slippers she sat in while watching a DVD of *Ice Age*. Before dinner a bellhop delivered her a complimentary banana split

A stunning suite in the Balmoral Hotel

and after dinner (see p. 52) we returned to the room to discover the turndown services – a Balmoral teddy bear under our daughter's covers in a dressing gown like hers and my whisky. The following morning I took our daughter on the Balmoral quiz that involved a fun scoot round the hotel while my wife indulged herself in the candlelit relaxation suite. For teens, there is a Play Station II, headphones for a PSII as well as a complimentary Internet card. Boys get a free baseball cap, girls a French manicure and pink polish. There are board games, a what's on newsletter, DVDs and books including the full Harry Potter series in honour of the fact J.K. Rowling completed *Harry Potter and the Deathly Hallows* here in the hotel (Room 522, if you fancy a snoop).

Rates *interconnecting classic rooms £360–880, deluxe suite (bedroom, lounge capable of sleeping two children plus a cot) £995. Executive doubles £180–440.* ***Credit*** *AmEx, MC, V.* ***Amenities*** *two restaurants, swimming pool, champagne bar, resident pianist* ***In room*** *TV, DVD player, Internet access, air conditioning.*

The Scotsman Hotel

20 North Bridge, 01315 565565, ***www.thescotsmanhotel.co.uk****.*

This hotel is so posh you don't even open the door to room service – your chocolate muffin is posted through a service hatch for you to retrieve when the bellboy you might otherwise have to speak to has scuttled away. Based in the grand old *Scotsman* newspaper building and still retaining much of its original charm – you can stay in an oak-panelled room that was the editor's office – this is a great place to treat your family. There are interconnecting rooms in the Baron's Suite and the Publisher's suite sleeps two adults and up to two children. Each room comes with the Edinburgh Monopoly boardgame encased into a coffee table and on the lower-ground floor, where printing presses used to shake the building's foundations, there's a fitness centre where middle-aged men now try and do the same with star jumps. There's a pool although children are admitted only between 9am–midday and 2–5pm. The 'Full Scottie' breakfast with Finnan haddock comes with a newspaper-style menu for your former sub-editor wife to scour for typos.

***Rates** Baron's Suite £820. Publisher's suite £520 per night. **Amenities** spa, two restaurants, brasserie and bar, pool. **In room** TV, DVD, Internet.*

INSIDER TIP

If you're here on a Saturday, wander down to The Meadows between 10am and 6pm where you'll find the **Cheesee Peasee** cheese van, selling French cheeses at French prices.

MODERATE

Aonach Mor Guest House

*14 Kilmaurs Tce, 01316 678694, **www.aonachmor.com.***

Nestled beneath the Salisbury Crags, this recent winner of the AA Egg Cup award for its breakfasts is near Prestonfield House Hotel, with its substantial grounds, highland cattle and roaming peacocks, among which your children are free to wander or chase fruitlessly after with a squeaky plastic hammer.

The guesthouse, with WiFi (and a laptop you can borrow), has one large family room on the first floor with oblique views of Arthur's Seat and two smaller rooms sleeping up to three. Fluffy towels and pamper products from Molton Brown provide a touch of luxury; the children's TV station CBeebies is available and games are kept behind reception, although it's the breakfast which sets this hotel apart. Black pudding, haggis, steamy porridge, smoked salmon, haddock, pancakes and chocolate chip rolls made by the owner, a professional chef, come with the room rate. In winter the lounge has a fire you can fall asleep in front of and/or discuss the best Cheesee Peasee van jingle you can think of.

***Rates** large family room (one double, two twin beds) £85–140, smaller family room £80–100. **Amenities** free on-street parking, gardens, WiFi. **In room** TV.*

The Inverleith Hotel

*5 Inverleith Terrace, 01315 562745, **www.inverleithhotel.co.uk.***

This elegant Georgian town-house with views across the Royal Botanical Gardens and close to The Meadows has a self-catering apartment on the first floor with two bedrooms, a lounge and a small well-equipped kitchen. There are also two family rooms, and two doubles with a sealable private corridor.

A supermarket is nearby for emergencies (wipes, formula, Pinot Grigio) and highchairs are available for the full Scottish breakfast in the beautiful dining room. Car parking is free on-street over weekends and overnight, and metered the rest of the time (£4.30 for nine hours).

Rates** self-catering apartment £89–175. Family room (one double two singles) £75–159 (one double, one single £69–149). Two doubles, private corridor £89–175. **Amenities

baby-sitting (£5 per hour), bar, parking (on-street), WiFi. ***In room*** *cot (£10), hairdryer, cable TV.*

INEXPENSIVE

A-Haven Townhouse

*180 Ferry Road, 01315 546559, **www.a-haven.co.uk**.*

This family-friendly B&B is a stone's throw from Victoria Park, where you'll find the best children's play area in the city. A 19th century semi-detached property, it has two family rooms each with a double and two single beds, although best is room 8 on the 2nd floor. It has views of Arthur's Seat and Castlehill. More importantly, if your toddler requires the following conversation about the Night Garden before bed: 'Iggle-piggle's going to sleep.' 'Shall we go to sleep?' 'NO!'... it's the only room with the CBeebies children's TV channel. Telephone numbers for registered child-minders (£5 per hour) are available or baby monitors are in range if you fancy hanging out child-free in the lounge, or taking a nip or two of Macallan single-malt at the resident's bar to unwind/fall asleep in after jibbering emotionally to two strangers from Dundee about the history of orange marmalade. Children's toys are behind reception and there's a back garden for that pre-bath tire-them-out-and-they'll-sleep- piece of wishful thinking. Full Scottish breakfast means just that.

Rates *£30 per person, (under-5s free).* ***Amenities*** *baby-sitting (£5 per hour), bar, free gated parking.* ***In room*** *TV.*

Drum Mohr Caravan and Camping Park

*Levenhall, Musselburgh, 01316 656867, **www.drummohr.org**.*

An excellent alternative to paying exorbitant festival rates, this campsite with views of the Firth of Forth even has two chalets with private Big Brother-style hot tubs. Family-run and within the walled grounds of a former monastery, its tranquil atmosphere survives.

Wooden chalets are six- or four-berth with TVs, DVDs, bed linen and everything except tea towels. There's a walk to the shingle beach about 1km away; although we didn't spot the seals often in the Forth, thrillingly for our daughter the campsite was over-run with rabbits which she got up especially early (5am) to shout at. There is a shop onsite selling everything from wine to fresh croissants, as well as home-baked bread for the sandwiches your children won't eat later because they've had too many Chocolate Gems again.

For the city centre take bus 26 (every 10 minutes, hourly after midnight); it's 40 minutes to Princes Street.

Rates *6-berth chalet (double, two twin rooms) £300–700 per week. 4-berths (double, one twin) £300–600. Short breaks Fri–Sun or Mon–Thurs for 6-berth chalets start at £200 and 4-berths £150.* ***Open*** *Mar–end Oct only.* ***Amenities*** *shop, TV/DVD, laundry, play area.*

The Original Raj Hotel

*6 West Coates, 01313 461333, **www.rajempire.com***

The first British hotel to be themed around the Indian Raj, this former Victorian house has a three-ton white marble elephant outside if you get lost looking for it. It is tastefully decorated in an Indian style (i.e no flock wallpaper) and there is a rickshaw in the front garden that children like to climb.

In the main family room, the Bollywood Suite, there's a double bed and two twins. The continental breakfast at weekends, if you can stomach it, includes onion bhajis and samosas. There's no bar or restaurant but the hotel does offer a free mehndhi service. Your children can get decorative flower designs painted with henna paste on their hands and feet (or even 'a big lion going ahh' on your leg – our daughter's request).

Rates *£60 for a double and a twin, £70 for a double with two twins.* ***Amenities*** *children's activities.* ***In room*** *cots, TV.*

University of Edinburgh Pollok Halls of Residence

*23 Warrender Park Crescent, 01316 512184, **www.edinburghfirst.com**.*

Student accommodation is different from when we slept in pokey dorms under posters of Che Guevara (although, politically naïve, my wife actually had one of Dennis Healy). Nowadays students live in modern self-catering apartments rented by tourists during summer term that provide a fantastic budget alternative during the festival. The university has several 3–6-bed flats throughout the city but best for families is the converted Victorian school a short walk from The Meadows, where in August circus acts practise their skills. The flats are carefully prepared so don't worry about Blu-tac marks on the walls or rotting maggi noodles under your bed.

All rooms are singles but an extra bed can be added for couples. Facilities include a living room with a dining table, and a basic kitchen (no microwave or washing machine). There's no TV, but they can be hired for £25 a week from local firm Tellycare and delivered well in time for that night's episode of *Taggart*.

There's no lift but ground floor rooms are available. To ensure accommodation in August, book by January.

Rates *per week for 3-bedroom apartments £340–530, 4-bed £360–570, 5-bed £380–610.* ***Open*** *June–Aug only.* ***Credit*** *MC, V.* ***Amenities*** *concierge 9am–10pm, emergency number after that, laundry, parking.* ***In apartment*** *cot (free), kitchen (basic), phone.*

FAMILY-FRIENDLY DINING

Brodie's Tavern

435 Lawnmarket, 01312 256531.

This traditional pub is named after its most famous drinker, William Brodie, who by day was a town councillor and deacon of the Cabinetmakers Guild and by night a thief and gambler.

Thought to be the inspiration behind Robert Louis Stevenson's *Dr Jekyll and Mr Hyde*, Brodie made wax key impressions while working in the homes of wealthy citizens so he could return at night to burgle them. When he was caught in 1788, he was sentenced to hang on the gallows he'd ironically designed and built himself.

The location makes this a noisy bar; the restaurant upstairs is quieter. On your way up check out the model of the fickle scoundrel in 18th century garb dressed half-respectably and half-disreputably. The pub is also, according to staff, haunted by a poltergeist, or at least that's what they claim when they smash a glass.

Try the haggis in a hoagie bun, my wife's was excellent, and although I cringed saying the word, so was my Ploughperson's. For a bit of fun during your meal wildly compliment its tastiness, and then change your tune when dessert arrives and claim it's absolutely disgusting. Staff will never have heard a Jekyll and Hyde gag before and will think you're hilarious.

Open *10am–midnight Sun–Thurs, 10am–1am Fri and Sat. Food served in the bar 10am–10pm, in the restaurant noon–10pm.* ***Credit*** *AmEx, MC, V.* ***Amenities*** *children's portions (noon–9.30pm), highchairs.*

Est Est Est

135a George St, 01312 252555, ***www.estestestedinburgh.5pm.co.uk***

Children 'make' their own pizzas here, or at least arrange in their very own artistic way their choice of toppings (always creating a human face with a pepper mouth). The idea of involving children in meal preparation is that they're less likely to complain when it arrives that 'it's disgusting', which worked with our daughter, who ate all the pizza face (bar the crusts) she'd made mainly with trumpet mushrooms. The concept backfired, however, when she then refused to take off the paper chef's hat that came with her Bambini Box and started bossing other diners on how they should consume pan-fried calves liver (with trumpet mushrooms arranged in the shape of a face) and tomato braised meatballs with fresh tagliatelle (with trumpet mushrooms arranged in the shape of a face).

Mick Jagger was famously turned away from here because the restaurant was full or maybe because there wasn't enough red pepper for him to make a likeness of his lips.

Open *daily noon–11pm (make your own pizza available until 6pm only).* ***Credit*** *V, MC, AmEx.* ***Amenities*** *baby-changing, children's menu (£5.95), highchairs.*

Hadrian's Brasserie

The Balmoral Hotel, 1 Princes Street, 01315 575000, ***www.thebalmoralhotel.com/dining****.*

Eating here gives you an idea of what it must be like being Beyoncé's mum and dad. At one point during our toddler's spaghetti bolognaise three members of staff surrounded

Hadrian's Brasserie at the Balmoral

her attentively as part of a management initiative that has seen staff trained to deal with children. Our daughter was asked how her food was, if there was enough, if she liked crayons, what she'd done that day, and planned to do tomorrow, leaving my wife and I to enjoy the excellent food (traditional Scottish mixed with contemporary European) served by Michelin-starred chef Jeff Bland.

Beyoncé loved her bolognaise.

***Open** 12pm–2.30pm Mon–Fri, 12.30pm–2.30pm Sat, 12.30pm–3pm Sat. Dinner 6.30pm–10.30pm Mon–Sun. **Credit** AmEx, MC, V.*

Henderson's

*94 Hanover Street, 01312 252131, **www.hendersonsofedinburgh.co.uk**.*

One of the oldest wholefood cafés in Scotland, this is a popular hang-out for young mums with children. Serving gluten-free, vegan, and vegetarian options as well as 12 different salads, under the 'eat better, live better' ethos, Henderson's location and self-service make it a great place for a quick family meal between sights. Children (not served after 8pm) can help themselves to games, jigsaws and colouring-materials by the door. The atmosphere is completed by soothing jazz and, when we were here, the murmur of sci-fi buffs discussing Scot Bakula's casting as the latest Captain of the Starship Enterprise ('what I like is his sense of wonder about the universe *and* he's a renegade like Kirk').

***Open** noon–midnight Sun–Wed, noon–10.30pm Thurs–Sat. **Main courses** £5. **Credit** AmEx, MC, V. **Amenities** children's menu (£4.95).*

The Mussell Inn

61–65 Rose St, 01312 255979.

A day after eating a half-kilo pot of mussels here, our daughter banged her knee in The Museum of Childhood and instead of crying for chocolate shouted, 'I want a musssssellllll.' Owned by two west-coast shellfish farmers, we expected to find the restaurant full of fishermen in threadbare jumpers...it actually resembled a modern All Bar One. When you get bored, read up about the health benefits of mussels – low calorie, life-enhancing minerals, vitamin B12 and Omega-3 oils, and learn bivalve facts to amuse (annoy) your friends. Such as: did you know mussels can live up to 50 years? Try the kilo pot of mussels in chillies and cumin or the oysters with Gruyère cheese and bacon (half-dozen £8).

No bookings in August.

Open *daily May–Sep noon–10pm.* ***Amenities*** *children's portions, highchairs*

Ndebele African Café

57 Home Street, 01312 211141.

Frequently voted one of Edinburgh's top three cafés, the Ndebele (appropriately pronounced 'in-de-belly', and named after a peace-loving faction of the Zulu tribe) is more than a place to eat great South Africa sausages or try something out of the ordinary such as an ostrich in ale stew. The café, and upstairs deli, is like stepping onto the African continent itself. Themed on an Ndebele hut, hessian coffee sacks cover the ceiling, traditional South African biltong dries on a shelf, and one wall is a mural of a tribeswoman painting her house. There are metre-high Ndebele dolls and drums that children can play with while parents tuck into the sort of meat that makes South African rugby players what they are. Visiting choirs from Soweto sing during festival time.

Sandwiches start at £3 (children £2), and staff will mix and match ingredients to make a children's meal. Try the boerewors sausages and the Ouma rusks – used for teething babies in Africa. The deli sells more than 700 products and has become a mini-market for Africans in Scotland, who come for anything from Burkina Faso fabrics to Swaziland candles, and even a particular type of deep fried doughnut (coek) that South Africans eat as children.

Open *9am–6pm Mon–Sat, noon–6pm Sun, Aug 9am–7pm Mon–Sat.* ***Credit*** *MC, V.* ***Amenities*** *highchairs.*

The Elephant House

21 George IV Bridge, 01312 205355, ***www.elephant-house.co.uk****.*

J.K. Rowling used to drag out long coffees here while writing her first Potter at table 10, so watch for fanatics loitering around carrying wands, while discussing the funny excerpt about Voldemort on page 187. Although famous as the birthplace of Harry Potter, this hip hang-out prefers to cast its spell with its coffee and snacks (try the delicious spinach and feta in filo pastry). Children are well looked after with half-pizzas, and for those not yet bitten by the Potter bug there's also an elephant theme with more than 600 pachyderm models lining the restaurant, including a giant

FUN FACT One Popular Dog

The most frequently photographed statue in Edinburgh is not of a king, or a writer, but of a small Skye terrier. Greyfriars Bobby's statue sits by the gates of Greyfriars Kirk reminding visitors of this famously loyal dog, who wouldn't leave the graveside of his owner, policeman John Gray, after he was buried in 1858. The dog died 14 years of grave-watching later, going on to be the inspiration for a Disney film.

one our daughter insisted she be fed upon. The contemporary interior (wooden tables) and music (gentle salsa) make this a relaxing place for a break. The café will heat milk and baby food, and if you ask, talk about the time 26 Potter fans arrived en masse and ordered three coffees between them to read the latest Potter from beginning to end in one sitting.

***Open** 9am–11pm daily. **Menu** sandwich and coffee £4. **Credit** MC, V. **Amenities** baby-changing, highchairs.*

The Filling Station

233–241 High Street, 01312 262488.

Expect the Filling Station to be full of families feasting over ribs in tight clusters like miniature prides of lions. I ate so much at this American-style diner I went to sleep on my bloated stomach with my arms and legs in the air like a penguin.

The restaurant plays unimaginative homage to the American motor car – fuel pumps and steering wheels on the walls – but the food (Tex-Mex mainly) is good, while the waitresses were so smiley I began to suspect that a) they fancied me, b) had mistaken me for Art Garfunkel (that happened once), or c) (as my wife pointed out the next morning) had just been politely humouring the way I was drunkenly whispering/shouting, 'When the children are older let's hire a huge Pontiac and drive to Reno.'

There is a children's menu (frozen yoghurt instead of ice-cream is a nice touch) and our daughter was presented with colouring packs and a helium balloon to play with/accidentally released to the ceiling. Prices are reasonable and so the evening won't be a wallet-breaker.

***Open** 12pm–11.30pm Mon–Sat, 12.30pm–10.30pm Sun. **Main courses** £7.50. **Credit** AmEx, MC, V. **Amenities** children's menu (£4.45).*

The Tower

*Chambers Street, Old Town, 01312 253003, **www.tower-restaurant.com**.*

This rooftop restaurant with spectacular views of Edinburgh Castle is great for lunch after visiting the New National Museum of Scotland downstairs. The restaurant's sister operation is the Witchery (see next page) and The Tower draws the same A-list crowds. Although Catherine Zeta Jones and J.K. Rowling have eaten here, youngsters are welcome too. A good bet for children is the lemon marinated chicken breast.

The museum downstairs includes the spooky Arthur's Seat coffins containing mysterious wooden figures unearthed in 1837 and made famous in an Ian Rankin *Rebus* detective novel. There's also Dolly the Sheep, the world's first cloned mammal, stuffed and donated to the museum after her death. If you're in a hurry, enter through the main door and you'll see her on your way to the glass lifts (the museum shuts at 5pm). It wasn't this or the views that kept our daughter amused, however, it was the statue of loyal canine Greyfriars Bobby. Failing all this, surrender the good parent handbook and order a chocolate and praline fondant (£6).

Open *daily noon–11pm.* ***Main courses*** *lunch £12.95 for two courses, à la carte dinner £35.* ***Credit*** *AmEx, MC, V.* ***Amenities*** *baby-changing, children's portions, highchairs.*

The Witchery By The Castle

352 Castlehill, The Royal Mile, ☏ 01312 255613, ***www.thewitchery.com.***

The most famous eatery in Edinburgh, perhaps Scotland, has received plaudits from as diverse a crowd as Sir Andrew Lloyd Webber ('the prettiest restaurant ever') to Dannii Minogue's ('it's the perfect lust den'). The restaurant, based in a former 16th century merchant's house at the gates of Edinburgh Castle, gets its name from the spot outside where witches were burnt up until the 18th century. Inside, the atmosphere is theatrically Gothic and entirely candle-lit, with Hogwarts-style oak panelling, tapestries and antiques. It's the setting that attracts the likes of Matt Groening and Michael Douglas. However, don't expect indulgent smiles if your toddler flips a soufle to the floor in front of TV news host Jeremy Paxman.

Under-11s aren't allowed in the restaurant after 7pm and there are no highchairs, children's menu or nappy-changing, so make it an evening treat if you find a sitter. Meals can be modified to suit younger palates and the chocolate tart is good 'behave yourself' bribing material. The set lunch menu doubles

FUN FACT

Did You Know?

In the 17th and 18th centuries Scotland, Europe's biggest witch persecutor, identified more than 4,000 of them, around one-tenth of which were executed often by strangling, their bodies normally burned at the stake. Methods to uncover a witch were: 1) Confession about their pact with the devil; 2) Neighbours' testimony of a quarrel with the suspect quickly followed by personal misfortune; 3) Getting dobbed in by other witches; and 4) Carrying the mark of the devil, i.e. having some bodily blemish or insensitive spot discovered by pricking with pins, often by itinerant witch-prickers.

as a theatre supper until 7pm and post-theatre dinner at 10.30pm.

***Open** 12pm–4pm, dinner 5.30pm–11.30pm. **Main courses** set lunch menu (£12.50 for two courses) doubles as a theatre supper until 7pm and post-theatre dinner at 10.30pm. At other times à la carte dinner £35. **Credit** AmEx, MC, V.*

Mobile Dining: The Bebetel Extra

*0845 313 3794, **www.bebetel.co.uk**.*

Available only online, this Swiss-made gizmo is probably the greatest £150 you'll invest if you have young children and are planning to stay with them for any length of time in hotels. Hotels were great before kids. You got a lie in, a slap-up breakfast with the papers and a meal out in the evening. As a parent, only one of these – the meal out – is now possible. And often this is denied to you if the hotel hasn't got a baby-listening service or your baby monitor won't stretch to the restaurant from the 10th floor your room is. At the risk of sounding like an advert, the Bebetel solves this problem. I do not want to know how it works, but it does work. This is what happens. You plug one of its sockets into the telephone line and another into an electricity point. After you've tapped in your mobile phone number you can set it to three levels of noise sensitivity. You then go downstairs, order an enormous three-course meal with wine and start carousing. If there is any noise in the room the Bebetel calls your mobile. When you answer it, you hear exactly what's happening in the room and can even talk reassuringly through your phone into the room or shout, "I said no ice-cream tomorrow if there was any talking. Now go to bed. My cheese, with grapes and celery, has arrived." I'm currently writing *Frommer's England With Your Family*. I'm in a hotel in Newquay researching for it, actually eating cheese, and writing this right now with the Bebetel on. We have used it maybe 45 times so far on this trip. In only one hotel that had a strange analogue phone system did it fail to work, and then the machine bleeped to let me know this. My only regret is that when we wrote this Scotland book we did not know about Bebetel.

4 Glasgow

GLASGOW

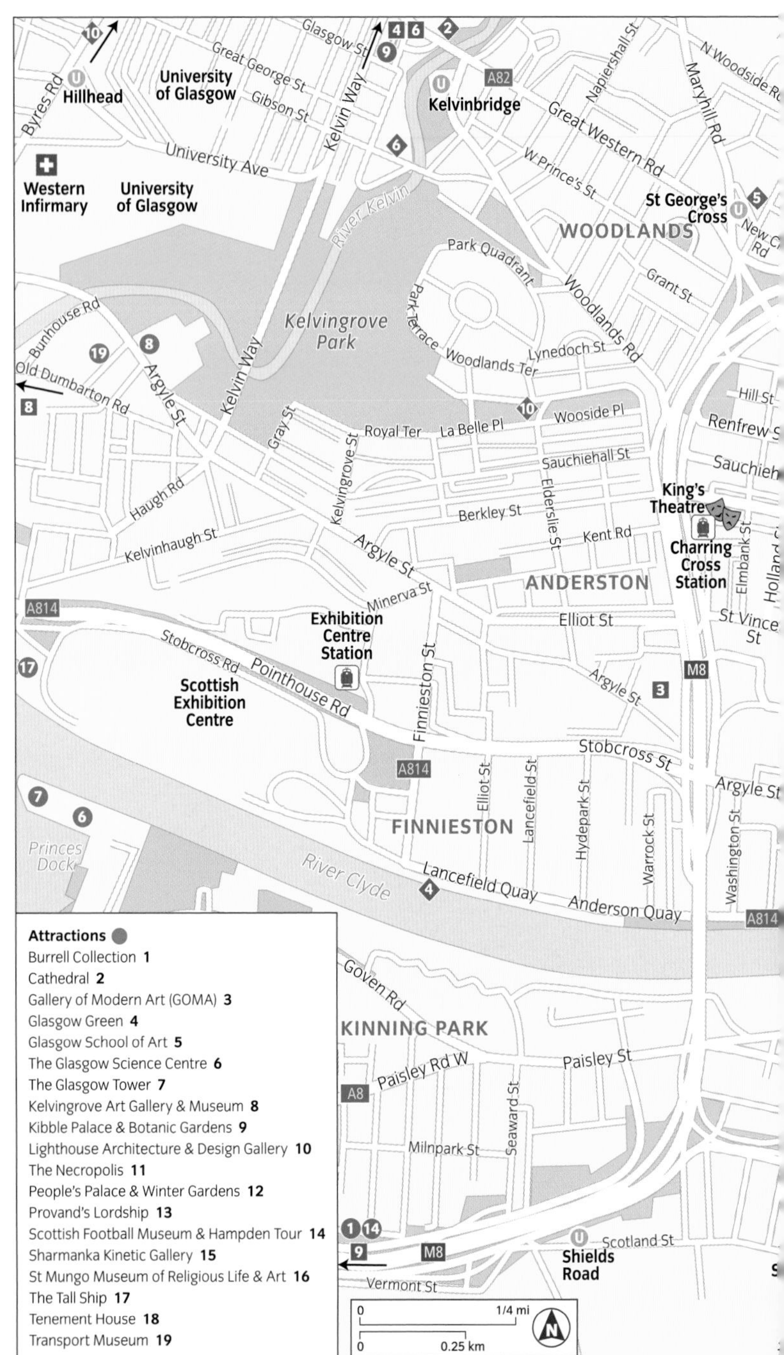
Attractions
Burrell Collection 1
Cathedral 2
Gallery of Modern Art (GOMA) 3
Glasgow Green 4
Glasgow School of Art 5
The Glasgow Science Centre 6
The Glasgow Tower 7
Kelvingrove Art Gallery & Museum 8
Kibble Palace & Botanic Gardens 9
Lighthouse Architecture & Design Gallery 10
The Necropolis 11
People's Palace & Winter Gardens 12
Provand's Lordship 13
Scottish Football Museum & Hampden Tour 14
Sharmanka Kinetic Gallery 15
St Mungo Museum of Religious Life & Art 16
The Tall Ship 17
Tenement House 18
Transport Museum 19
Hillhead
University of Glasgow
Kelvinbridge
Western Infirmary
University of Glasgow
St George's Cross
WOODLANDS
Kelvingrove Park
River Kelvin
King's Theatre
Charring Cross Station
ANDERSTON
Exhibition Centre Station
Scottish Exhibition Centre
FINNIESTON
River Clyde
Princes Dock
KINNING PARK
Shields Road
Byres Rd
Glasgow St
Great George St
Gibson St
Kelvin Way
University Ave
Great Western Rd
W Prince's St
Napiershall St
Maryhill Rd
N Woodside Rd
New City Rd
Park Quadrant
Grant St
Woodlands Rd
Park Terrace
Woodlands Ter
Lynedoch St
Bunhouse Rd
Old Dumbarton Rd
Argyle St
Gray St
Royal Ter
La Belle Pl
Wooside Pl
Hill St
Renfrew St
Sauchiehall St
Kelvingrove St
Haugh Rd
Berkley St
Elderslie St
Kent Rd
Kelvinhaugh St
Elmbank St
Minerva St
Elliot St
St Vincent St
Stobcross Rd
Pointhouse Rd
Finnieston St
Stobcross St
Elliot St
Lancefield St
Hydepark St
Warrock St
Washington St
Lancefield Quay
Anderson Quay
Goven Rd
Paisley Rd W
Paisley St
Seaward St
Milnpark St
Scotland St
Vermont St
A82
A814
M8
A8
0 1/4 mi
0 0.25 km
N

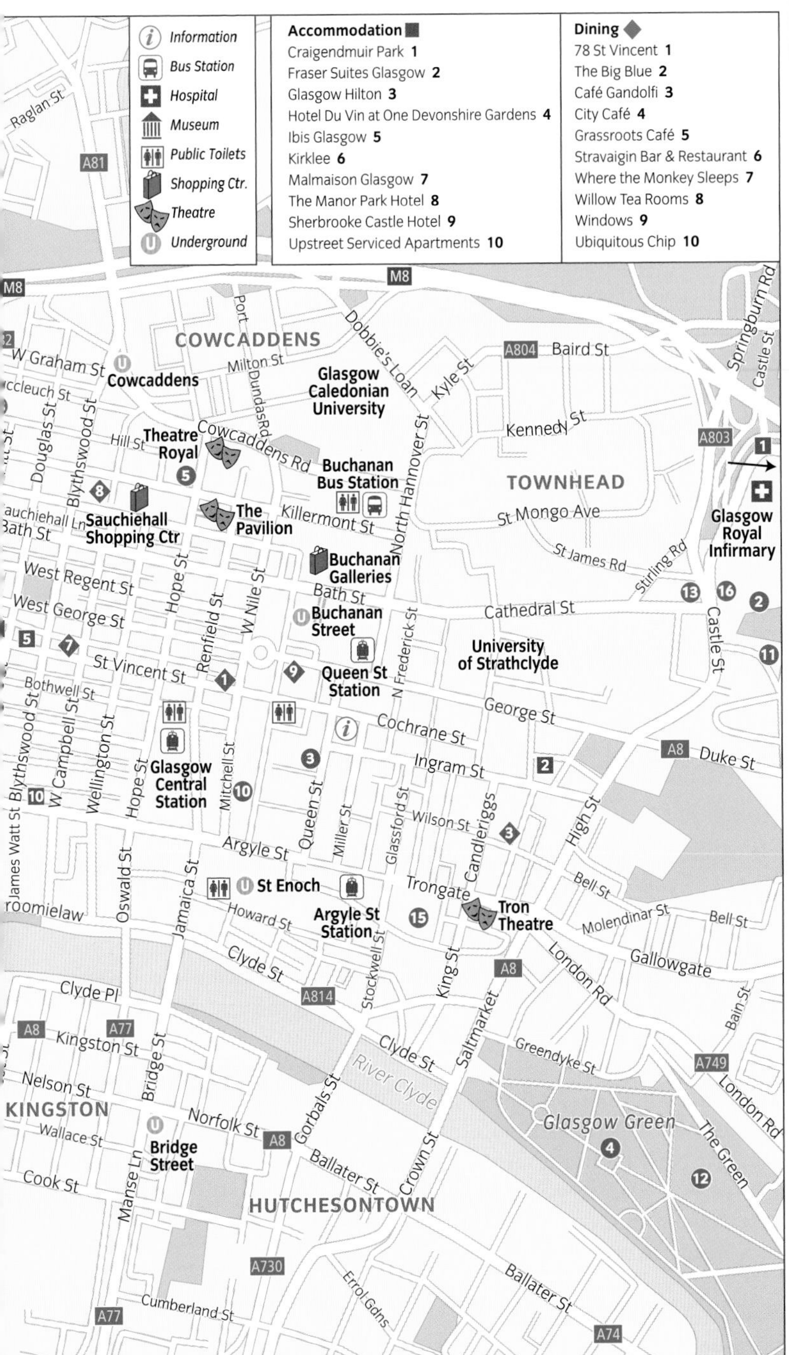
Information
Bus Station
Hospital
Museum
Public Toilets
Shopping Ctr.
Theatre
Underground
Accommodation
Craigendmuir Park 1
Fraser Suites Glasgow 2
Glasgow Hilton 3
Hotel Du Vin at One Devonshire Gardens 4
Ibis Glasgow 5
Kirklee 6
Malmaison Glasgow 7
The Manor Park Hotel 8
Sherbrooke Castle Hotel 9
Upstreet Serviced Apartments 10
Dining
78 St Vincent 1
The Big Blue 2
Café Gandolfi 3
City Café 4
Grassroots Café 5
Stravaigin Bar & Restaurant 6
Where the Monkey Sleeps 7
Willow Tea Rooms 8
Windows 9
Ubiquitous Chip 10
Raglan St
A81
M8
COWCADDENS
W Graham St
Cowcaddens
Milton St
Port Dundas Rd
Dobbie's Loan
Glasgow Caledonian University
Kyle St
A804
Baird St
Springburn Rd
Castle St
Buccleuch St
Douglas St
Blythswood St
Hill St
Theatre Royal
Cowcaddens Rd
Buchanan Bus Station
North Hannover St
Kennedy St
A803
TOWNHEAD
Sauchiehall Ln
Bath St
Sauchiehall Shopping Ctr
The Pavilion
Killermont St
St Mongo Ave
Glasgow Royal Infirmary
Buchanan Galleries
St James Rd
Stirling Rd
West Regent St
West George St
Hope St
Renfield St
W Nile St
Bath St
Buchanan Street
Cathedral St
N Frederick St
University of Strathclyde
St Vincent St
Queen St Station
Bothwell St
George St
Cochrane St
A8
Duke St
Ingram St
Blythswood St
W Campbell St
Wellington St
Hope St
Glasgow Central Station
Mitchell St
Queen St
Miller St
Glassford St
Wilson St
Candleriggs
High St
James Watt St
Argyle St
Bell St
Broomielaw
Oswald St
Jamaica St
St Enoch
Howard St
Argyle St Station
Trongate
Tron Theatre
Molendinar St
Bell St
Stockwell St
Clyde St
King St
A8
London Rd
Gallowgate
Clyde Pl
A814
Saltmarket
Bain St
A8
A77
Kingston St
Bridge St
Clyde St
Greendyke St
A749
Nelson St
River Clyde
London Rd
KINGSTON
Norfolk St
Gorbals St
Glasgow Green
The Green
Wallace St
Bridge Street
A8
Ballater St
Crown St
Cook St
Manse Ln
HUTCHESONTOWN
A730
Errol Gdns
Ballater St
Cumberland St
A77
A74

The fortunes of Scotland's most populous city – a thriving port in the 18th century and the shipbuilding and locomotive-building capital of the world in the 19th – were rescued from ruin in the 20th century not by a great leader, nor even by a government, but by Mr Happy, one of the *Mr Men* from the children's TV series. As the decline in shipbuilding and locomotive manufacture coincided with a housing shortage, Glasgow in the 1960s suffered job losses just as cramped tenements came down and rushed slum clearances fractured community spirit. The city's reputation became notorious. The desire to reinvent Glasgow in the 1980s culminated in the Glasgow's Miles Better campaign. Dogged by its dirty, dangerous image, a campaign featuring a smiling Mr Happy telling visitors that 'Glasgow's Miles Better' altered perceptions almost overnight. Optimism returned. The Scottish Exhibition and Conference Centre (SECC) opened, kicking off the redevelopment of the Clyde corridor. A year as European City of Culture in 1990 proved a further catalyst for change.

Now there are more theatres here per head than any other city in the UK. Eating out, too, has never been more popular thanks to an abundance of chic restaurants in the Merchant City area. Glasgow is also the second-largest shopping centre in the UK and sees more than four million tourists arrive each year to fill its 12,000 hotel rooms.

And what of Mr Happy, who kick-started it all? He left Glasgow after getting fed up with its complicated one-way streets north of the Clyde, and now lives back in Happyland with a fat grin on his yellow face.

ESSENTIALS

By Air Two airports serve the city. **Glasgow International Airport** (✆ *0870 040 0008*; ***www.glasgowairport.com***) is 13km southwest of the city off the M8 at Abbotsinch. Most British airports including Gatwick, Stansted, London (Luton), Heathrow, Southampton, East Midlands, Manchester and Leeds/Bradford connect here. From the airport get the 905 **Glasgow Citylink** bus to Buchanan Street Station (£3, from bus stops 1 or 2).

Glasgow Prestwick Airport (✆ *0871 223 0700*; ***www.gpia.co.uk***) is 50km south, near Ayr. Its main carrier is **Ryanair**. The airport has a rail station with regular services into the city taking 45 minutes (Monday–Saturday running half-hourly, hourly Sundays). Buses to Glasgow's Buchanan Street Bus station go from outside the terminal every half-hour and take 50 minutes (£4.20).

For more information on airlines flying to Glasgow call ✆ *0870 040 0008* or visit ***www.baa.co.uk/glasgow***.

By Rail The city centre has two main-line rail stations. Services from London's Kings Cross and Euston, and from anywhere south, arrive at Glasgow Central,

The Caledonian Sleeper

An alternative to flying if you have too much luggage for the plane is the overnight **First ScotRail** Caledonian Sleeper service from London Euston to Glasgow (*0845 755 0033*). Single- and twin-berth cabins are available as well as interconnecting rooms, each with blankets, sheets, bedside lighting, wash basins with shaver point and hand towels. There is a lounge car (only open to 1st class passengers when busy) serving snacks and drinks. In the morning you'll be woken (if the train pelting round tight corners hasn't done so already) with a light breakfast, tea or coffee and a complimentary newspaper. A toiletries pack is provided. Be warned: beds are very narrow (think ironing board) so if your child is a restless sleeper put him or her on the bottom bunk. There are no on-board showers, although they're available (at a charge) at Glasgow Central. Trains leave Euston at 11.45pm Monday–Thursday arriving at Glasgow Central 7.17am, and on Sundays at 11.21pm arriving 7.17am. Friday times vary. Bargain Berth single fares (available at ***www.firstgroup.co.uk/scotrail***) start at £19. Book three months in advance. APEX fares are £66 single, £99 return. Interconnecting fare is £172 one-way, £301 return.

sitting above Argyle Street. Anyone arriving from the north or Edinburgh disembarks at Queen Street Station on the corner of George Square.

By Road The main routes in are from England on the M74; from Edinburgh or Glasgow Airport on the M8; and from Stirling and points north and east via the M80. The city is approached from the West Highlands on the A82 dual carriageway. All routes converge on the M8, which runs into the city centre. There is no park-and-ride. Multi-storey car parks near the motorway in the centre are expensive, especially NCP ones. City council car parks in Concert Square (near the Royal Concert Hall), Cambridge Street (off the pedestrianised area of Sauchiehall Street) and Charring Cross are cheaper.

By Coach **National Express** (*0870 580 8080*) runs daily coaches from London's Victoria Coach Station to Buchanan Street Coach Station (from £21 single). Journey time is about 8½ hours. There are also services from Manchester and Birmingham, among others. **Scottish Citylink** runs frequent services from Edinburgh (£6 one-way). Tickets can be booked at ***www.citylink.co.uk*** or via *0870 550 5050.*

VISITOR INFORMATION

The Greater Glasgow and Clyde Valley Tourist Board, 11 George Street (*01412 044980*) is open in May from 9am to 6pm

(Sundays 10am to 6pm), June and September between 9am and 7pm (Sundays 10am to 6pm) and July or August 9am to 8pm (Sundays 10am to 6pm). Hours between October and April are 9am to 6pm (closed Sundays).

Orientation

Glasgow, built on steep hills punishing for buggy-pushers, has no obvious centre, making sightseeing challenging unless you break it up into chunks. Most transport facilities are around Argyle Street and nearby George Square, although Merchant City slightly to the east is also a focus, as are Sauchiehall Street's shops to the north. The city covers an area between Charing Cross and the M8 down to Glasgow Green in the East End. 1½ km from Central Station beyond the M8 lies the West End. The River Clyde is south and beyond the Gorbals and Govanhill is the national football stadium, Hampden Park, and Pollok Park, home of the Burrell Collection.

Getting Around

Run by Strathcylde Partnership for Transport (SPT), Glasgow's public transport system is one of the most extensive in the UK.

By Subway This operates in concentric circles around the city centre and a few inner suburbs. Interchanges with surface trains are at Buchanan Street, Queen Street and Partick stations. From Monday to Saturday trains run every 4 minutes at peak times, every 6 minutes during the day, and every 8 minutes in the evenings and on Sundays. The service operates from 6.30am to 11.30pm daily except Sunday (10am to 6pm). The flat fare for one journey is £1 (50p for children); it's £1.90 for unlimited daily use after 9.30am or all day at weekends. A 7-day season ticket costs £9 (children £4.50).

INSIDER TIP

Parents with buggies will find the subway hard. Pushchairs must be folded on all stairs, platforms and escalators, and inside trains.

By Bus Buses all over the city are run by the main operator **First Glasgow Bus Company** (*01414 236600*; ***www.firstgroup.com***). There's a bus within 10 minutes on most main routes; services taper off dramatically after 11pm. Buses in the city centre don't pull up automatically at every stop on their route, so check the bus stop you're waiting at. The main Buchanan Street Bus Station (*01413 333708*) is in Killermont Street. A single city centre fare starts at 75p. A FirstDay ticket for unlimited daily travel in all zones is £3 (children £1.60); FirstWeek 7-day ticket is £12.50. They're all purchased on the bus (no photos or ID necessary).

By Taxi Taxi ranks are at Glasgow Central and Queen Street stations, and Buchanan

Street bus station. Trips within the city cost £5–8; to the Burrel Collection about £11.

On Foot Glasgow is pedestrian-friendly with many shopping streets given over exclusively to foot traffic, although it can be hilly, especially between Argyle Street and Renfrew Street in the north. The underpasses around Cowcaddens can feel unwelcoming, although all the city centre and tourist areas are well policed and have information officers in red hats and jackets to assist. The Glaswegians are renowned for friendliness and will probably not only offer directions but come some of the way with you for a (sometimes indecipherable) natter (see 'Glasgow Patter', p. 79).

INSIDER TIP

If you're male, under 40 and in a group, it's not uncommon to be singled-out by beggars, especially on Buchanan Street. Forget prejudices about Glasgow being 'the murder capital of Europe', saying you're out of cash invariably ends the exchange and most are friendly (at least superficially) and usually only after £1 anyway.

By Car The city is a maze of one-way streets, bus lanes and pedestrian precincts, making it almost impossible to arrive at your destination without at least some harsh words being exchanged in the car's front two seats about who should have spotted that we'd crossed the Clyde again. Parking restrictions are fiercely enforced, and illegally leaving your wagon in a permit holder bay is not good. You'll be towed. There is metered parking (20p for 20 minutes) and car parks at Anderston Cross, Cambridge Street, George Street, Mitchell Street, Oswald Street and Waterloo Street.

City Sightseeing bus

01412 040444.

The best way to get about and orientate yourself is the hop-on/hop-off *City Sightseeing* bus. Open-top buses usually have guides pointing out sites and divulging quirky city history, although when there are too many other language speakers on board (this happens a lot) buses revert to multilingual headphones, which are hard to hear if you have youngsters screaming in your ears for another curry-flavoured rice cake. The distinctive red buses, running all year, stop at George Square, Glasgow Cathedral, the Radisson Hotel, the SECC, Glasgow University, Byers Road and the Willow Tea Rooms, among others. Drivers are friendly (we were helped off many times with our double-buggy), and compensate for the occasionally jaded guides. If you ask when first boarding, they'll provide felt-tip pens for youngsters in a small gift bag (not as washable as they appear). The tickets, valid for two consecutive days, provide some attraction discounts, and are £1 cheaper if you buy online (**www.scotsguide.com**), although whether you'll ever be asked to show them is another matter.

We weren't once. The service starts around 9.30am, you never wait more than 15 minutes for a ride; the last bus is between 5.30pm and 6pm depending where you are on the circular route. Fares are £9, children aged 5–14 £3, under-5s free; family (two adults and up to four children: £20.

INSIDER TIP

The round trip lasts one hour but it's best not to board near the Glasgow Science Centre around evening rush-hour.

Child-friendly Events & Entertainment

The Glasgow River Festival

www.glasgowriverfestival.co.uk.

Attracting 85,000 people a year in mid-July and based around the city's SECC, Glasgow Harbour and Science Centre, the festival includes a host of water-based activities including visiting Tall Ships, power-boat racing and dinghy rides, as well as live music and a fair near City Inn. The two-day finale concludes with thousands of plastic ducks released into the Clyde. A free shuttle bus from George Square takes visitors to the site.

The World Pipe Band Championship

www.seeglasgow.com/piping.

On Glasgow Green in August, 50,000 people flock to hear 200 bagpipe bands play (fortunately not all at once). The championship, which has been running since 1948, also features Highland dancing, a craft fair and a mini Highland Games with caber tossing.

FAST FACTS: GLASGOW

Business hours Most attractions open Monday to Friday between 9am–5pm, Thursdays until 7pm.

Dentist Accident and Emergency Department of the Glasgow Dental Hospital and School NHS Trust, 378 Sauchiehall St, ✆ *01412 119600*; open 9.15am–3.15pm.

Doctor The Royal Infirmary, 82–86 Castle Street, ✆ *01412 114000*.

Pharmacy Boots, 200 Sauchiehall Street, ✆ *01413 321925*; open Monday–Saturday 8.30am–6pm, Sunday 11am–5pm.

Internet Access EasyInternet Café, 57–61 St Vincent St, ✆ *01415 523200*; open Monday–Friday 7am–10pm, Saturday and Sunday 8am–9pm.

Post Office 47 St Vincent St, ✆ *01412 043689*; open Monday–Friday 8.30am–5.45pm, Saturday 9am–5pm.

WHAT TO SEE & DO

Children's Top 10 Attractions

❶ **Learn** how many galaxies would lie behind a hole in space the size of a 5p piece at the

Science Centre Planetarium. See below.

❷ **Listen** to quirky on-board commentary on the top deck of an open-top City Sightseeing bus. See p. 65.

❸ **Learn** how to speak in Glasgow Patter like Rab C. Nesbitt at the People's Palace Museum. See p. 77.

❹ **Find** Edie McCredie's bus from CBeebies' *Balamory* at the Transport Museum. See p. 72.

❺ **Feed** the geese in the River Clyde after a guided tour of Glasgow Green that includes the spot where condemned men were hanged. See p. 76.

❻ **See** how many children weigh as much as a baby elephant at the Kelvingrove Museum and Art Gallery. See p. 70.

❼ **Have the speed** of your kick logged at the Scottish Football Museum. See p. 80.

❽ **Enjoy** a delicious milkshake in Art Nouveau splendour at the Willow Tea Rooms. See p. 93.

❾ **Hang around** the secret back door of the Hotel Du Vin and get autographs of the famous (that you can sell later on eBay). See p. 84.

❿ **Pretend** to be a pirate aboard the Tall Ship in Glasgow Harbour. See p. 69.

Clydeside

The River Clyde was once the shipbuilding capital of the British Empire. Now the only shipyards left make warships for the Royal Navy. Recently, however, this once rundown area has been reborn. The 'Armadillo' concert hall, modelled on Sydney's Opera House, the Glasgow Science Centre and the Glasgow Tower and Tall Ship – reconnecting the city to its shipbuilding past – make it a popular destination with families.

To get here, walk a mile west out of the city along the riverside footpath or catch a train from Glasgow Central to the Exhibition Centre. Cross either footbridge for the Glasgow Science Centre.

The Glasgow Science Centre

*50 Pacific Quay, ☎ 0871 540 1000, **www.glasgowsciencecentre.org**.*

The best place for children in the city, the Glasgow Science Centre becomes so packed with youngsters that you have to remind yourself you're still among humans and not excitable chimps. At the planetarium you'll learn how to find the North Star and how many galaxies a 5p piece sized chunk of space might contain. In the Imax cinema – a distinctive egg-shaped building – 3D films tell the story of the dinosaurs, great fun for older ones, although a frighteningly lifelike T-Rex caused uproar with a few toddlers. Sit at the back for a quick exit or don't put the 3D glasses on and watch the movie in a blurry fuzz, as our toddler insisted on doing.

The Science Mall has more than 300 hands-on exhibits, and

Neurons at the Ready!

Children's TV favourite *Nina and the Neurons* uses the Science Centre as its backdrop. Resident scientists act as advisors to the show.

fills with school parties (displays are linked to the Scottish National School Curriculum), so time your visit for late afternoon. The gizmos here – good for most ages, adults included – include a giant chess board, displays on how muscles work, and driving a lunar buggy with radio signal delay. There's a game testing reaction-time that gets competitive if you're a couple who argue about who's the best driver under pressure (me) and in the climate change theatre the story of what we're doing to the planet is told via a talking sheep.

There's buggy access in a huge slow, hospital-porter-sized lift.

***Open** 10am–6pm daily. **Adm** one attraction £6.95, children £4.95, under-3s free (Planetarium, Science Mall, Imax or Glasgow Tower – see below). Any two attractions £9.95 (children £7.95). **Amenities** baby-changing, café.*

The Glasgow Tower

Looking like a giant motorcycle helmet on a stick, the Glasgow Tower at 127m is the tallest free-standing building in the world that can rotate 360°. Although it's not something to think about as you ascend in the slender glass lift on a windy day, the base of the tower resembles a ballpoint pen and is just 65cm in diameter, which means if you had a large enough crane you could lift it out of the cup it sits on like a quill from an inkpot. Powered by four 6-kilowatt motors (what it takes to operate an electric fan), the tower doesn't turn when winds exceed 40mph. The summit is a great

The Glasgow Science Centre

place for a lesson about the Clyde. With views of 65km taking in Loch Lomond and the Campsie Fells, the guided talks are adapted for youngsters, so alongside detailed answers about the *Titanic*, part of which was built nearby at the Harland and Wolff dry dock, expect to hear staff helping children find their 'red car in the car park,' or even fielding questions about Spiderman and his climbing abilities on titanium. Also popular (with our daughter anyway) was spotting helicopters taking off at the southern Scotland emergency services base on the north bank of the river.

***Open** 10am–6pm daily. **Adm** one attraction £6.95, children £4.95, under-3s free (Glasgow Tower or Planetarium, Science Mall, Imax – see above). Any two £9.95 (children £7.95).*

The Tall Ship

*Glasgow Harbour, Stobcross Road, 01412 222513, **www.thetallship.com**.*

For children into pirates, Glasgow's historic tall ship, the *S.V. Glenlee* built in 1896, is a must-see. One of only five Clyde-built sailing ships still afloat, and the only one remaining in the UK, its sides were painted with black squares that look like cannons to ward off buccaneers. Not quite so glamorously, the ship started life as a bulk carrier and its last voyage was transporting pigeon droppings. Seamen's voices ring out and you can see where the cook served up his slop.

Unfortunately, the tour is unfriendly for buggy-pushers (many stairs), there's no audio-guide, and there's nobody on board to answer youngsters' questions about walking the plank or why pirates like parrots so much (we heard a boy ask this). So to get your £10-worth, enthuse them with tales of rounding the Cape Horn in a gale or of sleeping under canvas in the idyllic calm of the Roaring Forties. If that doesn't work (it didn't for us) buy them chocolate-based treats at the

Peek into the kitchen at the tall ship, Glasgow Harbour

Pumphouse café after a whirl round its visitor centre (telling the story of Glasgow and the Clyde). There's a children's play area including dressing-up gear for wannabe sailors, books about the sea, a play boat and colouring-in station.

Open *daily Feb–Oct 10am–5pm, Nov–Jan 10am–4pm.* ***Adm*** *£4.95, children free with each paying adult (additional children £2.50).* ***Amenities*** *café, play area.*

The West End

In the 19th century, wealthy merchants established large estates out west, away from the grime of the city centre. Its focus now is Byres Road, in Hillhead, lined with trendy shops, restaurants, cafés, pubs and students wandering about in large scarves. Family-friendly attractions – the Transport Museum and Kelvingrove Museum and Art Gallery – straddle the river Kelvin, which snakes through the botanical gardens and Kelvingrove Park. Their sizes drive home the fact that Glasgow has more green space per head than any other city in Europe.

Kelvingrove Art Gallery and Museum

Argyle Street, ☎ 01412 872699, ***www.glasgowmuseums.com****.*

Kelvingrove Art Gallery & Museum

With more than 8,000 objects on display, including masterpieces by Salvador Dalí, Vincent Van Gogh, Claude Monet, Rembrandt van Rijn and Pablo Picasso, this is the city's most visited attraction. The lower halls include European Armour, Natural History, and a cute Mini Museum for children, where youngsters can try on animal feet and masks, compare their height against a giraffe's leg and see how many children weigh as much as a baby elephant. Meanwhile in 'Record-Breakers' they come up against the heaviest bird and the largest crab. They can handle bird wings, draw animals, and in the art gallery learn how artists such as John Constable used colour. It's pitched at two levels with parents encouraged to raise a

FUN FACT **Hello, Wendy**

People who live in the West End of Glasgow are called 'Wendys' (short for 'West End Trendies') by those outside the area.

Botanic Gardens

smirk. Look out for the explanation on Sir Roger, the stuffed elephant, who broke the arm of his keeper Mr Boston, 'who decided he must be put down so some soldiers and a man with an elephant gun shot Sir Roger one morning as he ate his breakfast'. Organ music wafting through the Victorian halls lends atmosphere and despite hundreds of little visitors, the museum never seems crowded. There's good buggy access (they can also be left in a park near the Mini Museum), baby-changing, free guided tours and a breastfeeding room.

FUN FACT Lord Kelvin, Comedian & Physicist 

Scots physicist William Thompson was made first Baron Kelvin (after the river that flowed past his home) for inventing the absolute scale of temperature measurement that bears his name. Kelvin was an eccentric who asked his second wife to marry him by ship signal and lived in the first home in Britain lit by electricity. He redesigned the interior of the *Great Eastern*, Brunel's ocean-going paddle steamer, and had the world's first fridges, Kelvinators, named after him. He also made several daft prouncements, claiming aeroplanes would never work and predicting that 'radio has no future'. Lord Kelvin also created the best (worst) physics joke ever. At Glasgow University, he was delivering a lecture in a room directly beneath a colleague whose students, at the end of the lecture, showed their appreciation in the customary manner – by stamping on the floor. 'Ah,' Kelvin remarked, as plaster fell from the ceiling, 'I see Dr. Campbell's conclusions don't agree with my premises.' Boom, boom!

FUN FACT Palace Escape

On 24th January, 1914, 20 panes of glass in the Kibble Palace were smashed by a bomb thought to have been planted by militant suffragettes. A second blast was averted when the lit fuse was snuffed out by a nightwatchman. Evidence that it was suffragetes included the impression of high-heeled shoes in soft ground and a lady's silk scarf found nearby.

***Open** Mon–Thurs and Sat 10am–5pm, Fri and Sun 11am–5pm. **Adm** free. **Amenities** café (children's food box £2.45).*

Kibble Palace and Botanic Gardens

730 Great Western Road, 01413 342422.

These gardens are a good place for a breather after shopping in nearby Byres Road (see p. 70). Full of students flicking frisbees, or revising (while surreptitiously checking each other out), it's ideal for people-watching and a picnic (if you haven't packed one already, try the Grassroots deli at 20 Woodland Road: lovely chilli-stuffed olives).

The Kibble Palace, a glasshouse with a musty, rain-foresty interior, is popular with office workers, children riding tricycles between its collection of exotic ferns, and older boys fascinated by the killer plants display including the Venus flytrap. After your picnic, wander through the park taking in the children's play area, the statue of Lord Kelvin (see p. 71) and work your way down to the river to try and spot a rare kingfisher; they're making a comeback here. I'm sure I saw one across the river perched behind a tree, although my killjoy wife maintained it was an empty packet of Walkers crisps.

Open** summer 10am–4.45 pm, winter 10am–4.15 pm. Gardens 7am–dusk. **Adm** free. **Amenities

Transport Museum

Kelvin Hall, 1 Bunhouse Road, 01412 872720.

The higgledy-piggledy assortment of classic cars, old buses, trams, steam trains, bygone bicycles, trucks, gypsy caravans and horse-drawn carriages under the roof of Kelvin Hall put you in mind of what an NCP car park might have looked like 100 years ago. The museum tells the story of transport by land and sea through the ages with a Glasgow

FUN FACT Testing, Testing

When Rolls Royce were designing jet engines for Concorde, there was concern that a bird strike would do more harm than on previous slower aircraft. So they fired frozen chickens at test engines to see what happened. The damaged engines ended up here at the Transport Museum.

twist. Children can imagine doing a paper round on the world's oldest pedal cycle, and the collection of Scottish-built cars include every granny's favourite, the Hillman Imp. There are lots more for youngsters here, although our daughter's favourite game was ducking under the guard ropes to wipe the remains of a Chocolate gem on the chassis of a vintage 1931 Rolls Royce Phantom Landaulette. Children can hare in and out of the traffic on a recreated cobbled 1930s road, although it did set our daughter's Highway Code training back a little. ('Yes you can run about this road, it's pretend. No, you can't run about the Clydeside Express Way, it's real'.) Elsewhere there's Edie McCredie's yellow bus from the children's TV show *Balamory*, racing cars for boys, an old-fashioned subway station, and in the hard-to-find Clyde Room (after the history of bikes) there are 300 ship models to take you back to those model-making days when the ends of your thumbs were permanently lengthened with globules of glue.

You can also send a postcard home: they have the oldest letterbox in the country.

***Open** Mon–Thurs 10am–5pm, Fri–Sun 11am–5pm. **Adm** free.*

Merchant City & City Centre

The Mediterranean spaciousness of Glasgow's set-piece public space, George Square, is dominated by the huge City Chambers. Right behind lies Merchant City, an 18th century warehouse district that has become home to trendy loft apartments, designer bars, chic cafés and family-friendly restaurants. To get a flavour for what this area once looked like take a look at Glasgow Cross, and the Tolbooth Steeple, now a traffic obstacle between London Road and the High Street.

South of the City Chambers, Royal Exchange Square's focal point is the Gallery of Modern Art, and tucked away nearby is the Lighthouse Architecture and Design Gallery. West from here, the city is laid out in a fairly strict grid system that American cities later copied, so faithfully that Glasgow is often used in movies to represent 19th century New York City.

The main shopping areas are Buchanan Street and Sauchiehall Street, where you'll find the Willow Tea Rooms and nearby The Glasgow School of Art. For more shopping ideas, see p. 83.

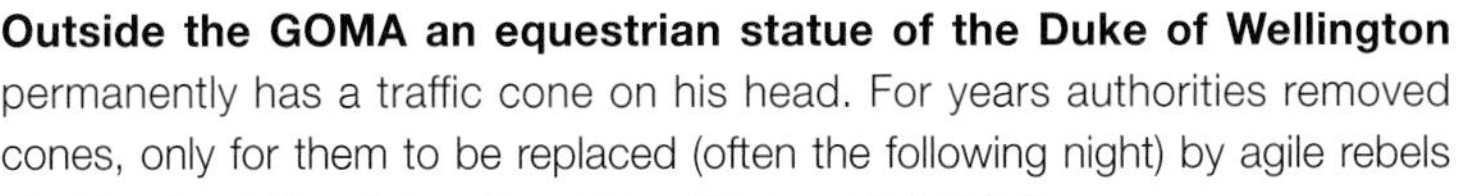

If You Can't Beat Them...

Outside the GOMA an equestrian statue of the Duke of Wellington permanently has a traffic cone on his head. For years authorities removed cones, only for them to be replaced (often the following night) by agile rebels climbing the 5.5m statue. Nowadays the cone is just left.

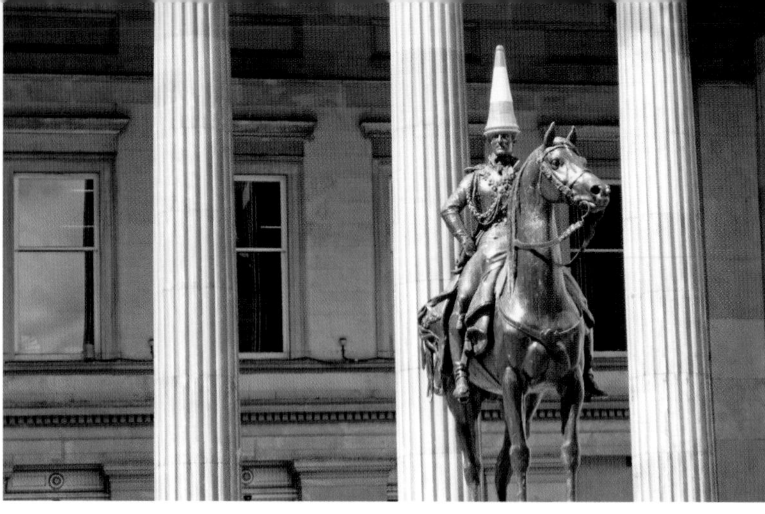

The Duke of Wellington statue outside the gallery of Modern Art

Gallery of Modern Art (GOMA)

*Royal Exchange Square, 01412 291996, **www.glasgowmuseums.com**.*

Housed in a neoclassical former mansion, the gallery represents the best of the city's contemporary art as well as symbolising Glasgow's light-hearted approach to authority (see 'If you can't beat them...', below). Exhibits include works by David Hockney, Sebastiao Salgado and Andy Warhol as well as Scottish artist Ken Currie.

Between 10am and 1pm on Saturdays there are free, drop-in children's art classes in the studio on the top floor with activities for 3–10-year-olds ranging from mobile making to sculpting. The gallery also houses a Learning Library in the basement, where there's children's storytelling on Friday afternoons at 2pm. The GOMA has also become a magnet for the city's youth. The gallery's environs, once a hangout for goths in Slipnot garb, are now a hub for skateboarders. Take a break at a nearby café and watch a scruffy handful practising their Ollies.

Open *Mon–Wed 10am–5pm, Thurs 10am–8pm, Sat 10am–5pm, Fri and Sun 11am–5pm.* ***Adm*** *free.*

Glasgow School of Art

*167 Renfrew Street, 01413 534526, **www.gsa.ac.uk**.*

The only way to see Charles Rennie Mackintosh's greatest architectural achievement is on a guided tour given by students at this working art college. The hourly tours (roughly one hour long) wind through the corridors of this magnificent 1896 building, ending at the Mackintosh library. It isn't geared for children, although the stylish student-guides (was it just our one, or did she really look a little like *she* had been designed by Mackintosh) don't mind if they run around touching things, or

Charles Rennie Mackintosh: A Potted History

Charles Rennie Mackintosh, Scottish architect, designer and artist, is celebrated as one of the leading creative figures of the 20th century. Born in Glasgow, the second of 11 children, he trained at the Glasgow School of Art, where he met J. Herbert MacNair and the Macdonald sisters, Frances and Margaret (he married the latter and credited her with three-quarters of his inspiration). The Glasgow Four, as they became known, collaborated on posters, metalwork, and on designing and furnishing a chain of tea-rooms established in Glasgow by Miss Cranston, in a campaign to combat daytime drunkenness. The fancy tearooms did little to wean drinkers from pubs, but did allow Mackintosh to create the Willow Tea Rooms; see p. 93. Mackintosh believed a revival of the Scottish Baronial style, adapted to modern society, would best meet contemporary requirements. His work, easily recognisable with its frequent use of motifs such as the stylised rose, fell from fashion quickly, however, and Mackintosh died forgotten aged 60 in 1928.

in our daughter's case say loudly and often in a way that sounded rude, 'What's that funny women talkin' about.' The tour covers ghost stories (one lives in the air vents, apparently) and hidden codes in the tilework, as well as the life and art of Mackintosh. Buggy-pushers have stair problems, and double buggyers worse if they try the lift (the doors are stiff, aggressive and only to be attempted with a detailed knowledge of your buggy's wheelbase).

Reserve tickets by phone or email or buy from the entrance shop.

***Open** daily Apr–Sep, tour times 10.30am, 11am, 11.30am, 1.30am, 2am, 2.30am; Oct–Mar (closed Sun) tour times 11am and 2pm. **Adm** £6.50.*

Lighthouse Architecture and Design Gallery

*11 Mitchell La, ☎ 01412 216362, **www.thelighthouse.co.uk**.*

Built by Charles Rennie Mackintosh in 1895, the Lighthouse is great for lunch away from shopping crowds on Buchanan Street, but even better for panoramic views across the city. Our daughter enjoyed hide and seek in the Mackintosh room as well as touching people's shoes from behind the Charles Rennie Mackintosh time-line. Once the headquarters of the *Glasgow Herald*, the building's chief attraction is the Mackintosh Tower accessed via a helical spiral staircase that reduced my leg muscles to soup and initiated a spell of dizziness that meant I temporarily forgot I had two children. The climb is well worth the 135-steps for the cityscape.

For buggy-pushers and those unable to abandon their wife with two children for 20 minutes (when they promised they'd only be 5), there's a buggy-friendly

The Barras Market at the weekend

viewing platform at the south of the building. After this, if peckish or in need of a little time to recover your legs (or explain yourself to your wife – 'I told you it's helical; I got dizzy'), the fifth floor Doocot restaurant has its own views. You needn't pay to use the restaurant; just tell the receptionist where you're going.

Open *Wed–Sat and Mon 10.30am–5pm, Tues 11am–5pm, Sun 12pm–5pm.* ***Adm*** *£3.00, (children £1), under-5s free* ***Amenities*** *restaurant.*

Tenement House

145 Buccleuch Street, Garnethill
01413 330183.

Just past the School of Art, children can learn through the preserved home of shorthand typist Agnes Toward what life was like in a middle-class Victorian tenement. Basically, straw mattresses, box beds, coal fires, and lots of doilies.

Open *daily 1st Mar–31st Oct, 1pm–5pm.* ***Adm*** *£5, children £4.*

The East End

Resembling the old Glasgow and bordered by Glasgow Green and the old university, tourists thin out here and although safe in daylight, it's like walking through Michael Jackson's

FUN FACT Grizzly Green

Between 1814 and 1865, 71 people were executed in Glasgow Green. Most notorious was Dr Pritchard, who murdered his wife and mother-in-law. His hanging drew a crowd of 100,000, and was the last public execution in Glasgow. People brought picnics, stalls sold snacks and whole families made it a day out, the spectacle serving as both cautionary tale and family entertainment.

Thriller video at night. Here you can buy anything from a tongue piercing to a Nazi uniform.

The Barras, Glasgow's weekend market (Saturdays and Sundays), is in Gallowgate, its 1,000-plus stalls selling rip-off designer goods and bric-a-brac. To the south is Glasgow Green, the oldest public park in Britain, housing The People's Palace and Winter Gardens, while the Sharmanka Kinetic Gallery hosts the strangest show in the city.

Glasgow Green

Greendyke Street, 01412 875064.

The best way to learn about the Green's claim to fame – James Watt came up with his steam engine brainwave walking here – is via a free park ranger tour. They leave from the steps of the People's Palace at 2.30pm every Saturday and Sunday. They'll tell you that this was where Bonnie Prince Charlie reviewed his troops before defeat at Culloden (see p. 153), and that both Rangers and Celtic football teams have their roots here. These ranger tours (1¼ hours) also include a walk down the banks of the River Clyde behind the Winter Gardens where youngsters can feed the geese (bring your own bread).

The Green has staged public executions, Victorian temperance rallies and Chartist protests. Its statue of temperance campaigner Sir William Collins is now a popular late-night rendezvous for local winos.

People's Palace and Winter Gardens

Glasgow Green, 01412 712962.

Fronted by the Doulton Fountain – the largest terracotta fountain in the world and maybe the largest terracotta anything – the People's Palace is the best place to get to know what makes Glaswegians tick. Check out Rab C. Nesbitt's help on how to say: 'Stop complaining, you've got yourself upset now' in Glaswegian ('Quit whingein ye've got yersl in a righ fankle'). There are displays on the city's love affair with alcohol and interactive exhibits on the rigmarole of cleaning clothes in a public washhouse. You can even see the banana boots Billy Connolly wore on stage in the

FUN FACT Glasgow's Kitty of Culture

During the 1980s, one employee at the People's Palace gained national fame becoming a member of the General, Municipal, Boilermakers and Allied Trade Union, after rival union NALGO had refused her blue-collar admission. This employee was Smudge the Cat, employed to ensure the Palace did not become home to mice. Smudge was so well known that Glasgow's Lord Provost made press appeals and police searches were carried out when she disappeared for three weeks in 1987, eventually reappearing half a mile away. When Smudge died in 2000, she received an obituary in the *Glasgow Herald*.

The People's Palace and Winter Gardens

1970s. In the Education Centre, youngsters aged 3 and over (check days on *01412 713951*) can manufacture bugs out of pebbles or make dolls from scrap.

Inside the adjacent Winter Gardens you can enjoy an ice-cream among tropical plants and chirping birds in this elegant Victorian glasshouse. On your way out, to the right, the turreted building of arched windows with elaborate mosaic-style patterns is Templeton's old carpet factory, modelled on the Doge's palace in Venice. It was designed to appear as though it were covered in an old Axminster carpet (quite why, nobody knows). It's now a business centre, which serves it right.

***Open** daily 10am–5pm, Fri and Sat 11am–5pm. **Adm** free.*

Sharmanka Kinetic Gallery

2nd Floor, 14 King Street, 01415 527080.

Genius, tinged with an invigorating madness: this show consists of a series of mechanical models made from scavenged metal from Barras market (including lawnmower blades) with intricate wooden figures atop turning to synchronised classical music. The 50-minute *Sharmanka* show (it means 'hurdy gurdy') is a synthesis of sculptor/mechanic Eduard Bersudsky's life in communist Russia with his sad childhood that saw him forced to make his own toys from nut shells. It's moving on the theme of life and death and the depth of the human spirit, although our toddler just enjoyed 'all the lovely mice' (actually rats).

If your child has nightmares (some contraptions are mounted with animal skulls) comfort or berate yourself with theatre director Tatyana Jakovskaya's words: 'De children is de mirror for de parents.' If you have a buggy, you'll have to ring the bell for help; but then you'll get to ride to the gallery in a huge clanking service lift of the sort featured in scary American serial killer films. Come in daylight.

***Open** Thurs and Sun 7pm, family matinees Sun 3pm (40 minutes). **Adm** £4, under-16s free.*

The Southside

This large area includes the deprived Gorbals and Govan districts where you might be head-butted for wearing the wrong colour shirt, although there are oases such as the Burrell Collection at Pollok Country Park and the Scottish Football Museum.

Burrell Collection

*Pollok Country Park, 2060 Pollokshaws Rd, 01412 872550, **www.glasgowmuseums.com**.*

Sir William Burrell, who in 1958 bequeathed 9,000 works to the city of Glasgow, started his famous collection as a boy, saving pocket money to buy art rather than the sherbet dib-dabs we preferred. His gallery houses medieval art, tapestries, stained glass English oak furniture and modern works by Edgar Degas, Paul Cézanne and Auguste Rodin.

The building in Pollok Park was recently judged Scotland's second-greatest build in post-war times and apart from a convoluted process reaching the mezzanine floor with a buggy (going through security ropes, using the staff lift), the museum is child-friendly. There's a quiz and treasure hunt, blown up artworks to which children can add personal flourishes and dressing up. In Chinese Art there's a mini-pagoda full of scatter cushions where weary under-5s can relax or smack each other round the head with (what our daughter preferred). The staff are scrupulously friendly with not an eye, nor even a nose, batted when our thought-to-be-potty-trained daughter had a little (major) accident in the Degas Room.

Its woodland setting also offers a children's play park, highland cattle-spotting and picnicking. If arriving by bus or train take the courtesy bus from just inside the park to the museum.

***Open** Mon–Thurs and Sat 10am–5pm, Fri and Sun 11am–5pm. **Adm** free (parking £1). **Amenities** café (children's lunchboxes £2.25), picnic and play area.*

Glasgow Patter

He couldn't kick his ain arse. He isn't particularly skilful at football
Harry Potter is pure mince. I don't like Harry Potter
Aw, that pure mintit that top. Your shirt is quite nice
Dad's mad wi it again. My father is drunk again
They're no makin jeans that'll go over that big bahookie. I'm afraid my bum is too big for these trousers

Scottish Football Museum and Hampden Tour

Hampden Park, 01416 166139, www.scottishfootballmuseum.org.uk.

The Scottish Football Museum has one of the world's most impressive collections of the game's memorabilia, and is a must for young footie fans and dads who, having stared at their fill of porcelain in the Burrell Collection, now fancy having the speed of their penalty kicks logged. The museum houses the world's oldest football letter: in 1868 Queen's Park wrote to Glasgow Thistle inviting them to play a game of 20-a-side. And the stadium tour of Hampden Park, home of lowly Queen's Park (and also the world's oldest national football ground), includes a chance to smack a ball in the warm-up area and have the speed of your kick electronically measured. If you make the top 100 (I didn't, but I had incorrect footwear, as I explained to my wife) your name is recorded on the museum's website. Visitors also tour the changing rooms and royal box and walk down the tunnel into the stadium to hear the famous Hampden Roar (or not, if it's Queen's Park at home). Don't get stung for a retro replica shirt in the gift-shop where, naturally, you can buy a video of Scotland's defeat of England in 1967 (incorrect footwear again).

Open *10am–5pm, Sun 11am–5pm (subject to events).* **Adm** *museum £5.50, under-16s £2.75. Stadium tour £6, under-16s £3, under-5s free.* **Amenities** *parking.*

Medieval City

Incorporates what little is left of the old city – the cathedral, St Mungo's Museum of Religious Life and Art and Provand's Lordship plus the Necropolis.

Cathedral

Cathedral Square, Castle Street, 01415 528198.

Glasgow Cathedral is mainland Scotland's only complete medieval church. Also known as St Mungo's, after the city's patron saint, the vaulted crypt holding his tomb was so prestigious that in 1451 the Pope declared a visit here as worthy as one to Rome. I'm not sure if that accounts for the children we saw pelting up the famous blackadder aisle shouting 'I have a cunning plan, My Lord' in their best Baldrick voices. Also of interest is the Millennium Window. Unveiled by Princess Anne in 1999, it's one of the most technically demanding stained glass windows ever produced, don't you know.

Open *Apr–Sep weekdays and Sat 9.30am to 5.30pm, Sun 9.30am to 5pm; Oct–March weekdays and Sat 9.30am–4.00pm, Sundays 1pm–4pm.* **Adm** *free.*

Provand's Lordship

3 Castle Street, 0141 5 528819, www.glasgowmuseums.com.

Although it sounds like the name of an exclusive brand of shortbread, this is in fact the oldest surviving house in Glasgow. Built in the 15th century as part of St Nicholas's Hospital, it was named after its former resident the Lord

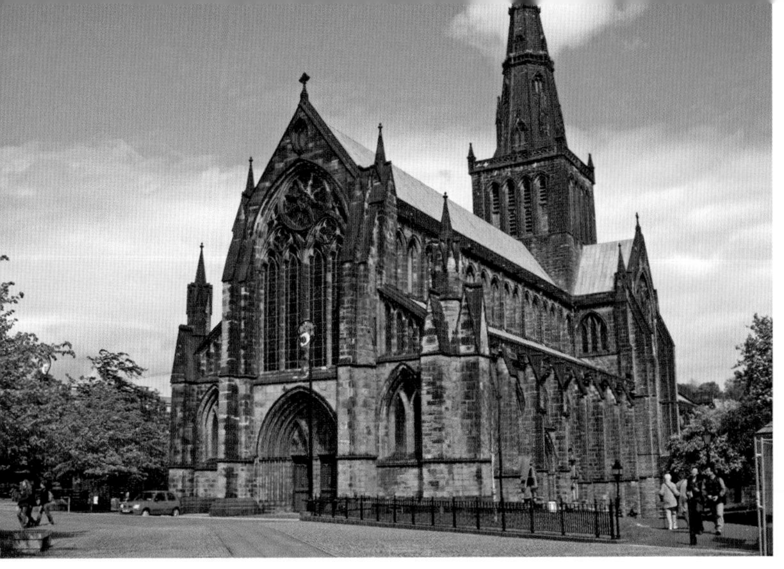

The Cathedral

of the Prebend of Barlanark, corrupted to Lord of the Provand. During years of decline it was used as a sweet shop, a drink factory, a junk shop and was even the home of the city's 18th century hangman. Scheduled for demolition, the city took over in 1978, and a local builder renovated it for 1p. (No, he won't do your attic conversion). Now, thanks to the donation of 17th century Scottish furniture by Sir William Burrell (see p. 79), children can experience a domestic interior from 1700.

There are stairs and no lifts for buggies.

***Open** Mon–Thurs and Sat 10am–5pm, Fri and Sun 11am–5pm. **Adm** free.*

St Mungo Museum of Religious Life and Art

*2 Castle Street, 01415 532557, **www.glasgowmuseums.com**.*

This unique museum sets out to explore the history and importance of religion across the world, and to promote respect between people of different faiths and those with none. It has sculptures of gods, pictures and displays of religious practices such as the Mexican Day of the Dead (not as morbid as it sounds: it involves eggy bread). Although the main reason to come is Salvador Dalí's awesome 1951 *Christ of St John of the Cross*. However, do take the elevator to the 1st floor and look through the floor-to-ceiling window – the view of the Necropolis (see p. 83) is superb.

On the top floor's hands-on area, children can try on religious headgear, as well as complete a brass rubbing of a Celtic cross. After this, why not contemplate life in the simplistic masterpiece of Britain's first permanent Zen garden, adjacent to the museum. I'll tell you why not...a two-month old in need of a boob feed and a

The Case of Oscar Slater

In 1925 William Gordon was released from Peterhead Prison in Scotland. He carried out a smuggled message from fellow prisoner, Oscar Slater, who 17 years earlier had been imprisoned for life for the murder of Miss Marion Gilchrist, now buried in the Necropolis. Written on waterproof paper and hidden beneath Gordon's tongue, the message was a plea for help to be delivered to Sir Arthur Conan Doyle. What followed is more extraordinary than any case that Conan-Doyle's famous creation Sherlock Holmes ever had to solve.

The facts, Watson, the facts

On 21st December, 1908, Helen Lambie, Miss Gilchrist's servant, went to buy a newspaper. Shortly after, Arthur Adams, who lived in the apartment below, heard knocking on his ceiling. Assuming his neighbour wanted assistance, Adams investigated and was at the front of the door when Helen Lambie returned. Together they discovered Miss Gilchrist bludgeoned to death. A diamond brooch was stolen. A public outcry followed and police quickly announced they were looking for Oscar Slater. Slater lived nearby, was known for running illegal gambling operations and had recently pawned a diamond brooch. More damningly, after the murder Slater left for America under an assumed name, although on hearing the allegations willingly returned. The brooch he pawned did not match Miss Gilchrist's. He had an alibi, but the police were unswayed. In addition to Slater's criminal history there were witnesses (after some police coaching) sure that they'd seen Slater leaving the murder scene. Found guilty at trial, Slater was sentenced to death, but this was commuted to imprisonment for life with hard labour. Slater's lawyers contacted Sir Arthur Conan Doyle and in 1912 he published *The Case of Oscar Slater*. After studying the evidence, he concluded that Slater was not the killer. Outraged when officials refused to budge, Conan Doyle pressed the issue again and again. Then in 1925 he received the message from Peterhead Prison. Containing no new evidence, it was just a desperate plea to Conan Doyle not to forget him. Conan Doyle wrote to influential friends, the press and the Secretary of State for Scotland. The turning point only came in 1927 when a book by Glasgow journalist William Park was published. Park, too, concluded Slater was innocent. Newspapers were full of the case. Witnesses came forward to talk about police coaching them into naming Slater and within weeks Oscar Slater was free, though never pardoned. Elementary, my dear Watson.

two-year-old who's just flung herself to the ground, rigid with anger, shouting 'I *want* a treat. I *want* a treat', with chocolate from the last treat still smeared over her face.

***Open** Mon–Thurs and Sat 10am–5pm, Fri and Sun 11am–5pm. **Adm** free.*

The Necropolis

50 Cathedral Square, ☎ 01415 523145.

Glasgow's cemetery, the Necropolis, was modelled on Père-Lachaise in Paris. At its centre is a monument to John Knox (see p. 36), erected in 1825, which denotes the status of every resident of the graveyard (the closer to Knox, the richer you were in life). Best for families is a ranger tour. They're free and start at the main gates (for times call ☎ *01412 875064*). The guides talk generally about Scottish history, Glasgow and the problem of grave-robbing prior to an act in 1832 allowing people to donate their bodies to medical science. You'll learn how Mary Shelley, who wrote *Frankenstein*, came up with her monster after a talk in Glasgow University given by Dr Jefferson on galvanism (shocking a corpse to produce movement), and an even stranger tale about Sir Arthur Conan Doyle (see 'The Case of Oscar Slater', previous page).

Shopping

Argyll Arcade

30 Buchanan Street, ☎ 01412 216680.

This ornate arcade has 32 jewellers under one roof.

Barras Market

Gallowgate, ☎ 01415 524601.

A mix of covered and open stalls selling everything from antique furniture to computer games. The market has a reputation for selling counterfeit videos, CDs and DVDs that are often available here before anywhere else in Europe.

Buchanan Galleries

Buchanan Street, ☎ 01413 339898.

The city's newest shopping centre at the junction of Sauchiehall Street and Buchanan Street has a 2,000-space car park and over 80 shops, including John Lewis, Habitat, Mango and Next.

Merchant Square Indoor Shopping

71–73 Albion Street.

Exclusive shops, restaurants and bars, as well as arts and crafts

FUN FACT Taggart

1 *Taggart* writer Glen Chandler drew inspiration for his characters' names from tombstones in Glasgow's Maryhill Cemetery.
2 The series, originally called *Killer*, kept the name *Taggart* even after the death of Mark McManus, who played Jim Taggart.
3 When character John Samson was murrrrrrderrrrrrred, the gaping wound left by the shotgun blast was made realistic with mince and chicken bones.
4 *Taggart* is the UK's longest running crime drama, having been on TV continuously for more than 20 years.
5 Ant and Dec once did a spoof *Taggart* sketch entitled *Tagg-fart*.

that make unique gifts to take home.

Prince's Square

48 Buchanan Street, 01412 210324.

A cosmopolitan selection of designer boutiques and trendy cafés under an Art Nouveau glass roof; it's also home to the Scottish Craft Centre.

Sauchiehall Street Shopping Centre

177 Sauchiehall Street, 01413 320726.

This centre on the north side of the city centre houses Superdrug and WH Smith, as well as TK Maxx and Primark.

St Enoch Shopping Centre

55 St. Enoch Sq, 01412 043900.

The largest shopping centre in Scotland, and Europe's largest glass structure, is family-friendly and includes department stores Debenhams, Boots, TK Maxx and BHS, as well as Scotland's largest food court with seating for more than 850.

FAMILY-FRIENDLY ACCOMMODATION

West End

EXPENSIVE

Hotel Du Vin at One Devonshire Gardens

*One Devonshire Gardens, Great Western Road, 01413 392001, **www.onedevonshiregardens.com**.*

If you fancy treating your family, the favourite city haunt of

Hotel Du Vin at One Devonshire Gardens

Pavarotti and Elizabeth Taylor is the smartest place to stay in Glasgow. It even has its own four-bedroomed, private-gardened, £950-a night luxury mews suite with a secret unmarked doorway at the back so you can escape the tiresome paparazzi on your way in and out. The sumptuous hotel, just a 10 minute walk to the Botanical Gardens, covers three classical terraces, but if you're jaded by city attractions or simply very shy, why not stay in your room practising holing a long one at The Old Course. Each individually styled room is equipped with a putter, a putter returner and balls, all of which can be purchased if you become attached to them (£70 for the lot). Another good idea is to badger the front desk to show you where the secret celebrity door is at the back of the hotel and then loiter around with your camera. Your snatched *Hello!* magazine pictures might help offset the cost of your stay.

Joking aside, the 35-room hotel is a great place to bring a

Some Useful Gaelic Phrases

Tha mi airson Gàidhlig ionnsachadh. (hah mee EHR-sawn GAH-lik YOON-sa-hugkh) I want to learn Gaelic.
De an t-ainm a tha oirbh? (Jeh un TAH-num uh HAW-ruv?) What's your name?
U toigh leam bracaist a ghabhail. (Boo tuh LUH-oom BRAH-kawsht uh GAH-ull) I would like to have breakfast.
An toir thu dhomh pòg? (Un TUH-r oo ghawnh pawk?) Will you give me a kiss?

family. Baby-sitters are available (£15 an hour). There is a spa (basic facial, £60), in-room yoga instruction, a whisky snug bar with more than 300 malts, and the restaurant is superb. Best for families are the Townhouse suites with pull-down beds in the lounge. Ask for 'Touques et Clochers' for a bit of fun. Access to its lounge is through a secret doorway in what looks like a bookcase. Cheaper alternatives are Classic Rooms or Grand Rooms.

***Rates** Classic £250 per night, Grand £305, Townhouse Suite £375, Luxury Townhouse Suite £496, Mews Suite £950. **Amenities** baby-sitting, WiFi, laundry, dry-cleaning, highchairs. **In room** cot (free), broadband Internet access, DVD/VCR, sat TV, newspaper, fridge.*

INSIDER TIP

Instead of booking the Townhouse suite, save £120 and ask for Classic Room Concha y Toro (rooms are named after wines). It has a small room between the main bedroom and the bathroom ideal for a youngster. Also, the hotel has an upgrade policy so always ask. Other offers are posted on the website.

MODERATE

Kirklee

*11 Kensington Gate, 01413 345555, **www.kirkleehotel.co.uk**.*

On a quiet road overlooking private gardens, this former Edwardian townhouse is just a short walk to Byres Road. High ceilings, and a full Scottish breakfast at your own bay window table, make it a good rest stop for families. Most rooms are within range of a baby monitor so you can stay in for takeaway in front of *Taggart* and the private gardens over the road are good for a picnic. On-street parking is unrestricted, but nearby roads are busy in the mornings. Off-season rates are flexible so haggle. Cots are free, buggies can be left at reception and there's no lift so if clobbered-up ask for Room One on the ground floor. It has a double-bed, a single and an additional chair-bed.

***Rates** from £72–100 per room. **Amenities** WiFi. **In Room** cot (free), TV.*

INEXPENSIVE

The Manor Park Hotel

28 Balshagray Drive, Glasgow, 01413 392143, ***www.manorparkhotel.com****.*

This is the B&B if you're interested in learning to speak a little Gaelic. Next to Victoria Park with its host of child-friendly amusements including a play park, a duck pond and a maze, this old terrace is run by Hebridean proprietor Angus MacDonald, who'll teach you to say *Is mise Ben* ('my name is Ben'), and also 'my hovercraft is full of eels' (*Tha mo bhàta-foluaimein loma-làn easgannan*) quicker than he can cook an *Is bean* (sausage). His hospitality has spilled into his Gaelic-speaking children who, if you ask nicely (*is mas e do thoil e*) will entertain you with bagpipe and accordion music. Highland dancing has also been known. There are 10 rooms, all named after Hebridean islands. Cots are free, though there is no lift and only one ground floor room. The three family rooms contain a double and a single, and one room has an extra foldaway bed.

Rates *double £60–70, family rooms £70–85.* ***Amenities*** *Scottish breakfast.* ***In room*** *cot (free), TV.*

City Centre & Merchant City

EXPENSIVE

Malmaison Glasgow

278 West George Street, 01415 721000, ***www.malmaison.com****.*

This ultra-modern hotel in a converted 19th century Greek Orthodox Church is the ideal stay if you've something to celebrate. A short walk to Buchanan Street's shops, the hotel has a Gothic theme (dark colours, rich velvet) and they like to dim the lights at night to create mood – good if you're on a romantic weekend (voted the sexiest place in the city in 2006), but not so great if you have children prone to run off and hide at check-in during a game of 'Be the monster, daddy'. Its highlight is the candlelit champagne bar where you can sip bubbly, hold your wife's hand and promise that tomorrow you won't lose your temper when you go wrong again driving around the Tolbooth Steeple.

The relaxed atmosphere sees staff hand out colouring-in books and pens to children at check-in and mealtimes, and extends to the informal breakfast in the brasserie (inside the church's vaulted crypt) where you're more likely to hear David Bowie than muzak over your full Scottish breakfast. All rooms are individually designed and have pay-per-view TV with youngsters' favourites such as *Shrek*.

Parking is awkward to say the least: it's 10 minutes away in a multi-storey, so drop bags off first and remember to get directions.

Rates *doubles £100–150, kingsize doubles (accommodating folding beds for children up to 16) £150. Interconnecting rooms £200–300.* ***Amenities*** *Scottish breakfast (£13.95), safe deposit box, doctor on call, gym.* ***In room*** *Internet, flat-screen TV, CD / DVD player.*

INSIDER TIP

If you want a good meal away from the children ask for atrium rooms 158, 159 or 160, where your baby monitors will work in the brasserie.

MODERATE

Glasgow Hilton

1 William Street, 01412 045555, ***www.hilton.co.uk/glasgow****.*

Initial impressions of this busy city hotel aren't great: it's near the expressway, there was a big queue at check-in and the lobby was packed with revellers at a Glasgow Rangers football do talking about Barry Ferguson. But they weren't borne out by the excellent service. Families get a good deal: children under 11 eat free from the children's menu at Minsky's carvery, and under-18s stay free in parents' rooms on sofa beds or get an interconnecting room for 50% off the rate. Rooms also have the Cartoon Network TV channel – where our daughter watched her first episode of *Scooby Doo* (she cried in the night, unsure about Fred) – Sony Playstations and there's a swimming pool, spa and steam room.

Forget eating at Cameron's however – the policy is only children aged 12 plus. Check the Hilton website for regular offers.

Rates *doubles £110, interconnecting rooms £165.* ***Amenities*** *Internet, parking, spa.* ***In room*** *free newspaper, sat TV, Sony Playstations.*

INEXPENSIVE

Ibis Glasgow

220 West Regent Street, Glasgow, 01412 256000, ***www.ibishotel.com****.*

This 141-room chain option is close to attractions, and has a talking lift our daughter had a long conversation with about Roly Mo (from *The Fimbles*). There are goodie-bags on arrival (containing colouring-in books and sweets), free cots and they have a children's menu, but no baths.

Rooms *141.* ***Rates*** *family rooms (£49–68) come with a double and a three-quarter size bed.* ***Amenities*** *restaurant, bar.* ***In room*** *TV, shower only, Internet.*

Southside

EXPENSIVE

Sherbrooke Castle Hotel

11 Sherbrooke Avenue, Pollokshields, 01414 274227, ***www.sherbooke.co.uk****.*

This Gothic-style hotel 5km south of the centre, once the residence of a Victorian tobacco merchant, is ideal if you're visiting the Burrell Collection (a few minutes' walk away). It's family-run and operates a baby-sitting service run by staff (£10 an hour), has spacious grounds, games behind reception, and baronial flourishes including suits of armour as well as fun-to-climb turrets.

Food is made from local ingredients and prepared on site.

The hotel has children menus, highchairs and cots, as well as two family suites.

***Rooms** 25. **Rates** £215 for a family of four, £185 for three. **Amenities** baby-sitting, two bars, WiFi, laundry, parking, restaurant. **In room** cots, flat-screen sat TV.*

Camping

Craigendmuir Park

*Campsite View, Stepps, North Lanarkshire, 01417 794159, **www.craigendmuir.co.uk**.*

This no-frills caravan park is a few minutes from bus and rail links into the city centre, and with great views of the Campsie Fells it's a scenic alternative to budget B&Bs. There are centrally heated chalets and two types of static caravan (the Holiday Home is warmer in winter). Most have TVs and many have DVD players. Bed linen is supplied; towels are not. All have either showers or baths. There is a large field for children and a play-park over the road. On site you'll find a token-operated laundry, but no shop, although the local Somerfield supermarket is open until 9pm. The Wee Pub is a few minutes away as is family-friendly restaurant Buchanan Gate.

Number 36 buses run every 20 minutes from Stepps (5 minutes away) to Glasgow's Buchanan Street (journey 30 minutes). Stepps train station has services to Queen Street (13 minutes).

***Rates** 4/5 berth chalets per week £235–310, 6/8 berth holiday homes per week £300–450, 4/6 berth static caravans per week £150–300. All can be hired for shorter periods (minimum stay three nights). Prices include gas and electricity.*

Serviced Apartments

As a popular family alternative to the one-room difficulties of hotels, serviced apartments give you extra space, greater comfort and the luxury of your own child-free zone to cosy-up in.

Upstreet Serviced Apartments

350 Argyle Street, Glasgow, 0845 257 1867.

Centrally located, these apartments have all the extras included in the price, and there's a nearby leisure centre for a free dip and sauna. The modern kitchens come with all the appliances you'd expect (including a dishwasher). The roomy lounge with laminate flooring has a TV with Sky+ and a DVD player. There's a dining table and broadband, but book ahead for highchairs. Although without a permanent front desk, there's a speedy response from the mobile number provided.

Staff shop before you arrive and so orange juice, tea, coffee, bread and cereal are in your cupboard for breakfast. There's also a handy Tesco Metro shop below. One irritation is getting from the underground car park to the room. You take a lift to the first floor, hump bags across an uncovered concourse (not great in the rain) and then ride another lift to the room.

***Rates** one bedroom apartment £95 per night, two bedrooms £145 per night; minimum two night stay.*
***Amenities** Internet, kitchen, parking (free), Sat TV and DVD.*

Fraser Suites Glasgow

1–9 Albion St, Glasgow, 01415 534288.

In the heart of the Merchant City these apartments are set in an old 19th century building with its original Victorian façade. Kitchenettes have just the essentials (strangely, no pans) and also, a nuisance when you've got mucky children, no washing machines (though there is a hotly contested self-service laundry in the basement).

There are three types of family room. The one-bed, the one-bed deluxe and two-bed deluxe (the difference being room size). There's a TV (and a DVD player) set up for broadband (although at £10 for 24 hours its cheaper using Internet cafés). There's a decent sound system, a lobby with free tea and coffee, a tiny fitness suite and continental breakfast on the first floor. A thoughtful extra – free coffee, tagliatelle, passata, tea, sugar and bread in your apartment. Parking beneath the building is £6 a day (£2.59 overnight).

***Rates** One bed £110, two-bed £160.*

FAMILY-FRIENDLY DINING

EXPENSIVE

Stravaigin Bar and Restaurant

*28–30 Gibson Street, 01413 342665, **www.stravaigin.com**.*

Stravaigin, a popular hangout for city bands including Snow Patrol, Belle and Sebastian and Franz Ferdinand, is named after an old Scottish word meaning 'to wander about'. It reflects the ethos of the menu – locally sourced produce given an international makeover. Try the Thai-spiced Aberdeen Angus beef. All ingredients are fresh, and the haggis – a favourite with Snow Patrol, apparently – is made from scratch. The restaurant (slate floors and exposed beams) recently removed its tablecloths and, much more relaxed now, they'll deep-fry a Mars Bar if you ask (don't). Staff will carry buggies downstairs and stow them in the cloakroom, colouring-in books and stickers are handed out, and the children's menu has traditional fish supper options and the west coast mussels with basil (£2.25) has the advantage of keeping young hands busy de-shelling.

The main restaurant is in the basement, and between 12 and 4pm at weekends children eat free. The restaurant and upstairs café (slightly cheaper) are popular, so book two weeks in advance for a weekend sitting and one week for a week night.

Open *café Sun–Sat 11am–midnight; Restaurant Tues–Thurs 5–1pm, Fri–Sun noon–2.30pm, 5–11pm.* ***Main courses*** *restaurant £12.95, café £8, children's dishes £2.* ***Credit*** *all major cards.*

Ubiquitious Chip

12 Ashton Lane, 01413 345007, ***www.ubiquitous chip.co.uk****.*

Crouched under twinkling fairy lights in a cobbled mews in the city's West End, The Chip has long been the favoured haunt of visiting celebs (Mick Jagger and Meryl Streep are fans) but staff at this celebrated hangout are just as happy to accommodate children, providing building blocks, colouring-in books and crayons to keep them amused while you crane your neck star-spotting. Children get their own menu – Weans' World – stacked with good food cleverly disguised as fun, and there are no chips unless you ask. The emphasis is on innovative local cooking given a sprinkle of magic by 2004 Scottish Restaurant Chef of the Year, Iain Brown. The Chip (opened in 1971) was ahead of its time sourcing local ingredients, so expect to be told almost to the nearest field or stream where every piece of meat and fish is from.

Open *Mon–Sat noon–2.30pm, 5.30–11pm, Sun 12.30–3pm, 6–11pm.* ***Main courses*** *lunch £21, dinner £32.50.* ***Credit*** *AmEx, MC, V.*

Windows

7th floor, Carlton George Hotel, 44 West George Street, 01413 545070, ***www.carltonhotels.co.uk****.*

Although fairly formal – white linen table covers, hushed ambience, lots of businessmen using words like 'facilitate' – the only rooftop restaurant in Glasgow is worth a visit for stunning skyline views. The large glass windows on the top floor of the hotel mean no diners miss out, and if you get bored of the cityscape there is the live cooking area. The restaurant offers updated Scottish fare including an excellent spinach and mushroom ravioli.

Although there is no children's menu or baby-changing, children's portions are available. There is a lift at the hotel reception and no steps. Between 5pm and 6.30pm the pre-theatre menu offers two courses for £15.

Open *Mon–Sun noon–2.30pm, 5–11.45pm (last orders).* ***Main courses*** *lunch (12pm and 2.30pm) £15 for two courses, dinner after 6.30pm (£18).* ***Credit*** *AmEx, MC, V.*

MODERATE

City Café

Finnieston Quay, 01412 271010, ***www.citycafe.co.uk****.*

Offering good food in one of the most beautiful settings in Glasgow overlooking the River Clyde and the city's emblematic Finnieston Crane, this café on the ground floor of the City Inn is ideal after a visit to the Glasgow Science Centre. Ingredients in the modern European cuisine are fresh and dishes are homemade. The interior is minimalist, but relaxed enough for children not to feel a nuisance. Their menu includes favourites such as burgers as well as healthier pasta dishes.

***Open** Mon–Sat noon–2.30pm, 6–10.30pm, Sun 12.30–14.30pm, 7–9.30pm. **Main courses** lunch £9.95 for two courses, £14.95 for dinner. **Credit** AmEx, MC, V. **Amenities** baby-changing, children's menu (£4.95), highchairs, parking (free).*

78 St Vincent

*78 St Vincent Street, 01412 487878, **www.78stvincent.com**.*

A sophisticated turn-of-the-century Parisian-looking restaurant with white linen table cloths, high ceilings and red velvet curtains doesn't seem the ideal place for a hungry toddler eager to get back to watch Tombliboos in the Night Garden. Yet 78 is a good and reasonably priced option for an early family dinner. It has secluded booths that provide ideal tantrum screening as well as make dining relaxingly private (especially for breast-feeders). The children's menu has chicken goujons and chips with fancier options such as salmon. Small portions from the adults' menu are also available.

Arrive between 4pm and 7pm to eat at lunch time prices.

***Open** Mon–Fri 8.30am–3pm, 5pm–midnight, Sat 9am–3pm, 5pm–midnight, Sun 10am–3pm, 5pm–midnight. **Main courses** set lunch (two courses) £12.95, pre-theatre (two courses) 4–7pm £12.95, dinner (à la carte) £20. **Credit** AmEx, DC, M, V. **Amenities** children's menu (£5.95), highchairs.*

INEXPENSIVE

Café Gandolfi

*64 Albion St, 01415 526813, **www.cafegandolfi.com**.*

More laid-lack than Des Lynam on a Barcalounger, this restaurant so relaxed our daughter into the whole dining-out experience she started imagining every piece of laminated paper was a menu. 'Now what shall I have...', she said the next day in Dixons. The restaurant occupies the offices of the old Cheesemarket and is named after a family of famous camera makers. The eponymous Gandolfi camera sits in a top corner overlooking diners. The very reasonably-priced food ensures a stream of regulars. A favourite is the haggis, baked neeps and tatties; specials include veggie options, but what sets this place apart is the treatment of children. Within seconds of arrival our daughter was slid into a highchair and a Café Gandolfi bib wrapped around her neck. Staff cooked half portions, brought food immediately, and there was an understanding attitude towards mess. A couple of regulars, so relaxed around children, even calmed her anguished cries for another 'choccy ice-cream', taking it in turns to play peek-a-boo with her until the bill arrived.

***Open** Mon–Sat 9am–11.30pm, Sun noon–11.30pm. **Main courses** lunch £10, dinner (£12. **Credit** AmEx, MC, V.*

Grassroots Café

97 St George's Road, West End, 01414 235628.

The city's best-known vegetarian restaurant, inside an old flour mill, is a great place to try something different. It's the sister company of Glasgow's biggest natural food store. We tried our daughter on the *mezze* platter (pitta bread, olives, spiked almonds, hummus) that had a sub-50% strike rate (plus she managed to rub a vine leaf into our two-month old's eye), until the Cajun fries came to the rescue. There's a reliable veggie burger, six salads, the sandwiches are good and chef's ingredients are nearly all organic. The cakes are all home-baked, organic wines are available (for under £10) and there's a toy box and baby-changing. Organic baby food is on sale, plastic plates and cutlery can be asked for, and table 6, tucked away, is best for those with more than one child.

***Open** Fri–Sat 10am–10pm, Sun–Thurs 10am–9pm. **Main courses** £7.50, children (half portions) £3.75. **Credit** AmEx, DC, M, V.*

The Big Blue

*445 Great Western Road, 01413 571038, **www.bigblue.glasgow.co.uk**.*

The best place for outdoor city eating, this Italian serves excellent crispy pizzas at tables overlooking the River Kelvin. The family favourite also has excellent tapas, seafood in a cavernous basement setting built around an aquatic theme and pizzas are too big for one. There's no children's menu, but for £4.50 they get half-portions, an ice-cream plus free drink, while our daughter loved the pizza sticks dusted with icing sugar. Crayons, drawing pads and highchairs are available, but there's no baby-changing. Buggy pushers can avoid the stairs entering via Kelvingrove Park. (Park at Kelvin Bridge underground station and cross the footbridge).

If you get really settled, order a flaming Sambuca from the cocktail bar, then the '*gamberoni* Big Blue', a starter of king prawns, and while staring at the 4.5m dolphin carving made in situ from a toppled 24m poplar, reprise your argument about whether you saw that kingfisher in the Botanic Gardens (see p. 72).

***Open** daily noon–10pm. **Main courses** lunch £4.99, dinner £7. **Credit** V, M.*

Where the Monkey Sleeps

*182 West Regent Street, 01412 263406, **www.monkeysleeps.com**.*

This trendy café serves great food to office workers, media/arty types and families at Saturday lunchtimes, but is most popular with metal-heads (you'll see). The panini and soups are regarded as the best in the city, attracting couriers from miles around (their bikes obscure the front of the café, in the basement of a 19th century townhouse).

The diverse clientele is matched by a menu that sees many of its dishes (like 'Taxi for Gary') named after customers and the stories attached to them. This café doesn't tick all the family-friendly boxes. There's no highchairs, baby-changing or children's menu, but staff happily assist in lugging pushchairs, nappies can be changed in the staff area, half-portions are served along with combinations of almost everything on offer, and most children roam the three interconnected rooms anyway, teasing out an assortment of toys (from soldiers to model lizards) embedded in an exposed wall.

And then there's the metal. Myself, I am not a big fan, but the music was low-volume and Judas Priest isn't all that bad. Check out the toilet. It's a rock shrine, decked floor-to-ceiling with music posters signed by band members from Anthrax and Iron Maiden among others.

***Open** Mon–Fri 7am–5pm, Sat 10am–5pm. **Main courses** panini from £4.30, £3.30 take-away. **Credit** all major cards.*

Willow Tea Rooms

217 Sauchiehall St, 01413 320521, www.willowtearooms.co.uk.

The city's famous tearooms, hidden above a jewellers on Sauchiehall Street, is a mecca for Charles Rennie Mackintosh fans. Once you've scaled the stairs (no lifts), it's like entering a time warp. From the leaded windows to the high-backed Argyle chairs and the waitresses' dresses, everything is as it was 100 years ago. The sumptuous purple and silver décor and its Japanese-influenced Art Nouveau make the tearoom an illuminating refuelling stop. Bag a table by the window for the views, order one of 25 blended teas and marvel at Mackintosh's attention to detail (he designed everything from the outside of the building to the teaspoons). Our daughter was kept amused with colouring-in sheets, word search puzzles, quizzes, crayons and by standing on her seat to lean over and blow bubbles into her milkshake through a straw. Staff are unfazed by tantrums (even ones close to the original leaded mirror frieze).

***Open** Mon–Sat 9am–5pm, Sun 9am–4.45pm. **Main courses** toasties from £3.95, children's lunchboxes (£4.50). **Credit** all major cards. **Amenities** baby-changing.*

5 The Central Highlands

THE CENTRAL HIGHLANDS

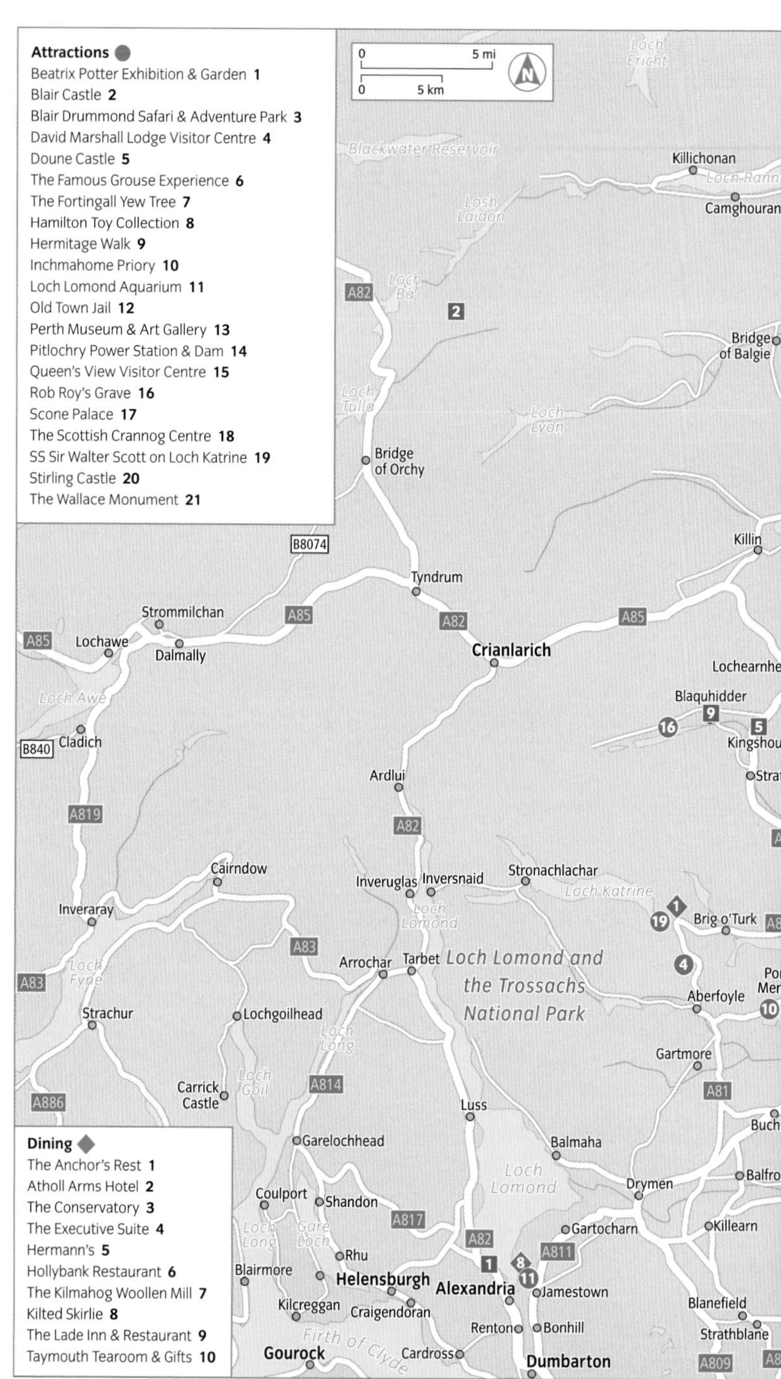

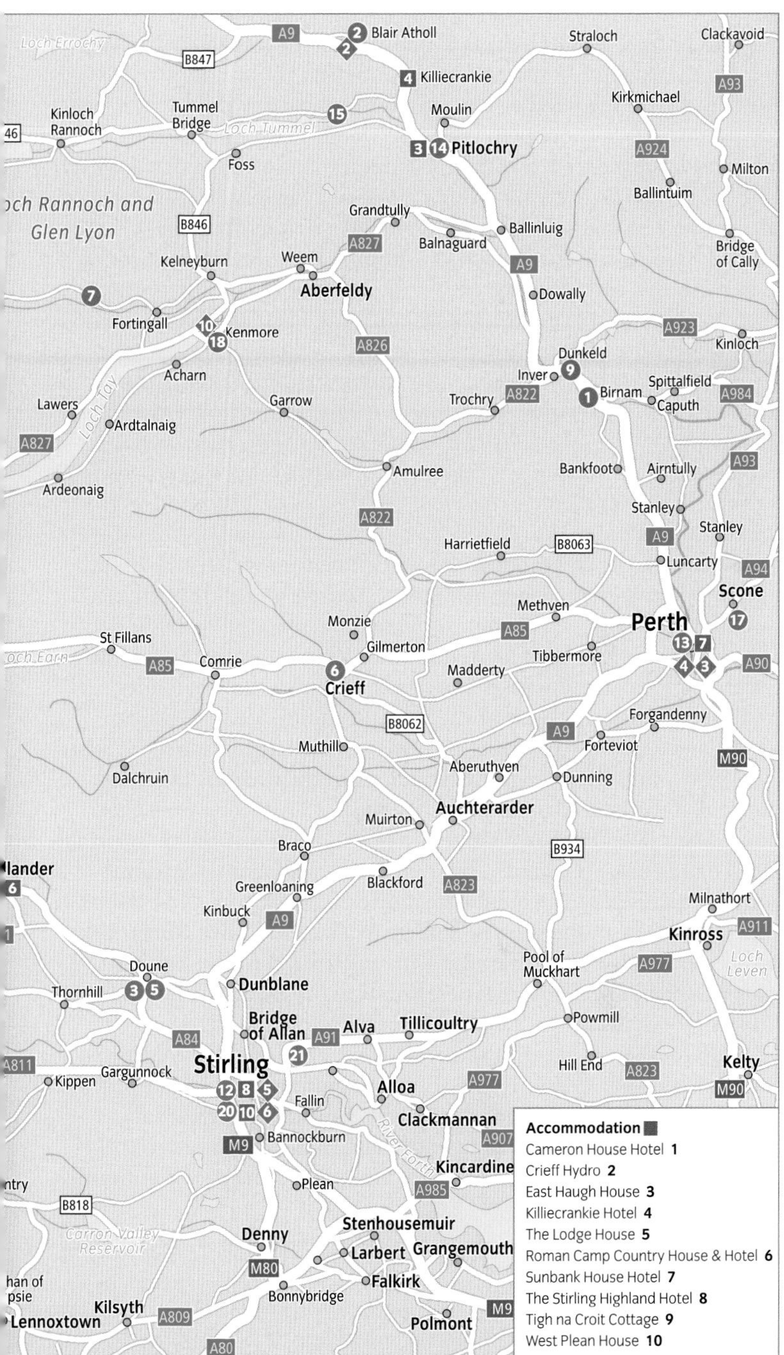
Loch Errochy
A9
B847
Blair Atholl
Killiecrankie
Straloch
Clackavoid
A93
Kirkmichael
Kinloch Rannoch
Tummel Bridge
Loch Tummel
Moulin
Pitlochry
Foss
A924
Milton
Ballintuim
Loch Rannoch and Glen Lyon
B846
Grandtully
A827
Balnaguard
Ballinluig
Bridge of Cally
Kelneyburn
Weem
Aberfeldy
A9
Dowally
Fortingall
Kenmore
A826
A923
Kinloch
Acharn
Dunkeld
Inver
Spittalfield
Birnam
Caputh
A984
Lawers
Loch Tay
Ardtalnaig
Garrow
Trochry
A822
A827
Ardeonaig
Amulree
Bankfoot
Airntully
A93
A822
Stanley
Stanley
Harrietfield
B8063
A9
Luncarty
A94
Scone
Methven
Perth
St Fillans
Monzie
Loch Earn
A85
Comrie
Gilmerton
A85
Tibbermore
Crieff
Madderty
A90
B8062
Forgandenny
Muthill
A9
Forteviot
Dalchruin
Aberuthven
Dunning
M90
Auchterarder
Muirton
Braco
B934
Callander
Greenloaning
Blackford
A823
Milnathort
Kinbuck
A9
Kinross
A911
Doune
Pool of Muckhart
A977
Loch Leven
Thornhill
Dunblane
Bridge of Allan
Alva
Tillicoultry
Powmill
A84
A91
Stirling
Hill End
Kelty
A811
Kippen
Gargunnock
A977
A823
Alloa
M90
Fallin
Clackmannan
M9
Bannockburn
A907
Kincardine
River Forth
Plean
A985
B818
Stenhousemuir
Carron Valley Reservoir
Denny
Larbert
Grangemouth
M80
Falkirk
Bonnybridge
Kilsyth
Lennoxtown
A809
Polmont
M9
A80
Accommodation
Cameron House Hotel 1
Crieff Hydro 2
East Haugh House 3
Killiecrankie Hotel 4
The Lodge House 5
Roman Camp Country House & Hotel 6
Sunbank House Hotel 7
The Stirling Highland Hotel 8
Tigh na Croit Cottage 9
West Plean House 10

The Central Highlands' pivotal centre is Stirling, on the south-western edge of the Trossachs, where Scotland is said to draw in her waist from the Clyde in the west to the Forth in the east. Monarchs have fought long and bloody wars for control of this gateway to the north. On the upside it means that the area now teems with attractive medieval towns, castles, royal palaces and historic battle sites where your children can wave wooden swords about. Part of the area has become a favourite leisure destination for Edinburghers and Glaswegians, who are a short jaunt away by car. In 2002 they helped make a huge chunk of it Scotland's first national park – the Loch Lomond and the Trossachs National Park. Recognised for its beauty in the 18th century, early visitors came here in their bustles and breeches to marvel at its lochs, pleasing hills, and birch and pinewood slopes. Romantic poets such as William Wordsworth (1770–1850) sang its praises, although it was Sir Walter Scott (1771–1832) who really put the area on the tourist map. His dramatic 1810 verse *The Lady of the Lake* set here ('In deep Trossach's wildest nook, his solitary refuge took...') was a huge success: visitors arrived in droves to trace the events of the poem, just like *Da Vinci Code* tourists today.

Meanwhile Loch Lomond, whose rich hedgerows become brooding woods and crags, is just half an hour's drive away. Over the centuries the loch has come to encapsulate the essence of Scottishness. The song, 'The banks of Loch Lomond', written by an 18th century Jacobite prisoner, epitomises a particular Scottish sentimentality, resulting in the popularity of the 'bonnie bonnie banks' across the world and especially in towns and cities where large numbers of Scots are to be found late at night with a drink in their hands. Even on home soil the loch stirs nationalistic blood. The rousing pipe band tune 'Scots Wha He Wi Wallace Bled', roughly translated to 'we're all now very drunk', is regarded by some as the real Scottish national anthem and is played around here at the drop of a Tam O'Shanter. The Wallace from the song is William Wallace who, like Robert the Bruce, fought the English in the 13th and 14th centuries in these parts. While in nearby Callander, Rob Roy MacGregor, Scotland's Robin Hood, lived (and terrorised) his way into legend.

Different in character to the north-west of Stirling lies Perthshire, or Big Sky Country as it is known in recognition of its large tracts of ancient forest. One of Scotland's largest counties, it contains the country's former capital, Perth, and is also home to remote countryside along with distilleries, castles, of course, and the very definition of a picture-postcard village – Kenmore.

CHILDREN'S TOP 10 ATTRACTIONS

❶ **Shout** catch phrases from *Monty Python and the Hold Grail* from the ramparts of Doune Castle. See p. 102.

❷ **Cycle** 23km from Stronachlachar to Trossach Pier around Lake Menteith, after a cruise on Scotland's oldest working steam ship. See p. 106.

❸ **Dress up** like 19th century prisoners on a tour of Stirling Old Town jail. See p. 112.

❹ **Sunbathe** with Vietnamese pot-bellied pigs at Blair Drummond Safari Park. See p. 100.

❺ **Stamp** on moving jigsaw pieces in the interactive room at the Famous Grouse Experience. See p. 122.

❻ **Visit** the Hamilton Toy Museum and see if you can find that Captain Scarlet Spectrum Pursuit Vehicle you lost in your best friend's sandpit in 1976. See p. 103.

❼ **Pony trek** at Crieff Hydro. See p. 125.

❽ **Find** your Scottish ancestry and which rival clans you're currently feuding with, after a bacon sandwich at the Kilmahog Woollen Mill. See p. 134.

❾ **Get the remains** of your delicious breakfast licked off your face by the friendliest Jack Russell in Scotland at the East Haugh House hotel. See p. 129.

❿ **Pretend** to be Mrs Tiggywinkle pegging out laundry at the Beatrix Potter exhibition at the Birnam Institute. See p. 117.

THE TROSSACHS

Originally the name of the narrow gorge between Loch Achray and Loch Katrine, the term **The Trossachs** now applies to the whole miniature Highlands north of Glasgow. These sparkling lochs and heather-clad hills were eulogised by Sir Walter Scott, not only in *The Lady of the Lake* but also his great work, *Rob Roy*. His novel and poem helped kick-start the whole concept of tourism back in the 19th century. Centring on the small town of **Callander,** Scotland's first national park contains the UK's largest forest, the Queen Elizabeth Forest Park, and is central to many Scottish fairy legends. The town itself is also a good place to explore the area's highlights, which include Inchmahome Priory, Lake Katrine and the famous 'Monty Python castle' at Doune. Stirling and Loch Lomond are no more than half an hour and an hour away, respectively, by car.

Essentials

The bus and train aren't ideally suited to exploring this area. The main and most central base is Callander, around 24km from

Loch Lubnaig

Stirling on the A84, about an hour by car from Glasgow (M80, M9, then A84). Meanwhile Perth is about an hour and half along the treacherous A9. From Callander the Trossachs themselves are easily accessed via a network of smaller roads woven through Loch Venachar, Loch Ard, Loch Lubnaig, Loch Katrine, Loch Lomond and the Lake of Menteith, as well as around the vast Queen Elizabeth Forest Park.

Roads are fairly clear and the only hazard will come from the countless times you pull over to take yet another picture of a beautiful loch framed on both slopping banks by forest. If you are using smaller roads, usually marked white on road maps (like the one from Kinghouse to Balquhidder), allow longer because they'll be single track with occasionally passing bays. Note: the road around Loch Katrine marked on some maps is a **private road** belonging to The Strathclyde Water Board. It is open only to walkers and cyclists.

Visitor Information

The **Callander Tourist Information Centre** (*01877 330342*) is at Ancaster Square, Callander, open daily 10am–4pm in January, February, November and December, daily 10am–5pm in March, April, May, June, September and October and daily 10am–6pm in July and August. The **Queen Elizabeth Forest Park Visitor Centre** (*01877 382383*) is off the A81 by Aberfoyle.

A useful website for information about the area is ***www.incallander.co.uk***.

What to See & Do

Blair Drummond Safari and Adventure Park ★★ ALL AGES

Callander Road, 01786 841456, www.blairdrummond.com. Off the A84.

Blair Drummond Safari and Adventure Park

Here children can boat around an island of chimps, drive through a Big Cat enclosure, feel the coat of a llama and lose their precious sleep-teddy (Nelly – a soft blue elephant) sunbathing carelessly with Vietnamese pot-bellied pigs. Throw in a small fairground, sealion and bird of prey shows, a giant slide, and the fact I accidentally lowered my wife's electric window in the tiger area, and it can make a pretty interesting family day out. After the safari section (also lions, bison, rhino), you park up in the fairground section where children get out and race around filling out activity sheets and beg you to go on rides while, if you are me, your wife says over a nerve-calming sausage roll, 'So tell me again. You just happened to put your elbow on the down button and then panicked and instead of pressing up you pressed down again. Ben, they were actual tigers, can you *please* be more careful.' Food is of the burger and fries variety but there's a barbecue area (staff provide, and light, coals, although bring utensils and meat) and the Trading Post café serves homemade dishes.

Slightly annoyingly, fairground rides including dodgems and slow revolving tea-cups, cost extra. However, there is always the four-times-daily sealion show and a falconry demonstration. Our daughter's best moment (apart from being lifted off the tea-cup: 'Too fast, Daddy. Too fast') was in the petting area, where debilitated by the earlier alarm of the tea-cup, she lay in a muddy puddle beside a pig. Our low-point was the loss of the aforementioned Nelly, which we only realised was missing a few hours later at bedtime. Nelly, however, (a kind of David Blane of the soft toy world: he has previously survived a night in our fridge, getting lost in Glasgow Primark and two nights under a suitcase in a flooded cellar) turned up, unscathed, beneath a pot-bellied pig.

***Open** daily 15th Mar–20th Oct 10am–5.30pm. **Adm** £10.00, children (3–14) £6.50, under-3s free. **Amenities** BBQ area, café.*

INSIDER TIP

Print off a voucher from the safari website for one child's free entry.

David Marshall Lodge Visitor Centre ALL AGES

Queen Elizabeth Forest Park, Aberfoyle, 01877 382258. Duke's Pass on the A821.

Here you can walk to a beautiful waterfall then try and spy red squirrels in a hide, while your toddler sings *Put The Little Pancake Into The Pan* through the wooden opening at the top and throws pine cones randomly. Through live webcams at the visitor centre you can watch baby ospreys feeding and have a picnic at one of the most scenic spots in the Trossachs, with views to Ben Lomond and the Campsie Fells. The best time to visit is July and August for the osprey chicks. On the Waterfall Trail (half a mile, flat for buggies), highlighted with yellow markers, look out for falcons, buzzards, red kite, eagles and signs of red squirrel activity (chewed pine cones, scratches on tree bark and a strange chuk-chuk noise).

If that's too *Springwatch-with-Bill-Oddie* for you, try next door's **Go Ape adventure course** (*0870 444 5562, **www.goape.co.uk***), where you can impress/embarrass your wife pretending to be Tarzan on the UK's longest zip wire (almost half a kilometre). There's a gorilla course for over-18s, and two 'baboon' courses for 10–15s and those aged 16–17. The course, a series of rope ladders, tree-walks and trapeze swings ending in a zip-wire over the gorge, is not for under-10s or anyone under 1.38m (4 feet 7 inches).

***Open** daily Feb–May 10am–5pm, June–Aug 10am–6pm, Sep–Oct 10am–5pm, Nov–Dec 10am–4pm. **Adm** free. **Amenities** children's playground (over 6s), craft shop, picnic area, café (with highchairs, baby-changing, children's lunchboxes).*

Doune Castle ★★ ALL AGES

*Doune, 01786 841742, **www.historic-scotland.gov.uk**. Off the A84.*

As the famous setting for *Monty Python and the Holy Grail*, 14th century Doune Castle is a mecca for comedy fans who flock here to practise John Cleese impressions, shouting down from the ramparts: 'I fart in your general direction. Your mother was a hamster and your father smelled of elderberries.' Others enjoy hunting for sword impressions made in the stonework during the filming of a movie they've learnt way too much about from the DVD *Holy Grail* extras. Historic Scotland lend coconut shells from its shop (although most visitors bring their own) to enable the mimicking of King Arthur approaching the castle in the movie's opening sequence, and in September there's a Monty Python Day that attracts 1,500 fans in period costume

FUN FACT Pragmatic Python

When *Monty Python and the Holy Grail* was filmed, permission from National Trust for Scotland to film scenes at other castles had been obtained. But as filming neared, Trust managers panicked and changed their minds, leaving Python producers with no choice but to use different parts of Doune Castle to depict all the fictional castles in the film. They relied on tight framing to maintain the illusion they were somewhere different.

from as far away as New York (£15, children £12).

For youngsters not into this brand of silliness, there's a mile-long nature trail taking you to a scenic spot flanked by meadows where the river Teith meets Ardoch Burn. Look out along the way for hidden sculptures of animals, although there's plenty of real wildlife including rabbits, squirrels and otters. Oh, and a nasty horsefly that bit my elbow, caused it to swell to the size of an avocado necessitating antihistamine and worries about a 'general neurological seizure', which my wife had so little truck with that she practically did fart in my general direction when I called NHS Direct. Leave buggies in the shop. And take a fly swat.

***Open** 1st Apr–30th Sep Mon–Sun 9.30am–5.30pm, 1st Oct–31st Mar Sat–Wed 9.30am–4.30pm (closed Thurs–Fri). **Adm** £4.00 (children up to 15 £2.00), under-5s free. **Amenities** baby-changing, shop.*

Hamilton Toy Collection ★

ALL AGES

*111 Main Street, Callander, 01877 330004, **www.thehamiltontoycollection.co.uk**.*

If you never grew up, stayed a child forever and had too much pocket money, this is how your house might eventually look, if social services didn't get to you first. Stuffed with more toys than I've ever seen in one place, its real market is nostalgic adults (like me) who never quite got over losing their Captain Scarlet Spectrum Pursuit Vehicle in Paul Harris' sandpit circa 1973. From teddy bears and dolls, through model trains and sci-fi figures all the way to soldiers, children can check out all the bygone choking hazards in the Edwardian Nursery, while parents roam to the chorus of 'I remember that'.

Buggy-pushers should use papooses — the collection is over several floors.

***Open** 1st Apr–end of Oct, 10am–4.30pm Mon–Sat (Sun noon–4.30pm). **Adm** £2, children 50p.*

Inchmahome Priory ★★

ALL AGES

Port Menteith, 01877 385294. 13km south of Callander on B8034 off A81.

Set on an island in the middle of Scotland's only lake (actually a loch, they just forgot to call it one), it was the mysterious *Famous Five*-style access to this former Augustinian retreat that

FUN FACT Inchmahome: Did You Know...?

1 Buried at the abbey is adventurer, scholar and politician Robert Bontine Cunninghame Graham (1852–1936), a pal of Buffalo Bill, H.G. Wells, George Bernard Shaw and novelist Joseph Conrad. He was the first ever MP to be suspended from the House of Commons for swearing (he said 'damn'), and later became president of the Scottish National Party. He is buried next to his beloved wife, Chilean poet Gabriela, whose grave he had dug with his bare hands 30 years earlier. They met after he knocked her down with his horse.

2 According to legend the Earl of Menteith, who built the Priory, was driven mad by loch-side fairies who pestered him, as only fictional gobliny-type people can, until he gave them Coire nan Uruisgean on Ben Venue as a meeting place. The fairies are said still to meet there, which is situated half-way up the mountains west of Lake Menteith, where they enjoy salsa nights and competitive games of canasta.

3 Scenes in the title song of the biggest-ever Bollywood movie *Kuch Kuch Hota Hai* were filmed at the Priory.

convinced us to visit. To get to the priory you must catch a boat from Port Menteith (a small stone pier), which you call by turning a metal board so the white side faces the island. Somehow an unseen boatman then chugs over to collect you, the board being turned back to the black before you leave. Although our female skipper, disappointingly, didn't try to involve us in a smuggling conspiracy or enlist our support in restoring the Stuart line, she did point out an osprey, and tell us

Exploring Inchmahome Priory

she preferred remote parts to the city, possibly implying she thought cities were evil.

The priory was founded in 1238 by Walter Comyn, the Earl of Menteith, and has been visited by Robert the Bruce and Mary Queen of Scots, who stayed here in 1547 aged 4 after her side's disastrous (and rather camp sounding) defeat at the Battle of Pinkie, near Edinburgh. Although we were slightly unhappy not to be clandestinely bringing ashore barrels of rum, the roofless priory and the huge old oaks dotted about were great for our daughter to clamber over and play hide and seek. There is a small kiosk where the friendly staff will tell you more fascinating history about the island, as well as pointing out a good spot where children can catch small fish. Awash with bluebells in May, the island gets busy in summer, attracting birdwatchers who come for the crested grebes, tufted ducks and herons in regular attendance.

Open *1st Apr–30th Sep Mon–Sun (9.30 am to last outward sailing at 4.30 pm).* ***Adm*** *(including crossing) £4.50, children £2.25.* ***Amenities*** *shop.*

Rob Roy's Grave AGES OVER 12

Balquhidder Church, Balquhidder. 16km north of Callander.

You can't visit the Trossachs without a trip to Balquhidder, where the legendary cattle-rustler, intrepid outlaw and Jacobite, Rob Roy lived, died and is buried in the graveyard of the village's tumbledown 17th century church. Romanticised by Daniel Defoe (1723), Sir Walter Scott (1818) and two Hollywood movies, Rob Roy lies under a headstone reading 'MacGregor despite them'. Robert MacGregor was known as Rob Roy due to the red ('roy') colour of his hair. He also had disproportionately long arms, giving him a great advantage with the Highland Sword and also meaning he could, if he wanted, tie the garters of his Highland hose without breaking stride. The statue designed by the Queen's sculptor Benno Schotz above the

FUN FACT Witching

The last person tried for witchcraft in the UK was 22-stone medium Helen Duncan from Callander, convicted under the 1735 Witchcraft Act in 1944. She'd embarrassed the government in 1941 by talking in a séance to a dead sailor from *HMS Barham*, a ship the War Office did not reveal had been torpedoed, with the cost of 861 lives, until several months later. On the night of 19th January 1944, the medium, with ectoplasm 'issuing from her mouth', was apparently arrested because of fears she'd reveal the date of D-Day landings. Tried at the Old Bailey, Duncan received nine months in London's Holloway Prison.

Albert Hall in Stirling shows Rob Roy looking about as disproportionate as your average cereal-packet figurine.

Also buried in Balquhidder is the wife of Robert Kirk (see below), whose story has amazed as many generations as Rob Roy's.

***Adm** free.*

SS Sir Walter Scott on Loch Katrine ★ ALL AGES

Trossachs Pier, Loch Katrine, Callander, ☎ 01877 376315. Off A821 at the end of Loch Achray.

The best way to see the crystal-clear waters of Loch Katrine and its setting against Ben Venue is on Scotland's oldest surviving screw-driven steamship, the *SS Sir Walter Scott*. Departing from Trossachs Pier, the 19th century boat sails 13km to Stronachlachar on the loch's south-western shore, the trip including on-board commentary (if you can hear it above the coal-fired engine) pointing out Glengyle, where Rob Roy was born, stories about evil loch-side goblins and the fact the loch was Sir Walter Scott's inspiration for his famous poem, *The Lady of the Lake*. The cruise lasts 1½ hours and apart from the thrill of staring out of portholes ('Look daddy, the windows are round'), and getting in people's way as they ferry Rob Roy Specials (hot drinking chocolate beverages containing slugs of brandy) up and down the stairs between decks, there isn't a lot for children after they've tried to fall overboard between the gaps in the railings.

The best way to make this a family occasion is to hire bikes at

SS Sir Walter Scott, Loch Katrine

FUN FACT Rev. Robert Kirk

The Reverend Robert Kirk, the David Icke of his day, was minister of Balquidder until 1685, until he was transferred to Aberfoyle. There he became the first man to translate the Bible into Gaelic before a strange change saw him abandon pastoral visits to explore nearby Doon Hill, where he became convinced the fairy legends of the hill were real and that he'd been chosen to interpret their thoughts. By 1690 he began writing *The Secret Commonwealth of the Elves, Fauns and Fairies*, a manuscript explaining that the 'wee folk' communicated through a system of whistling. When visible they wore plaid and could be mischievous, he concluded, often stealing milk from cows.

One moonlit night in May 1692 walking near Doon Hill, Kirk died of a heart attack. That would have been that if after his funeral, particularly sad as his wife was expecting a child, the minister's first cousin hadn't shocked the neighbourhood by claiming Kirk had materialised before him and pressed him to tell the local laird, Graham of Duchray, that he wasn't dead but had been carried off by fairies. To bring Kirk back to life, Graham of Duchray had to attend Kirk's son's baptism and at the moment of Kirk's appearance throw a knife, which would break the spell. Kirk's wife eventually gave birth and despite his doubts Graham of Duchray did duly arrive at the baptism carrying a knife. The ceremony went smoothly until incredibly Rev. Kirk strode into the room (although not in a turquoise tracksuit). The story goes that Graham of Duchray was so stunned he forgot to hurl the knife, and Kirk left the room by another door never to be seen again. Theories of Kirk's church dissapearance, witnessed by so many it beggars belief, have included time travel, because Aberfoyle lies in an area where electromagnetic forces are strong. So could the Aberfoyle minister have been centuries ahead of his time (and ours) in understanding the earth's magnetic field, and have intended the metal knife to create a short circuit? Kirk's fairy manuscript, now preserved at Edinburgh University, was rediscovered in 1815 and so intrigued Sir Walter Scott when he came to the Trossachs that he made his headquarters at the old manse at Aberfoyle.

Katrinewheelz at the pier (adults £10, covered trailer for toddlers £7) and cycle back from Stronachlachar along a private road (no cars) around the loch. The 23km ride is on tarmaced surfaces but gets hilly and the trailers are low to the ground meaning our daughter kept shouting 'No Daddy, no', every time I went over a cattle grid. Along the way you'll pass Glengyle House (no public access), the clan Macgregor graveyard, become a little worried about evil goblins as it gets dark, and eventually have a small argument about whether you'll make it back in time to the cycle hire place (bikes are rented for 4 hours). A good bribe if your daughter starts to shout 'My don't like it. My bottom hurts', is the £1-a-go bouncy castle back

FUN FACT **Katrine: Did You Know...?** 

You cannot throw coins in, or fish, or bathe in Loch Katrine because it became Glasgow's main water supply in 1859. Interestingly, although its pure water rid the populous of typhus in the 19th century, because of the lack of calcium in the loch (burned off in violent earthquakes) it caused children to be born bandy legged with rickets.

at the pier. There are no bikes with stabilisers for under-6s, although you can hire a tag-along. Katrinewheelz is open daily 9am–6pm, although phone ahead between October and March.

Fare *£6.50 (45 minutes sailing) £7.50 (1½ hour sailing), under-16s £4.50 and £5.50, respectively.*

INSIDER TIP

If planning to cycle back, book tickets **at least a day in advance** because there are only 20 bike spaces on the boat that fill up quickly in the summer.

LOCH LOMOND

Probably the world's most famous lake, **Loch Lomond** is renowned for its beauty and tranquillity. Dotted with picturesque touring boats and families of swans along its edge, its main shoreside centres are approached on its western bank via the A82. They include the quaint village of Luss, where *Take The High Road* (a Scottish soap opera) is filmed, and and the Vale of Leven (between the A82 and the A813), a loose term for the five villages of Balloch, Renton, Jamestown, Bonhill and

Sir Walter Scott (1771–1832)

The novelist and poet Sir Walter Scott was revered throughout the world in his time. His most famous poem is *The Lady of the Lake*, and best known among his novels are *Ivanhoe* and *Rob Roy*. Scott's eventful life saw him find the lost Scottish Crown Jewels in Edinburgh Castle, invent the modern historical novel, and rehabilitate the public perception of Highland culture after years in the doldrums following the Jacobite revolts. His organisation of King George IV's visit to Scotland in 1822 led Edinburgh tailors to invent many new clan tartans and resulted ultimately in a return to fashion for both the kilt and playing the bagpipes. Scott, who has a central railway station in Edinburgh (Waverly) named after one of his novels, was also responsible, through a series of letters in the Edinburgh Weekly News, for retaining the right of Scottish banks to issue their own banknotes, reflected today by his continued appearance on the front of all Bank of Scotland paper money.

Loch Lomond

Alexandria that have merged over the years into one. You'll find locals here confusingly talking about 'goowin doon the Vale' or 'goowin up the Vale.' Don't worry, it's not a term of abuse because you're wearing a brightly coloured bumbag and don't know the way to the aquarium.

The loch itself is a bit of a record breaker. At 44 square kilometres, it is the largest inland waterway in Britain. It's perhaps most notable for the 1841 song *The Banks of Loch Lomond*, written by a captured Jacobite and including a chorus all Scots can sing after a few drams:

'Oh, ye'll tak' the high road, and I'll tak' the low road,

And I'll be in Scotland afore ye;

But me and my true love will never meet again.

On the bonnie, bonnie banks o' Loch Lomond.'

Because the loch is crossed by the Highland fault boundary it exhibits characteristics of both high- and lowland Scotland, and has 38 islands, one of which, Inchconnachan, is home to a colony of wallabies. Loch Lomond also harbours 200 species of birds, and 25% of British plant life has been recorded in the area.

Essentials

By Bus From Stirling there are hourly services to Callander (45 minutes), and to Doune (six a day, 35 minutes). For more information contact **Scottish Citylink** (📞 *0870 550 5050*, ***www.citylink.co.uk***).

By Car It is car country here, if you want to see all there is. Loch Lomond is approached via the A82 from Glasgow (journey time: one hour). From Edinburgh the M9 takes you into Stirling, where you pick up the A811 (journey time: two hours). From Perth it's the A9 and then the A811 (journey time 1¾ hours).

Although the loch is beautiful from almost every road circling it, it is best seen from one of two cul-de sacs by way of Drymen at the southern end via the A911, taking you through Balmaha and on to Rowardennan. Alternatively, if you're more pressed for time or your children are rebelling about the amount of time they're strapped in their car seats re-reading a *Koala Brothers* book, west from Aberfoyle you can reach Loch Lomond near its northern end, at Inversnaid, via the B829.

Visitor Information

The **National Park Gateway Centre** (*0870 720 0631*) is based at Loch Lomond Shores, Ben Lomond Way, Balloch. The **Balloch Tourist Information Centre** (*0870 720 0607*) is at Balloch Road, Balloch. The **Balmaha National Park Centre** (*01389 722100*) is unmissable in Balmaha. The **Drymen Tourist Information Centre** (*0870 720 0615*) is at Drymen Library, The Square, Drymen, and the **Luss National Park Centre** (*01389 722120*) is next to Luss village.

What to See & Do

Loch Lomond Aquarium ★

ALL AGES

Ben Lomond Way, Balloch, Arygll, *01389 71500,* ***www.sealifeeurope.com.***

Based in the cylindrical Drumkinnon Tower, modelled on a medieval Scottish castle (minus the ramparts, the moat, the drawbridge and almost everything else that makes a castle), the aquarium's highlight is an ocean tunnel where on alternate days at 1.30pm either sharks or rays get fed. The aquarium also has touch pools where staff teach youngsters interesting facts about sea creatures. (Did you know starfish push their stomachs out through their mouths to eat?) Other species on display include Asian short-clawed otters, octopuses and slightly duller fish native to Loch Lomond such as trout and perch, while a unique sea-horse breeding centre allows youngsters to learn about their lifecycle (they're born, bob about, give birth, bob about and then die). The aquarium has fascinating sealife facts on the walls to keep younger teens interested, such as one about the dwarf seahorse moving at 0.00016 kph, roughly the speed we peeled our toddler away from the *Finding Nemo* display. A yellow route delineates a path involving no stairs, although beware: when we reached the café the lift system became so chaotic we couldn't get down in the same lift we ascended in, and although there was apparently another lift, it was impossible to find it, so we were marooned hopelessly for more than 10 minutes, queuing eventually at the tills in the café to throw ourselves on the mercy of the girl serving, who eventually radioed somebody like it was an emergency on Ben Nevis to re-programme the lift to allow us to exit with our buggy but very little dignity. However, there are worse places to be stranded; the views across Loch Lomond are stunning.

After the aquarium it's worth popping next door to the **National Park Gateway Centre**, a useful ranger-staffed information area that gives tips on attractions in the Trossachs, while in the Jenners shopping centre opposite there is a **Ceramic Experience** for children, where for £5 our daughter painted a porcelain dinosaur (and herself and the table and her chair and also two strangers from Fife), while we enjoyed a cup of a tea pretending to the strangers from Fife that she wasn't our daughter.

At the waterfront you can also arrange **boat trips** of the loch (Sweeney's Cruises, ☎ *01389 752376*), or pedalo hire (☎ *01389 602576*).

Open *daily 10am–4pm.* ***Adm*** *£7.95, children £5.50, family ticket (two adults, two children) £22.* ***Amenities*** *café.*

STIRLING

This small-scale Edinburgh is famous for a stunning hilltop castle and its status as the centre of the battles of Bannockburn (Robert the Bruce beats the evil English in 1314) and Stirling Bridge (William Wallace beats the evil English in 1297). More recently, a terrible statue of Wallace looking exactly like Mel Gibson from the Oscar-winning epic, *Braveheart*, has made headlines ('They may take away lives, but they'll never take our... *historical authenticity*!').

Stirling, which comes from an old Gaelic word for strife, had its golden age between the 15th and 17th centuries. It was the main residence of the Stuart monarchy and the setting for the 1543 coronation of Mary, Queen of Scots. In the 18th century its location was of strategic importance in the Jacobite rebellions of 1715 and 1745. Nowadays this historic old market town with its winding cobblestone streets, is best explored on foot (the hills are fairly steep however), although it lacks the cosmopolitan edge of neighbours Edinburgh and Glasgow.

INSIDER TIP

The open-topped 'hop on, hop off' **City Sightseeing Bus** (☎ *01786 446611*) runs every 30 minutes from 9.30am till 4.10pm between April to October and includes the Wallace Monument. Tickets cost £7, children £3.

Essentials

By Train There are links to Stirling from Aberdeen (hourly, 2¼ hours), Dundee (hourly, one hour), Falkirk (hourly, 30 minutes), Glasgow (hourly, 30 minutes), Inverness (three daily, 2½ hours) and Perth (hourly, 30 minutes). For more details: **National Rail Enquiries** (☎ *0845 748 4950*, ***www.nationalrail.co.uk***) or **First ScotRail** (☎ *0845 755 0033*, ***www.firstgroup.com/scotrail***).

By Bus There is one daily **National Express** (*0870 580 8080*, ***www.nationalexpress.com***) coach direct to Stirling from London; the journey lasts nine hours. There are regional services into Stirling's bus station at Goosecroft Road (behind the Thistle shopping centre) from Glasgow (hourly), St Andrews (three daily, two hours), Dundee (hourly, 1½ hours), Inverness, Edinburgh (hourly, 1¼ hours), Falkirk (every 40 minutes, 25 minutes) and Perth (hourly, 45 minutes). From Stirling there are also services hourly to Callander (45 minutes), and to Doune (six a day, 35 minutes). For more information contact **Scottish Citylink** (*0870 550 5050*, ***www.citylink.co.uk***), **First Ltd** (*0870 872 7271*) at Stirling bus station or **Stagecoach** (*01738 629339*, ***www.stagecoachbus.com***) at Ruthvenfield Road, Perth.

By Car Coming from Edinburgh, the M9 runs to within sight of Stirling Castle. The journey takes around 1½ hours. From Glasgow it's the M80, A80, which becomes the M80 again, then the M9. It will take about an hour. Perth, via the M9 and A9, is about an hour away.

Visitor Information

The **Stirling Tourist Office** (*01786 475019*) is at 41 Dumbarton Road. Hours are April–May Monday–Saturday 9am–5pm; June and September Monday–Saturday 9am–6pm, Sunday 10am–4pm; July–August Monday–Saturday 9am–7pm, Sunday 9.30am–6pm; October Monday–Saturday 9.30am–5pm; November–March Monday–Friday 10am–5pm, Saturday 10am–4pm. **The Royal Burgh of Stirling Visitor Centre** (*01786 479901*, ***www.visitscottishheartlands.org***) at Castle Esplanade is open daily April–October 9.30am–6pm and November–March 9.30am–5pm.

What to See & Do

Old Town Jail ★

*St John Street, Stirling, 01786 450050, **www.oldtownjail.com**.*

Children can dress up like 19th century prisoners during tours conducted by actors telling the gruesome story of life behind bars in Victorian times. At the jail, opened in 1847, you'll meet Jock Rankin, the town's hangman, from the days when prisoners were branded, as well as other costumed characters including a warden, an escaped prisoner and a Victorian reformer. 'Coarse food; a dress of shame; hard, continual, irksome labour; a planned and regulated and unrelenting exclusion of happiness and comfort' was the Victorian prescription for prisoners, and coincidentally pretty much mine when I left behind our baby's gro-bag.

These former times are brought back to life through echoey sound effects of slamming doors, shuffling feet and keys jangling so convincingly it reminded my wife we'd gone away without

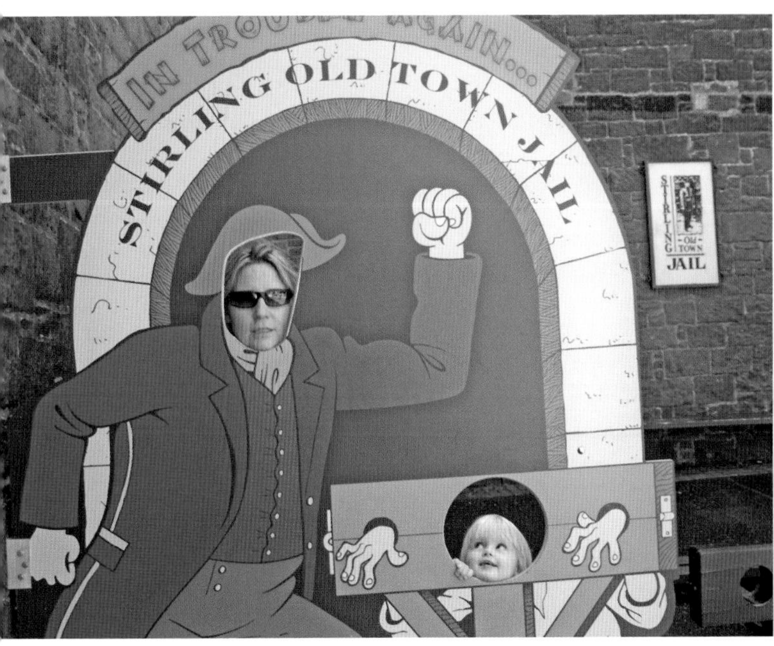

Old Town Jail, Stirling

renewing our TV licence. Children are given their own audio headsets to ensure they are only appropriately scared for their age group and our daughter also got to draw a picture of a cat on a piece of slate with some chalk. Elsewhere there is an exhibition where you can learn prison talk (see 'Prison Slang', below) while the not-to-be-missed exhibit is the dreaded crank – a lever that prisoners were forced to turn more than 14,000 times a day as a punishment. Arguably the main attraction is the view. Take the glass lift to the 5th floor where you can gaze out on the **Forth Valley** and see the battlefield of **Bannockburn** as well as the distant **Wallace Monument**.

INSIDER TIP

The lift to the top floors is blocked for descents, but staff will bypass the controls if you ask.

FUN FACT Prison Slang

Jailers could make turning the crank handle harder by tightening a screw. Hence the phrase 'turning the screw,' and also the slang term of 'screw' for prison warder. Other useful prison slang includes:

Dinghy – a lie
Dig out – (alleged, of course) victimisation of prisoners by staff
Suitcase – The anal cavity (as in 'I got the drugs stashed in me suitcase')

***Open** Apr–May 9.30am–5.30pm, June–Sep 9am–6pm, Oct 9.30am–5pm, Nov–Mar 10am–4pm (guided tours run daily Apr–Oct and Sat and Sun Nov–Mar). **Adm** (with actor) £5.95, children £3.80, family ticket (two adults, two children) £15.70; tours without actors £5, children £3.20, family ticket £13.25. **Amenities** audioguides.*

Stirling Castle ★★ ALL AGES

*Castle Wynd, Stirling, 01786 450000, **www.historic-scotland.gov.uk**.*

Stirling Castle towers over some of the greatest battlefields in Scotland's history, including William Wallace's triumph at Stirling Bridge in 1297, Robert the Bruce's defeat of the English at Bannockburn in 1314, and my victory over my wife about the best way to connect the in-car DVD player. (You have to use the yellow jack, of course). The castle's strategic importance has seen it besieged more than 16 times, and many great events from Scotland's past are associated with it, including the 1452 murder of the Earl of Douglas by James II, the 1543 coronation of Mary, Queen of Scots in the Chapel Royal, the baptism of the future James VI, and my wife finally admitting 'OK, OK – you're probably right – I didn't see the yellow jack.' Packed full of history for adults, children will also have fun on the children's trail, although our daughter preferred trying to lose me in the Royal Palace and then sitting astride a cannon in the grand battery overlooking the Wallace Monument, eating her children's lunchbox and ignoring me when I told her, 'It's dangerous to run off. I need to see you at all times. You're eyes have gone glazy. Do you need a wee? You need a wee, don't you?

Other attractions to enjoy after you have mopped toddler wee from an ancient cannon include a re-creation of the 16th century kitchens with interactive exhibits, and the hammerbeam roof of the

View of Wallace Monument from Stirling Castle

FUN FACT An Unfortunate Resemblance

The statue of Sir William Wallace beside the Visitor Centre caused controversy when it was unveiled because many thought it bore an uncanny resemblance not to Wallace, but to Mel Gibson who played him in the 1995 Hollywood epic *Braveheart*. Wallace's shield even bears the legend 'Braveheart'. This led to calls for its removal, which were refused, but the statue has been subject to regular vandalism. As a result it was enclosed by a security fence, a touch embarrassing for a sculpture emblazoned with the word 'freedom'.

Great Hall (the biggest ever built in Scotland) that reminded our daughter of my step-mother's barn conversion.

Open *daily Apr–Sep 9.30am–6pm, Oct–Mar 9.30am–5pm.* ***Adm*** *£8.50, children (5–15) £4.25, under-5s free.* ***Amenities*** *café (with highchairs), parking £2.00 (maximum two hour stay).*

The Wallace Monument

ALL AGES

Abbey Craig, Stirling, 01786 472140, ***www.nationalwallacemonument.com****.*

If they climb the 246 steps to the top of this monolith, children get a certificate to mark the achievement that they can rip into small pieces in the car for you to clear up later. The Monument was built in 1869 and has commanding views on a clear day (rare) to the Forth Bridge. It marks where Scottish hero, Sir William Wallace(c. 1272–1305), ordered his attack against the English at the Battle of Stirling Bridge in 1297. This famous Scots victory ultimately ended in defeat for Wallace, who on 23rd August 1305 was dragged to Smithfield in London then hanged and disembowelled while still alive. His entrails were burned before his eyes, he was decapitated and his body divided into four parts.

The highlight here is Wallace's huge sword on the first floor. Preserved in a glass case, its blade is over 1.5m long while on the floor below there's a re-enactment of Wallace defending himself at his trial in Westminster. On the floor above at the Hall of Heroes (marble busts of significant 19th century Scots) you can vote for your modern day Scottish hero (I chose Ricky Ross from Deacon Blue to annoy my wife). Afterwards, if your knees have not fused into lifeless bones, there are short signposted woodland walks.

Open *July–Aug 9am–6pm, Sep 9.30am–6pm, Oct 10am–5pm, Nov–Feb 10.30am–4pm, Mar 10am–5pm, Apr–June 10am–6pm.* ***Adm*** *£6, children £4.* ***Amenities*** *parking.*

INSIDER TIP

There is a **shuttle bus** that runs from the Visitor Centre car park to the top of the Abbey Craig. The hill is steep. Take it.

PERTHSHIRE

Perthshire's importance in the history of Scotland stems from its border location between the unruly Highland peoples and their slightly less scruffy lowland neighbours. It is home to Scone Palace where Scottish monarchs were once crowned and Perth, the former capital of Scotland. The county is also full of record-breaking trees, including the tallest tree in Britain and also the oldest tree in the world. Apart from all these record-breaking trees (there is also a famous hedge, but we'll leave it there), the county offers distilleries, great scenery and the fine Georgian city of Perth, accessed via the beautiful Smeaton bridge over the River Tay and home to two vast public parks called Inches. One of the largest counties in Scotland, its southern parts are mainly lowland, aside from the Ochil Hills, while further north sees the start of the Highland boundary faultline from Dunkeld in the east reaching westward to Crieff. These are a different kind of highlands, less rugged and instead full of shimmering lochs and villages nestling in peaceful grassy glens amid gentle tree-clad slopes.

Essentials

By Train On the Inverness–Perth line there are stops at Blair Atholl, Pitlochry and Dunkeld. For more details contact **National Rail Enquiries** (☎ *0845 748 4950*, ***www.nationalrail.co.uk***) or **First ScotRail** (☎ *0845 755 0033*, ***www.firstgroup.com/scotrail***.

By Bus There are direct links to London; the journey lasts 11 hours: **National Express** (☎ *0870 580 8080*, ***www.nationalexpress.com***). There are regional services from Stirling bus station to Perth (hourly, 45 minutes). For more information contact **Scottish Citylink** (☎ *0870 550 5050*, ***www.citylink.co.uk***) and **First Ltd** (☎ *0870 872 7271*) at Stirling bus station or **Stagecoach** (☎ *01738 629339*, ***www.stagecoachbus.com***) at Ruthvenfield Road, Perth.

By Car Perth is best approached from Edinburgh via the A90 and M90 over the Forth Bridge; from Glasgow via the A80 and M80 and then M9 to Stirling, and from there via the A9.

Visitor Information

The **Perth Tourist Office** (☎ *01738 450600*, ***www.perthshire.co.uk***) is at Lower City Mills, West Mill Street. There are other offices at **Pitlochry** (☎ *01796 472215*, ***www.perthshire.co.uk***); on 22 Atholl Road, Aberfeldy (☎ *01887 820276*, ***www.Perthshire.co.uk***); in The Square, **Crieff** (☎ *01764 652578*, ***www.perthshire.co.uk***); at Town Hall, High Street, Crieff, Dunkeld (☎ *01350 727688*, ***www.perthshire.co.uk***); at The Cross, Dunkeld, **Auchterarder** (☎ *01764 663450*, ***www.perthshire***); in the High Street, **Blairgowrie** (☎ *01250 872960*, ***www.perthshire.co.uk***); and at 26 Wellmeadow, **Blairgowrie**.

FUN FACT Beatrix Potter Trivia

1 *The Tale of Peter Rabbit* started as a letter Beatrix Potter wrote to the eldest son of her governess about her own pet rabbit that she took everywhere on a lead.
2 In 1881 Beatrix Potter started a journal recording her thoughts and feelings in a secret code not cracked until 1958.
3 Beatrix Potter popularised the practice of producing smaller books that were easier for children to hold.
4 Beatrix Potter was a renowned mycologist who came up with the theory that a lichen is a fungus and an algae living in a symbiotic relationship, which was dismissed at the time but which (as we all know) has since been proven true.
5 When she quit writing, Potter became one of the country's greatest sheep farmers.

What to See & Do

Beatrix Potter Exhibition and Garden ★ AGES UNDER 7

*Birnam Institute, Station Road, Birnam, 01350 727674, **www.birnaminstitute.com**.*

Beatrix Potter, the beloved children's author, was brought up when kids were supposed to be seen and not heard. Rarely seeing her parents, and not sent to school because her mum worried she'd catch germs, she spent her free time upstairs drawing and making up stories about the animals she'd smuggled into the house (hedgehogs, frogs, mice, etc.). Also a renowned mycology expert (that's fungi) and artist, this exhibition tells her story, identifies her inspirations (Mr MacGregor was based on their postman, Mrs Tiggywinkle on the family's washerwoman), while entertaining children with Beatrix Potter-related games, activities and puzzles. Our daughter (and my wife, overcome with nostalgia for Harlington Primary) got to draw acorns and pine cones from a nature trolley. Children can dress up like Peter Rabbit, pretend to be Mrs Tiggywinkle pegging out laundry on a miniature clothes line and colour pictures of Benjamin Bunny at a small desk set up to resemble the ones Potter sat at when she

FUN FACT A Beatrix Potter Quiz

Who tricked Jemima Puddle-Duck in Beatrix Potter's 9th book? **A whiskered gentleman.**
What is the name of Tom Kitten's sister? **Miss Moppet.**
What is Mrs. Tiggy-winkle? **A hedgehog.**
What happened to Peter's father? **He was put in Mrs McGregor's pie.**

was taught by a governess (and my wife claimed she sat at in Mrs Boileau's English classes, where she was also bullied for using long words such as purloined).

In the foyer of the Birnam Institute there is an excellent café where you can buy delicious carrot cake and try and turn a deaf ear to more of your wife's ludicrous memories of the consequences, for instance, of using the word discombobulated during morning break. (Susan Lardlow gave her a Chinese burn). Afterwards, visit the Beatrix Potter garden full of statues of Potter characters.

Open *daily mid-Mar–Nov 10am–5pm, Dec–mid-March Mon–Sat 10am–4.30pm (Sun 11am–4.30pm).* ***Adm*** *£1, children free.* ***Amenities*** *café.*

Blair Castle ★ ALL AGES

Atholl Estates, Blair Atholl, Pitlochry, ☎ 01796 481207, ***www-blair-castle.co.uk****.*

Despite the fact that the Duke of Atholl has the only private army in Europe (the Atholl Highlanders), we somehow managed to accidentally sneak in here without paying, after accidentally entering via the estate's private road. The castle, dating from the 13th century, was the last to be besieged in Britain. Highlights include the **Entrance Hall**, where there's a Scottish broadsword from Culloden that when discovered still had a severed hand attached to it. In the same room there's a mark in the floor left by a cannonball during the Jacobite siege of 1745. The Duke was granted his own private army by Queen Victoria in 1844; it gathers on the Duke's return from South Africa on the Saturday of the last bank holiday weekend in May, and at the Blair Atholl Highland Games the following day. Our worst moment came in the Grand Ballroom, overhearing two women discussing the admission fee, we

Blair Castle, Blair Atholl

suddenly realised we hadn't paid. The best – overhearing two Slovaks talking about the Picnic Grove. They thought it was the last resting place of Princess Diana rather than an 18th century forest garden named after the Roman goddess of hunting.

Children aged over 12 can join parents on hour-long pony trekking excursions round the estate (leaving at 10am and 2pm) for £20 a head; between April and June (Tuesday to Sunday).

***Open** daily 21st Mar–24th Oct 9.30am–4.30pm, Nov–Mar Tues and Sat 9.30am–1.30pm. **Adm** £7.90, children £4.90, under-5s free, family tickets (two adults and unlimited children) £20.50. Grounds-only £2.30. **Amenities** baby-changing, children's quiz.*

Hermitage Walk ★★ ALL AGES

1½ km north of Dunkeld on A9

Laden as we are with a baby and a shilly-shallying toddler, you might as well tell us that through the trunk of that oak tree is a secret porthole to Narnia as point us towards a woodland walk. That said, we rather enjoyed this stroll along the rhododendron-clad banks of the River Braan to an idyllic waterfall overlooked by Britain's tallest tree – a 65m Douglas Fir. This 1km walk, once part of the **Scottish Grand Tour**, has been enjoyed by nature lovers (such as Wordsworth and Mendelssohn) for more than 200 years. It's even ideal for buggy-pushers, apart from the last few metres of stubborn tree roots before the stone-arched bridge for which you'll need caterpillar tracks. The focal point, the **Black Linn Falls**, is next to **Ossian's Hall**, a Victorian folly with a concealed door and an echoey chamber our daughter had fun inside. After you've waited in vain for some of the gung-ho walkers posing on the waterfall's slippery rocks to plummet into the raging torrent, turn to look at the woodland pool the other side of the bridge. Bathed in white petals, it looked so like the Elysian backdrop of a Roman epic that we half expected to encounter Narcissus rather than the group we actually saw from Dumfries eating Ecclefechan buttered tart in Queen of the South football shirts.

Britain's tallest tree (presently under dispute; there's a rival near Inverness) is unmarked, to save trophy hunters hacking off chunks, so you'll have to guess. If you're buggy-free, a little further along the bank you'll find **Ossian's Cave**, basically a roof over some large rocks, appearing to be the makeshift home of a hermit, thus giving the walk its name.

***Open** all year. **Adm** free.*

Perth Museum and Art Gallery ALL AGES

*78 George Street, ☎ 01738 632488, **www.pkc.gov.uk**.*

Here youngsters can dress up in Roman armour, answer quizzes and compete to see who can guess what various indigenous stuffed animals sounded like when alive including red deer, squirrels, owls,

FUN FACT Scotland's Stone

Legend says the Stone of Scone (pronounced *skoon* and basically a block of sandstone) was (rather daftly) Jacob's favourite pillow in Biblical times. Also known as the Stone of Destiny, it was used from the 9th century in the coronation of all Scottish monachs. Captured in 1296 by Edward I, it was taken to Westminster Abbey, where it was fitted into the base of St Edward's chair, on which all subsequent English sovereigns except Mary II were crowned. It remained there until Christmas Day 1950 when four Scottish students bunked off tutorials and with nothing better to do decided to steal it. The stone wasn't returned for four months. Far-fetched rumours have circulated ever since that a copy was made, and that the returned Stone (now in Edinburgh Castle) is not the original.

woodpeckers and a scary badger whose cry is like a cross between a roaring lion and cavalcade of galloping horses. The museum has two permanent exhibitions on the human and natural history of Perthshire and a duller display about gold, silver and glassware. There are some fun-days where children can take part in mask-making, painting and other gluey-sticky events. Check dates ahead of your arrival.

***Open** all year Mon–Sat 10am–5pm, and 6th May–26th Aug Sun 1–4.30pm. **Adm** free.*

Pitlochry Power Station and Dam AGES OVER 12

Pitlochry, ✆ 01793 473152.

Although unfathomably in every guidebook for this area, the **Scottish Hydro Electric Visitor Centre** is actually dull for any child or adult without a geeky fascination for hydroelectric power. There is supposedly a salmon ladder built to help the fish swim upriver, and thus bypass the slab of hideous concrete that constitutes the dam, but don't expect to see them springing out of the water; they swim through pipes underneath small dirty looking troughs of water full of empty Coke bottles and rubbish. Oh, and the staff were unfriendly, refusing to allow our daughter to use their toilet so she wet herself. Thanks.

***Open** Apr–Oct Mon–Fri 10am–5.30pm; Sat and Sun 10am–5.30pm in July and Aug. **Adm** £3, under-16s free.*

Queen's View Visitor Centre ★ ALL AGES

Tay Forest Park, Strathtummel, (✆ 01796 473123). 10km west of Pitlochry on B8019.

From a vantage point 100m up a short hill from the Visitor Centre, perched high above Loch Tummel, you can see all the way up the spine of Scotland to the Glencoe mountains. Named after Queen Isabella, Robert the Bruce's wife, it was popularised by Queen Victoria who came here in 1866. There are big drops without railings in some places, so if your children are small, curious or have the sense of balance of a three-legged chair (our daughter) keep your wits about you. You can get a cup of tea in a little outside café here, where you can argue with your wife about why humans enjoy views. My theory: our caveman genes appreciate them not because of their beauty but because from high up we could see enemies approaching. My wife's view – 'Shut up and change his nappy – he's done a pooh.'

Open *end of Mar to mid-Nov 10–6pm (although you can see the view any time).* ***Adm*** *free.* ***Amenities*** *café, parking (£1).*

Scone Palace ★★ ALL AGES

01738 552300, ***www.scone-palace.co.uk****. 3km north of Perth off A93.*

Scone Palace was the capital of the Pictish kingdom, the centre of the Celtic church, the seat of parliaments and the crowning place of kings. It has also been home to the Stone of Destiny, as well as being where Queen Victoria was taught curling on the polished floor of the Long Gallery (the longest room in Scotland). On display here you can see, among other highlights, needlework by Mary, Queen of Scots and an old desk belonging to French queen Marie Antoinette. The palace also has the largest orchid collection in the country, the only maze in Perthshire and one of the 50 most notable trees in Britain – a Douglas Fir grown from the original American seed sent to Britain in 1825. It has Highland cattle in its grounds, an adventure playground and roaming peacocks. Although, of course, what our daughter most enjoyed was sitting on a replica of the Stone of Destiny on Moot Hill in front of Scone Abbey and bursting into hysterical shouting, 'I doing a big pooh pooh, daddy'. My highlight was the star-shaped maze where I accidentally (deliberately) lost my wife pushing the double buggy, and snuck off to stand contemplatively alone on Moot Hill at the spot Charles II and Robert the Bruce were crowned, after which I nipped off to the café for a bun before I was missed.

The palace is ideal for buggies and guides in each room pitch their information for children (check out the stuffed bears and baby sedan chair).

Open *daily 1st Apr–31st Oct, 9.30am–5.30pm.* ***Adm*** *£7.50 (just grounds £4), children £4.50 (just grounds £2.75).* ***Amenities*** *playground, café.*

Scone Palace

FUN FACT Mouse Catcher *Extraordinaire* 

Towser the cat, who lived at the Famous Grouse distillery for 24 years, is the *Guinness Book of Records* World Mousing Champion, having killed an estimated 28,899 mice. Although, somewhat dubiously, (sorry, Norris) this figure was arrived at by Guinness officials witnessing Towser in action over a few days and then extrapolating his three kills a day average over his life at the distillery (although if records can be broken this easily, presumably I can now lay claim to the world 100m record by extrapolating the speed I took my first three steps towards the front door when my new iPod docking station arrived from Amazon). Towser's number of kills is high because mice are fond of the barley used in whisky making, and because a nip of whisky in Towser's milk turned her, like many before, into a violent lunatic.

The Famous Grouse Experience ★ ALL AGES

Glenturret Distillery, The Hosh, Crieff, ☎ *01764 656565,* ***www.thefamousgrouse.co.uk****.*

Scotland's oldest and most visited working distillery was a surprisingly fun place for our 2-year-old, mainly because on the way back to our hotel, mentally weakened by four free drams, I passed her a whole packet of toffees because I was tired (drunk) and needed to concentrate on map reading (fall asleep snoring). There are four tours, starting with the basic 30-minuter that teaches you how the barley is ground, mashed, fermented and then distilled using words such as condenser, wort and draff that are hard to concentrate on when you're thinking about how maybe you should have chosen the Warehouse and Distillery Tour that sees you locked in a bonded warehouse sampling direct from the cask. Best bet is the mid-range, 70-minute malt tasting tour, which as well as educational stuff in the smelly rooms full of giant copper vats, nets six free drinks. It includes identifying important whisky smells from a scratch and sniff card (surprise, surprise, our daughter and my wife got the chocolate one) and the Grouse Room where, as part of an interactive display, Gilbert the Grouse flies over Scottish landmarks before the screen disintegrates into a jigsaw, whose pieces fall to the floor. As the pipe music gets louder, you must chase after and stamp on the jigsaws pieces moving faster and faster round the room. It's *Celebrity Squares* meets a drunken wedding, and with free booze inside you and a pungent whisky aroma pumped into the room (or was that me?) it's maybe best that you walk to the adjacent play-park afterwards for fresh air and a quiet stare at the horses in the field behind.

On the way, check out the statue of record-breaking Towser the cat (see 'Mouse Catcher *Extraordinaire*', below).

Open *daily Jan–Feb 10am–4.30pm, Mar–Dec 9am–6pm.* **Adm** *distillery* *tour (30 minutes, one dram) £5, children (10–17) £4, under-10s free.* ***Amenities*** *restaurant (with children's menu), baby-changing, play area.*

The Fortingall Yew Tree

ALL AGES

Fortingall Parish Church, Fortingall. 16km west of Aberfeldy.

There are numerous record-breaking trees in the aptly named **Big Tree Country** of Perthshire, but none rivalling this one's claim to fame: it was already 6,000 years old when the Romans ruled England. Impossible to age accurately because its trunk has hollowed with age (and so not all that impressive to look at) it's estimated to be up to 9,000 years old, making it the Earth's oldest living organism after Sir Menzies Campbell. The massive trunk, which measured 15.6m in 1769, has fragmented into separate stumps thanks to 19th century souvenir hunters. Now protected by a fence – though you can still touch branches and if you're our daughter, rip off leaves – the tree would characteristically have had a second wind when it reached 500. According to local legend Fortingall is reputed to be the birthplace of **Pontius Pilate**, the son of a local woman fathered by a Roman ambassador, who played under the Yew before rising through the Roman ranks and crucifying Jesus Christ.

There's no visitor centre and not much information about the tree, making it surprisingly quiet with just a few elderly tourists making jokes about getting their own second winds at 80. After you've contemplated being 9,000 years old and told your daughter off for stealing leaves, wander around the graveyard of the parish church (early Christians, revering the yew tree for its longevity, often built churches near old trees) feeling sorry for humans living out our paltry three score years and 10.

Open *daily all year.* ***Adm*** *free.*

The Scottish Crannog Centre, Kenmore

The Scottish Crannog Centre

★ **ALL AGES**

Kenmore, Loch Tay, Aberfeldy, *☎ 01887 830583,* ***www.crannog.co.uk****.*

At this re-created 5,000-year-old crannog on Loch Tay, children learn how Iron Age life in Scotland wasn't all bad. Although it meant no language, surviving off hazel nuts and

FUN FACT **Crannogs**

Today, thousands of ancient crannogs survive as tree covered islands in the middle of lochs. They rose above the water level thanks to the litter-bugging of ancient Celts who chucked debris over the side, which built up over time.

sleeping with smelly animals, they did trade, ate cheese toasties and had already invented the butter dish. Costumed guides give informal fireside talks inside the Crannog, and afterwards our daughter got to try on a slightly smelly skin tunic, while older children had a go at ancient bushcraft skills such as wood-turning, wool-spinning, making fire without matches, using wooden bows to drill holes and hitting each other over the head with sticks.

***Open** daily 15th Mar–31st Oct 10am–5.30pm, Nov weekends 10am–4pm. **Adm** £5.25, children £3.50.*

FAMILY-FRIENDLY ACCOMMODATION

EXPENSIVE

Cameron House Hotel ★

*Loch Lomond, Dunbartonshire, ☎ 01389 755565, **www.devere.co.uk**.*

Beautifully set on the banks of Loch Lomond, this resort-style country house is a children's paradise, and with a free crèche for under-5s (1½ hours per day), possibly a parental one as well. Family rooms with plasma tellies (children's TV and pay-per-view family movies) contain a children's den (bunk beds) within the main double that can be sealed off to enable you to move freely after the children are asleep. Attractions include a 9-hole course (the Wee Demon) and an 18-holer (children's lessons available via the pro), woodland hawk walks (£30), a haggis hunt (£10) and quad-biking (£45 per hour for 16s and over, £30 for 6–15-year-olds). There's a large swimming pool including a kids' pool with a flume, mountain bike hire, an outdoor play area plus tennis and squash courts. The hotel's cruise ship, The Celtic Warrior, runs thrice daily providing 90-minute guided trips on the loch (£35, £20 for children) including a glass of champagne and orange juice for youngsters. There is also a child-free spa area (spa bath, sauna, steam room, gym, hair salon) and four restaurants, the most informal being the Cameron Grill (£35 for three courses, children £15) with views of Loch Lomond, a children's menu and open kitchen. Fine-dining at Escape (£60 for three à la carte courses) is possible because child-minders are available.

***Rates** family rooms B&B £150–260. **Credit** AmEx, MC, V. **Amenities** baby-sitting, children's activities, parking, pool, spa, restaurants. **In room** Sat TV.*

FUN FACT **Two Johns**

When The Beatles stayed at the Roman Camp Hotel in 1963 (their hideaway retreat after a concert in Edinburgh) John Lennon was photographed with a young boy who also happened to be called John Lennon. The two John Lennons went on to become friends.

Crieff Hydro ★★★

Crieff, Perthshire, ☎ 01764 655555, ***www.Crieffhydro.com.***

Hydros were the 19th century equivalent of health spas, only instead of back massages the Victorians thought the best way to relax was with goose-pimples in freezing natural spring water. Today Crieff Hydro is a family resort with dozens of activities from water-skiing and quad-biking (6–11-year-olds: £20 for 13 minutes; 12s and over: £30/hour) to quieter pastimes such as table tennis. The stylish hotel in the shadow of Ben More and Ben Vorlich has a crèche for under-12s (three age groups, 2–4s, 5–7s, 8–12s) including indoor soft-play and a trampoline, but the emphasis is on educational play – baking, origami and science. For older children (13–17) there is air hockey, table football, an Xbox, pool tables and plenty more besides. Two free crèche sessions per day (three hours long) are, wonderfully, included in the room rate (pre-book) and additional sessions are £15, although we never used this properly as our (possibly over-sensitive) daughter came out in floods of tears with a number pinned to her chest talking about being pushed into some netting. Also popular are treasure hunts and family quizzes. There's pony trekking (a quick scoot – £2) and horse rides (an hour round the 360 hectare estate is £30), a swimming pool, badminton and pitch-and-putt competitions.

They have a fine dining restaurant, a brasserie, other casual cafés and The Hub, which sells children's packed lunches for £3.50.

Rates *family room (double bed with two single beds) £170. Interconnecting rooms £200.* ***Amenities*** *crèche, spa, parking, pool, restaurants, sports facilities.* ***In room*** *TV.*

Roman Camp Country House and Hotel ★

Off Main Street, Callander, ☎ 01877 3300033, ***www.romancamphotel.co.uk.***

Children can learn to fish, pet Shetland ponies and hide in a secret chapel in this beautiful 17th century former home of Lord Esher. The hotel has hosted two prime ministers (A.J. Balfour and Ramsay Macdonald), The Beatles and Peter Pan creator J.M. Barrie. Set in eight hectares, the hotel is on the banks of the River Teith, across the road from one of the most famous walks in the Trossachs, to Bracklinn Falls (drive to the car park beyond the golf course; it's 30 minutes there and back). As well as ponies, budgies, horses and peacocks for children to see, the hotel offers fishing tuition (£50 for an adult and one child, equipment included). The restaurant, with three AA Rosettes, is listed as one of the top 20 places to eat in Scotland but doesn't allow under-2s in the dining area, although families with babies can eat in the lounge or the spillover restaurant next door. The hotel provides baby-monitoring via its reception but there's no children's menu, although meals of the pasta and chicken variety (no goujons) are made on request.

Best for families is the Stary suite with a sitting room containing a sofa bed capable of sleeping two. It is the also the only room with an en suite attached to the bedroom, so no need for that midnight creep past sleeping children. Before checking out, visit the secret chapel accessed via a camouflaged door in the library. According to legend it was built to appease the ghosts of two monks.

***Rates** B&B in a family suite (two adults) £205, children (aged over 12) an extra £25, 5–12 £20 and under-5s free. **Credit** MC, V, AmEx. **Amenities** bar, library, parking, restaurant (£55 for three courses). **In room** TV (with children's TV channel), DVD player, Internet.*

The Stirling Highland Hotel ★

29 Spittal Street, 01786 2727227, ***www.paramount-hotels.co.uk****.*

Five minutes from Stirling Castle and half a mile from King's Park, this former high school has a swimming pool with special children's splash-times (Saturday 3–4pm and Sunday 10–11am and 3pm–4pm) plus the Bear Brigade Club (youngsters get goodie bags on arrival). The hotel has a health and leisure club, where my wife claimed she fell asleep in the steam room, although later admitted she'd

Roman Camp Country House and Hotel, Callander

just been reading *Hello!* magazine and eating a strawberry bun. Family suites include a double room and children's rooms, with bunk beds and their own TV. Child-minder numbers are available, there are games in the library and the Scholars restaurant has a children's menu.

***Rates** family suite £150. **Amenities** free parking, pool, restaurant (adult main courses £12.95), bar. **In Room** cot, WiFi, complimentary refreshment trays.*

MODERATE

Killiecrankie Hotel

*Pass of Killiecrankie by Pitlochry, 01796 473220, **www.killiecrankiehotel.co.uk**.*

Favoured by artists and photographers who come to paint and snap the nearby lochs and mountains, this small hotel has 1.5 hectares of secure gardens and woodland for children to explore. Nice touches include towels made into different animals each night, a games room and although the hotel has fine dining, its children's menu also features pizza and burger options. Best for families is either the ground floor family suite with an adjoining sitting room or two first floor rooms (7 and 8) that can be sealed off.

The hotel is 5km north of Pitlochry and within walking distance of Soldier's Leap at Killiecrankie Pass, where a desperate soldier from William of Orange's defeated army leapt more than 6m across the River Gary to flee pursuing Jacobite Highlanders after the Battle of Killiecrankie (1869). The **Killiecrankie Visitor Centre**, (*01796 463233*) marking this feat, is open 31st March to 31st October (daily 10am–5.30pm), and there's a touch table for children featuring various animal remains including a fallow deer skull, roe deer antlers, a squirrel's tail and the sticky entrails of vole (the last one is a lie).

***Rates** £130 per room, plus any children aged 5–16 £25, under-4s free;*

Killiecrankie Hotel by Pitlochry

Tigh na Croit Cottage, Balquhidder

family suite (two adults, two children) £180. ***Amenities*** *dining room, bar, games room.* ***In room*** *Sat TV, DVD player (with children's films).*

Sunbank House Hotel

50 Dundee Road, Perth, ☎ 01738 624882, ***www.sunbankhouse.com****.*

This hotel close to city centre attractions (including both North and South Inch parks, with crazy golf and a boating pond) has fine views over the River Tay. The best family room is on the ground floor with a double and a single bed. Extra z-beds and cots can be provided. The hotel has a front garden and games in its TV lounge. A baby-listening service means you can eat at the restaurant (£27.50 for three courses). If eating *en famille*, children are half price.

Rates *family room B&B £100–150.* ***Credit*** *AmEx, MC, V.* ***Amenities*** *parking, restaurant, laundry, DVD player in lounge.* ***In room*** *TV, cots.*

Tigh na Croit Cottage ('House on the Hill') ★★★

Balquhidder, ☎ 0208 5685466 or 07885 103353, ***www.cottage-in-scotland.co.uk****.*

Our scariest experience in Scotland occurred along the single-track, windy road through Balquhidder when, looking for a telephone box landmark to find this cottage, we were stopped by an old man, who stood menacingly in front of our car, waved a stick at the mountains and said, as I wound down the window, 'If yer stayin' at Gail's place, better shut the gate tonight.' It was only the next morning, after a long restless night worrying about escaped axe murderers, that the mystery was cleared up. 'It's because deer get in and eat all the azaleas,' we were told by the caretaker. 'And everyone knows Gail. The house has been in her family for years.'

The cottage, set in beautiful countryside with panoramic views, feels like a luxurious version of the cottage from the cult film *Withnail and I*. It has three large bedrooms and a great size bathroom with a claw-foot bath and a window you can see the clouds through. The kitchen-diner comes with a microwave, fridge-freezer and highchair and there's a laundry room with washing machine and dryer. The lounge, with an open fireplace, has a TV and DVD player and a selection of movies for adults and children. This is proper countryside, where you can get fresh venison and lamb delivered to your door and, with no streetlights for miles, venture outside after dark to admire the starry night sky. For groceries, the village store in Strathyre is 3km away.

A wonderful, unforgettable little place.

***Rates** £450–900 per week. **Amenities** bed linen and towels, highchairs, garden, kitchen, mountain views, TV/DVD player. **Open** all year.*

INEXPENSIVE

East Haugh House ★★

Pitlochry ☎ 01796 473121, ***www.easthaugh.co.uk****.*

It's a toss up who's most friendly here: owner Leslie McGowan, who did our washing and cooked porridge specially for our daughter, or pet dog Lucy, the wire-haired Jack Russell who licked whatever was left of it off our daughter's face. This hotel (as well as saving you a fortune in wipes) is set in almost one hectare of garden (badminton racquets, footballs, etc. available) and is a haven for fishing fans, with the River Tummell just half an hour away. The hotel has rods and children's waders and can arrange for a day (£85) or morning's trout fishing. All rooms are named after fishing flies; the best options for families, Red Drummond and Silver Wilkinson are opposite each other on the 2nd floor and have their own spa bath that at first terrified our daughter ('Daddy, the water's gone mad') but that she grew to love ('Daddy, make the water go mad'). Families eat together in the bar area where (to fit in) you must periodically murmur 'I like to use multiple hook and floating worm harnesses, myself.'

If you want to eat in the acclaimed Two Sisters restaurant (£39.95 for four courses; no children), the baby monitor is in range. Try the gently Warmed Craigellachie smoked Scottish salmon; chances are it was caught by Leslie's husband, Neil.

***Rates** B&B £45 (winter midweek) to £69. Children in travel cots free, using a bed £15. **Credit** MC, V. **Amenities** restaurants (main courses from £9.95). **In room** Molton Brown accessories.*

The Lodge House

***Crianlarich, Perthshire,* ☎ *01838 300276, www.lodgehouse.co.uk*.**

This quiet, family-friendly B&B overlooking the River Fillan is a great base for visiting Loch Lomond (13km away) and also good because you get to say the word Crianlarich a lot while you're here (surely the most Scottish-sounding word in the world). The best bet is the chalet off the main house. It has a double with en suite and a sitting room with a sofa-bed capable of sleeping two more. There's a garden for children and, behind reception, a box of games. If you fancy a dram of whisky ask for the 'wee magic cupboard'. You'll be taken to the famous whisky cupboard, where there are more than 40 varieties of single malts. Drink one or two in the lounge after dinner (24-hours notice required, ingredients locally sourced) and, as you admire the open fire, you can compete with your wife through saying the word Crianlarich in different contexts ('Where are you from? Crianlarich'. 'Where are you going next? Crianlarich'. 'How would you best describe yourself? Crianlarich') to see who sounds the most Scottish. The cooked breakfast (with the room rate) includes scrambled egg and smoked salmon.

'Crianlarich': I had to say it once more.

Rates *adults £27.50, children aged 12 and under £15, under-3s free.* ***Credit*** *AmEx, MC, V.* ***Amenities*** *DVD player, two lounges, bar.* ***In room*** *TV, WiFi.*

West Plean House ★

Denny Road, by Stirling, 01786 812208, ***www.westpleanhouse.com****.*

Children might see a calf being born and can have their picture taken on top of a combine harvester at this working farm with a family room. The room, with a double and two single beds, overlooks the farm and has a secure large front garden, great for youngsters' play (rounders' bats and balls available). There are board-games and puzzles, and a duck pond (at certain times of the year) full of Mallards. Run by Moira Stewart (not the newscaster), the best times are May (for the calving) and September (when children can pose on the combine harvester). The breakfast is vast and home-cooked. There is a TV room for after the young ones are in bed, and a drawing room where you might turn to your wife after a few glasses of wine and say something rather stupid like 'I'd like to run a farm one day – I've always rather liked cattle.'

Rates *B&B adults £32, children aged over 10 £10, under-10s free. Minimum stay two nights but negotiable.* ***Credit*** *MC, V.* ***Amenities*** *parking, TV room.* ***In room*** *TV, cot, highchair.*

FAMILY-FRIENDLY DINING

EXPENSIVE

Hermann's ★

58 Broad St, Stirling, 01786 450632, ***www.hermann's.co.uk****.*

Despite its formal appearance, this former 19th century

townhouse (a stone's throw from Stirling Castle) is well used to messy children. Colouring books and pens are available for impatient youngsters who insist on shouting 'Let's be lions and scare mummy. Raaaaaah. Daddy, I said be a lion.'

Named after its Tyrolean owner Hermann Aschaber, there's a clean-cut alpine feel to the place. A roaring fire welcomes you in winter and there's a sun-flooded conservatory in summer looking onto a walled garden. Quality Scottish ingredients are used to create Austrian classics such as strudel, with a Scottish twist (try the chicken breast with haggis in whisky cream sauce). The children's menu includes dishes such as melon with raspberry coulis. The service is as efficient as you'd expect from a place owned by a man named Hermann.

***Open** daily noon–2.30pm and 6–9.30pm. **Menu** £18.95 (for three courses). **Credit** AmEx, MC, V. **Amenities** highchairs, children's menu (£5–6.50).*

The Lade Inn and Restaurant

*Kilmahog, 01877 330152, **www.theladeinn.com**.*

Based on the slopes of Ben Ledi, children can run about in the beer garden, see small frogs in the undergrowth and, if they're terribly lucky/unlucky (our daughter thought they were rats and cried), water voles in a fenced-off pond. There are three areas to eat, but best for families is The Children's Room, containing a large toy box. The restaurant doesn't believe in children's menus, and so smaller portions are served from the adult menu at two-thirds the cost. Afterwards, wash your food down with the Inn's own ales, Waylade, Ladeback and Ladeout (be careful of this one if driving, operating heavy machinery or getting involved with you wife in a debate about whether you turn right or left to Tigh Na Croit after Rob Roy's grave off the A9).

On Friday and Saturday nights between 8.30pm and 11.30pm there's Scottish folk songs in the main bar.

***Open** daily noon–9pm. **Menu** £15 (three courses). **Credit** MC, V. **Amenities** baby-changing, highchairs.*

MODERATE

Kilted Skirlie ★

*Loch Lomond Shores, Balloch, 01389 754759, **www.kiltedskirlie.co.uk**.*

Sitting on the terrace here, you can watch the sun setting against the backdrop of Loch Lomond and Ben Lomond while sipping a razmopolitan cocktail (raspberry and vodka), the only danger being you might bump into Sir Alex Ferguson flinging a shoe into the kitchen if his beef stroganoff is under-done. He and Rangers' Walter Smith are regulars. That said, the restaurant is handily placed for the aquarium (see p. 110) and there is a good children's menu including fishfingers and sausage beans and chips, as well as healthy salad options. Adult food is traditional Scottish (think venison).

If your children get bored of the view and start rocking dangerously back and forth in their highchairs while you and your wife noisily debate (did we really do this?) which otters in the Loch Lomond aquarium we preferred (short or long clawed), attentive staff will encourage them to doodle chalk pictures on their wipe-clean slate place mats.

Open *daily noon–5.30pm, 6–9pm (Fri and Sat 6–10pm).* ***Main courses*** *from £12.* ***Credit*** *AmEx, MC, V.* ***Amenities*** *children's menu (£3.75). highchairs.*

The Anchor's Rest

Trossachs Pier, Loch Katrine, by Callander ☎ 01877 332008, ***www.lochkatrine.com****.*

A great place for lunch after a steamship cruise on Loch Katrine, this restaurant's perch overlooking the *SS Sir Walter Scott* enables you to watch unsuspecting fools wheeling their bikes aboard (see p. 106). There is a lift for buggy pushers and Nipper portions on the menu (£5 for a cheese and baked bean toastie, chocolate cake and juice). Children get colouring books and crayons to keep them amused after their father's array of funny faces (one bug-eyed one, one huge witless grin) run out. Boating pictures decorate the walls and the menu is adorned with (semi) interesting details about the origins of phrases such as 'The Cut of his Jib', which, since you ask, originated in the 18th century when sailing navies could determine the nationality of a sailing vessel by the shape of the jib (a triangular sail at the front) long before her colours would be seen.

Open *daily 10am–7pm (8.30pm when busy).* ***Menu*** *£10 (three courses).* ***Credit*** *AmEx, MC, V.* ***Amenities*** *baby-changing, children's menu.*

The Conservatory

Hunting Tower Hotel, Crieff Road, Perth, ☎ 01738 583771, ***www.huntingtowerhotel.co.uk****.*

This stylish conservatory (wicker chairs, linen tablecloths, men in panamas looking unflappable) gives on to the Hunting Tower Hotel's immaculate lawns, so children can run about and feed ducks at the nearby pond (fenced) with the macaroni cheese they refused to eat at lunch. The children's menu also features pasta and sausages, while freshly prepared adult options range from lamb to smoked salmon. On your way out, check out the two goldfish behind the reception desk (not a cruel jibe about the staff – they are real goldfish) in a strange wine glass styled tank.

Open *daily 7am–10am, noon–2pm and 6pm–10pm.* ***Menu*** *£12.95 (two courses).* ***Credit*** *AmEx, MC, V.* ***Amenities*** *baby-changing, highchairs, children's menu (£9.95).*

The Executive Suite

St Johnstone FC, McDiarmid Park, Crieff Road, ☎ 01738 459090, ***www.mcdiarmidparl.co.uk****.*

Football fans can eat at this memorabilia-stuffed restaurant in the ground of St Johnstone FC. The walls are adored with pennants from famous matches as well as old team photos, and before you sit down you can look across the hallowed ground (well, they once played Monaco in the Champions League) from the Main Stand and try to imagine Derby-day when 4,000 Scots pack in to shout colourful abuse at their Dundee rivals. Try the salmon or braised lamb.

Smaller portions are served for youngsters and other meals can be requested (pizza, burger, etc.).

Open *Mon–Fri noon–2pm.* ***Menu*** *£11.25 (three courses), £8.95 (two courses).* ***Credit*** *AmEx, MC, V.* ***Amenities*** *highchairs, children's portions (£5.95).*

INSIDER TIP

If the waiters go on about Scotland's 3–2 Wembley victory over England in 1967 under ex-St Johnstone manager Bobby Brown, casually bring up the Saints' relegation from the Scottish Premier League in 2002.

INEXPENSIVE

Atholl Arms Hotel ★

Blair Atholl, Pitlochry, ☏ 01796 481205, ***www.athollarmshotel.co.uk****.*

We'll always remember the Bothy Bar of this hotel because it was where our 2-year-old, midway through her excellent bangers and mash, turned to two old ladies behind us and asked: 'So where are you from then?' Startled by her precocious urbanity they were about to reply when our toddler maddeningly ruined it by discarding her teaspoon and beginning to eat her mashed potato using her hand like a bear paw. For us, the Bothy Bar was much better than the more formal (and expensive) Baronial Dining Hall (suits of armour and yellowing deer skulls on the walls) because children get a treasure map to colour in and pens while they wait.

Outside there's a children's play area with lovely views of the Tulloch Hills, although there is one bugbear: children aren't allowed past an invisible line near the fireplace because of some strange licensing law/health and safety directive/ancient witch's prophecy (who knows?) involving rules about a child's physical proximity to a bar. 'What line?' 'It's invisible'. 'What's invisible, Daddy?' 'It means you can't see it.' 'Daddy, what can't I see?' 'The line.' 'What line?' 'You can't see it.' Etc until there are tears. The children's menu features a main and ice-cream sundaes; adults should expect steak, venison and salmon to feature.

Open *noon–9.30pm daily (Baronial dining hall 7–9pm).* ***Main courses*** *from £7.95.* ***Credit*** *MC, V.* ***Amenities*** *children's menu (£3.35).*

Hollybank Restaurant

58 Glasgow Road, Stirling, ☏ 01786 812311.

This is a good budget option for families looking for a pick-me-up after the disappointment of the Bannockburn Heritage Centre next door (a big field with a flag in it). The restaurant, with old pictures of Stirling, serves freshly prepared, traditional Scottish food, while its children's menu includes burger and chips along with pasta and breaded haddock. Youngsters can also select smaller portions of adult meals, which include veggie options.

Open daily noon–2.30pm and 5–9pm (Sat and Sun 4.30–9pm). ***Main courses*** *from £7.* ***Credit*** *MC, V.* ***Amenities*** *children's menu (£4), highchairs, baby-changing.*

Taymouth Tearoom and Gifts

Old Kirk, Aberfeldy Road, Perthshire, ☎ 01887 8302285.

Friendly staff gave our daughter dry crusts of bread to feed the ducks at this former church on the banks of Loch Tay, little knowing that she'd eat them herself then hide behind a picnic table to vomit them up like a shy cat. This tearoom is an ideal lunch stop on your way to see the oldest living organism in the world (see p. 123) or the Crannog Centre (p. 123). The café, with highchairs and baby-changing, doubles as a buy-anything-gift-shop-cum-jewellers so it is possible to go in for a cheese toastie or baked potato and walk out £200 lighter but with an emerald crusted chain round your wife's neck and nothing left of your accommodation budget. There's no children's menu, but if youngsters don't like what's on offer staff will make jam sandwiches (£1) or simple meals such as beans on toast.

The outdoor picnic tables are a good perch to watch kayakers on Loch Tay practising their wet exit strategies, making you feel all the better for being on dry land.

Open *daily 10am–6pm.* ***Menu*** *cheese toastie £3.50, baked potato £4.50.* ***Credit*** *MC, V.* ***Amenities*** *picnic area, baby-changing, highchairs, shop.*

The Kilmahog Woollen Mill

Callander, ☎ 01877 330268, ***www.foreverscotland.com****.*

At the adjoining Clan Tartan Centre we discovered my wife (née Robinson) is descended from the warlike Clan Gunn, famous for maintaining a 500-year feud with the (implausibly named) Clan Keith, a falling-out that helps explain why my wife is still arguing with me six years after we married about the correct way to load knives in the dishwasher tray. The 72-seater café serves all day breakfasts and other homemade snacks plus soups and sandwiches. Children's portions are available and a filled roll (bacon, sausage or egg) is a thrifty £2.30 (extra fillings 50p) while a full breakfast costs £4.25. The mill is a mecca for coach parties who come to buy kilts and single malts from the large whisky shop (two free drams if you pretend to be interested in buying).

Open *daily Feb–Sep 9.30am–5.30pm, Oct–Nov 9.30am–5pm, Dec–Jan 9.30am–4pm.* ***Main courses*** *from £4.25.* ***Credit*** *AmEx, MC, V.* ***Amenities*** *baby-changing, highchairs, children's snack boxes (£2.75).*

6 Highlands & Islands

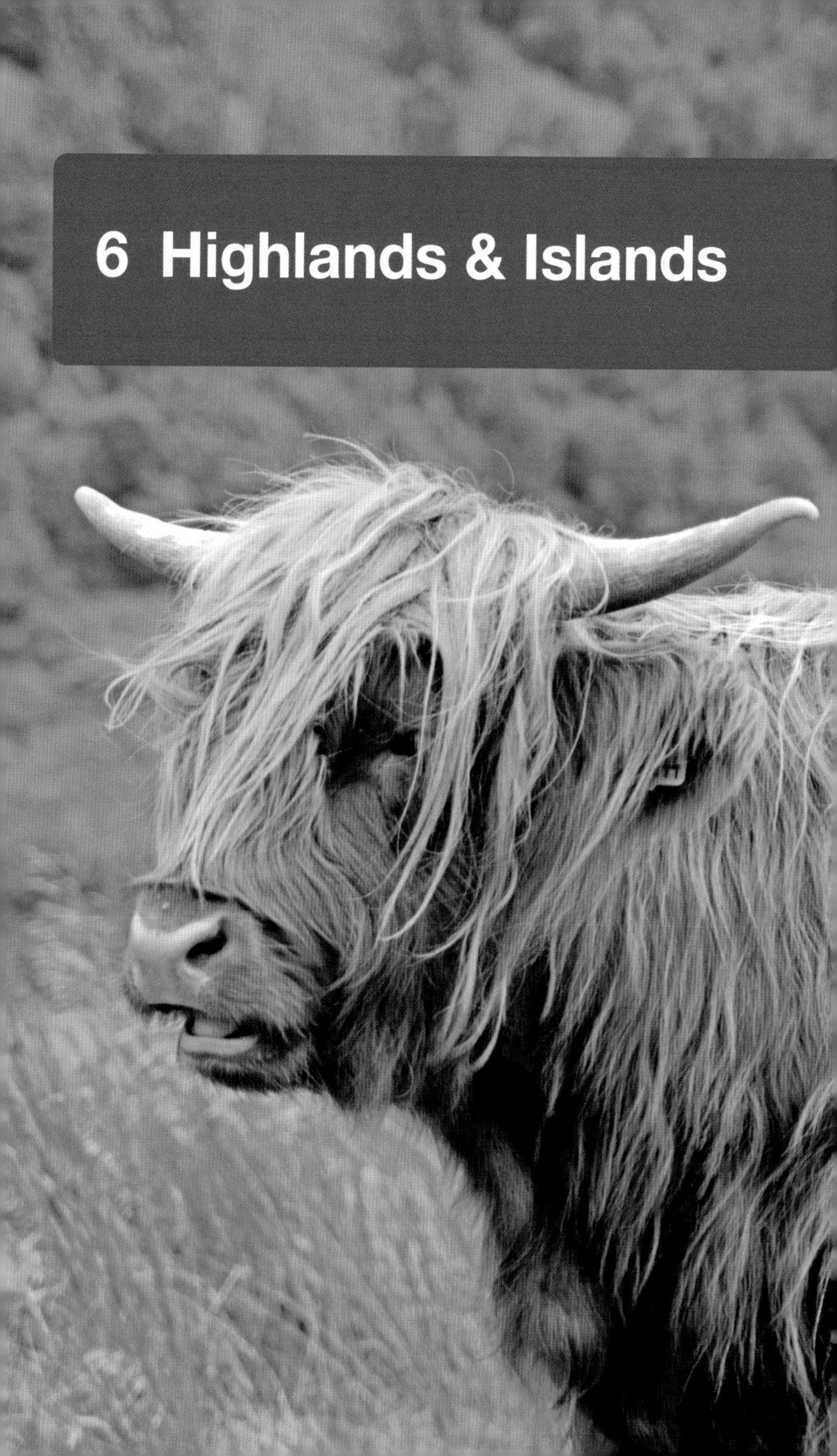

HIGHLANDS & ISLANDS

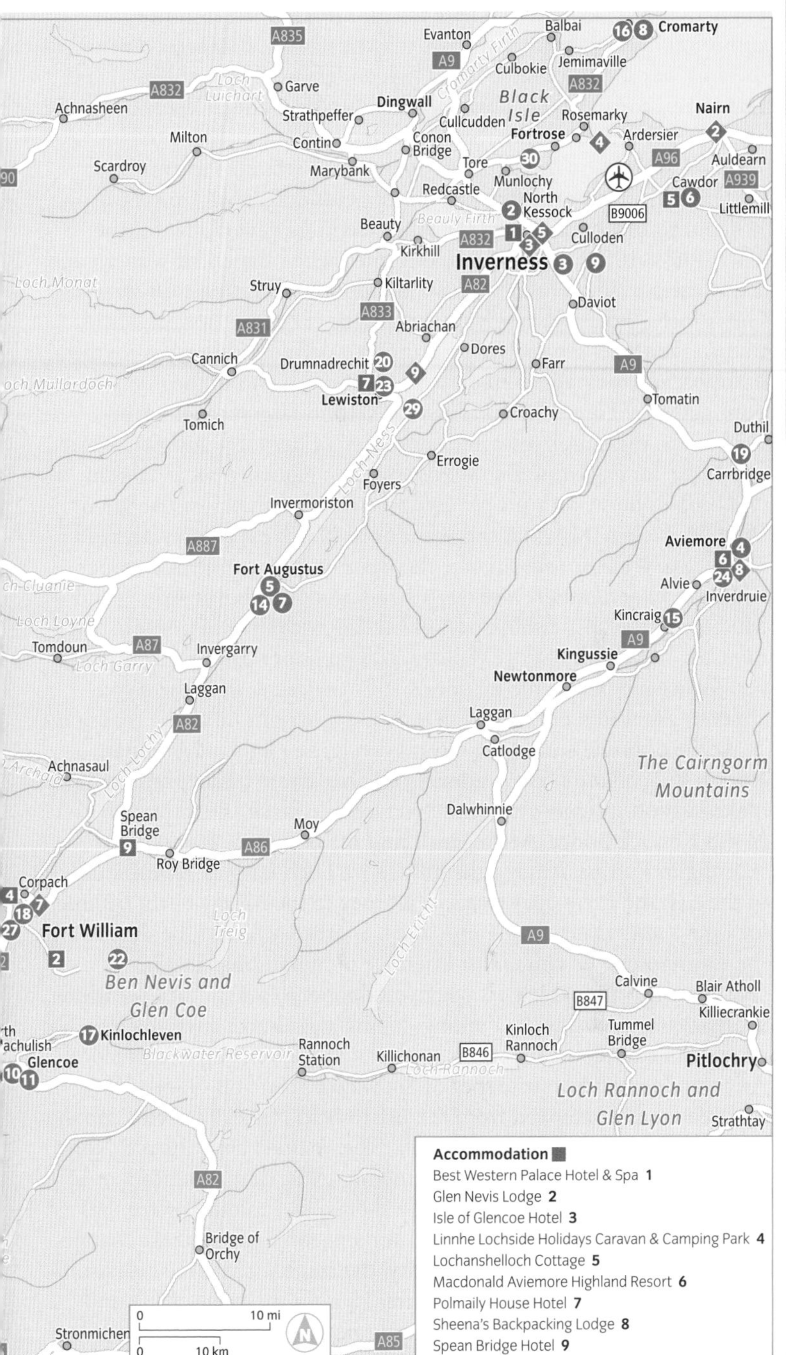
Cromarty
Balbai
Evanton
Culbokie
Jemimaville
Cromarty Firth
Black Isle
Dingwall
Garve
Loch Luichart
Achnasheen
Strathpeffer
Cullcudden
Rosemarky
Nairn
Fortrose
Ardersier
Milton
Contin
Conon Bridge
Tore
Auldearn
Scardroy
Marybank
Munlochy
Cawdor
Redcastle
North Kessock
Littlemill
Beauty
Beauly Firth
Kirkhill
Culloden
Inverness
Loch Monat
Struy
Kiltarlity
Daviot
Abriachan
Cannich
Drumnadrechit
Dores
Farr
Loch Mullardoch
Lewiston
Tomatin
Tomich
Croachy
Duthil
Loch Ness
Errogie
Carrbridge
Foyers
Invermoriston
Aviemore
Fort Augustus
Alvie
Inverdruie
Loch Loyne
Kincraig
Tomdoun
Loch Garry
Invergarry
Kingussie
Newtonmore
Laggan
Laggan
Catlodge
Achnasaul
Loch Lochy
The Cairngorm Mountains
Dalwhinnie
Spean Bridge
Moy
Roy Bridge
Corpach
Loch Treig
Fort William
Loch Ericht
Ben Nevis and Glen Coe
Calvine
Blair Atholl
Killiecrankie
Kinlochleven
Kinloch Rannoch
Tummel Bridge
Glencoe
Blackwater Reservoir
Rannoch Station
Killichonan
Loch Rannoch
Pitlochry
Loch Rannoch and Glen Lyon
Strathtay
Bridge of Orchy
Stronmichen
A835
A9
A832
A96
A939
B9006
A82
A833
A831
A887
A87
A86
B847
B846
A85
0
10 mi
0
10 km
N
Accommodation
Best Western Palace Hotel & Spa 1
Glen Nevis Lodge 2
Isle of Glencoe Hotel 3
Linnhe Lochside Holidays Caravan & Camping Park 4
Lochanshelloch Cottage 5
Macdonald Aviemore Highland Resort 6
Polmaily House Hotel 7
Sheena's Backpacking Lodge 8
Spean Bridge Hotel 9

The average population density of Scotland's Highlands and Islands is lower than in Papua New Guinea. And although the Highlands has never been a base for cannibalism (though the consumption of deep-fried Mars bars may be worse), for many centuries the area was so inaccessible that Highlanders were thought by Londoners to have tails. Finally opened up by General Wade's planned road system following the First Jacobite Uprising in 1715, the entire area is described by towering mountains and secluded lochs.

The fault-line of the Great Glen that cuts diagonally from Fort William to Inverness is the Highlands' defining geographic feature. This almost 100km rift valley was formed when the north-western and south-eastern sides of the fault slid in opposite directions. Of the Great Glen's lochs, Loch Ness is the most famous. The area swarms with tourists, zoom lenses ready to capture that defining shot of its mythical humpbacked monster. While the south-western end of the Glen is dominated by Fort William. This, the second-largest town in the Highlands, dubs itself 'the outdoor capital of the UK', and makes a good base for exploring Ben Nevis, Britain's highest peak at 1344m. (If climbing it, do so with proper equipment rather than just the bag of Woollies Pick 'n' Mix that the abandoned Hatch expedition packed.) From Fort William you can take the steam train into one of Europe's last great wildernesses before reaching unspoilt beaches at Arisaig and Morar, and the busy fishing port of Mallaig with its own non-existent monster. Just south of Fort William, half an hour's drive along the A82, lies Glencoe, home to the infamous 1692 massacre, and where your children can watch out for red deer, who graze right up to the roadside.

At the opposite end of the Great Glen is the Highlands' capital, Inverness. Scotland's fastest growing city has severe traffic problems, but makes a good springboard for the picturesque Black Isle across the North Kessock bridge, where you'll find the best place for dolphin-spotting in Europe. Among the hills above Loch Laggan, 64km south of the city, the River Spey starts its journey to the Moray Firth. Famous for forests and ospreys, the upper river, Strathspey, lies in the shadows of the Cairngorms, Britain's most extensive mountain massif. The Cairngorms National Park is where outdoor enthusiasts flock for winter sports, water sports, rock climbing, hiking and almost anything else that can be done outdoors in Gortex. A useful base here is ugly (if practical) Aviemore, once a favourite spot of Sir Walter Scott and Queen Victoria.

Even further removed from the urban belt, but still tail-less, are the main western isles of Skye and Mull. Skye, named after the old Norse word for cloud, amazes with plummeting cliffs, dramatic headlands, white coral beaches and black sandy shores. Its capital, Portree, has colourful houses, a traditional harbour and some of the most changeable weather in Scotland. Tobermory, the real life children's television *Balamory* with a Womble named after it, is on the Isle of Mull and worth a visit for either of these reasons alone. It has been turning its tourist spotlight away from TV characters such as Josie Jump in recent years, towards wildlife attributes that include eagles, whales and dolphins.

CHILDREN'S TOP 10 ATTRACTIONS

❶ **Pay homage** to classic children's TV series *Balamory* on the island of Tobermory, visiting the homes of characters such as Miss Hoolie, Spencer, Josie Jump and PC Plum. See p. 165.

❷ **Annoy** professional Nessie spotters at Urquhart Castle by telling your toddler 'that they proved it was a giant sturgeon years ago.' See p. 152.

❸ **Ride** quad bikes and electric go-karts, and take penalties against a goalkeeping dog, at the Bogbain Adventure and Heritage Farm outside Inverness. See p. 149.

❹ **Pretend** to be Harry Potter on the Jacobite Steam Train. See p. 143.

❺ **Get attacked** by greedy goats at the Black Isle Wildlife and Country Park in North Kessock, and then hold/try not to drop small furry animals. See p. 156.

❻ **Spot** dolphins at Chanonry Point. See p. 159.

❼ **Hand-feed** reindeer and deliver your Christmas list to Santa at Aviemore's Cairngorm Reindeer Centre. See p. 162.

❽ **Climb** a sheer ice wall in a giant refrigerator at Ice Factor in Kinlochleven. See p. 141.

❾ **Spend** an afternoon making castles on the warmest white sand beach in Scotland, in Nairn. See p. 154.

❿ **Get caught** by the Countess Dowager of Cawdor weeing in the moat of her beautiful castle and maze. See p. 155.

GLENCOE & AROUND

Just two hours' drive from Glasgow, Glencoe, the country's most famous and scenic glen, is home to some of Scotland's most rugged and unpronounceable peaks (try saying 'Buachaille Etive Beag' or 'Bidean nam Bian' after a pint of beer). The glen is still notorious for the massacre of 1692 (see p. 141), remembered in the village with a stone memorial to the Macdonalds. Around Glencoe, in almost any direction, are some of the best drives in Scotland. Clouds appear as shadows on the mountains and wild deer roam close to the road. There are pull-ins for camera stops almost every few metres, remote white cottages in the foothills of mountains and picture-postcard lochs. The BBC Gaelic station got us so into the mood, weaving our way along the A82, my wife said the language could almost make you 'feel like you've slaughtered a few Macdonalds'. To get children interested, though, tell the little heathens that scenes from *Harry Potter and the Prisoner of Azkaban* were filmed at the bottom of Clachaig Gully.

Essentials

Forget the train or bus, you're in the Highlands now: the only option is the **car**. The best approach from the south is the M8 and A82 from Glasgow. The journey of around 130km will take up to two hours. From Edinburgh the best way is the M9, A84, A85 and then the A82. The journey is around 160km and will take about 2½ hours. Fort William is around 32km away; allow 30 minutes.

Visitor Information

The Ballachulish Tourist Information Centre (*01855 811866*, ***www.glencoetourism.co.uk***) is unmissable in tiny Ballachulish. It is open in the summer 9am–6pm daily, and in the winter 9am–5pm Monday–Saturday and 10am–5pm Sundays.

What to See & Do

Glencoe and North Lorn Folk Museum ★ ALL AGES

Glencoe, 01855 811664, ***www.glencoemuseum.co.uk****.*

A fun museum of priceless artefacts sitting beside car-boot fare that's a favourite haunt of eccentric TV personality Sir Jimmy Saville, who has a house up the road. Exhibits include the wedding chest of the head of the clan Macdonald saved from the Glencoe massacre, and Bonnie Prince Charlie's cuffs, bizarrely displayed alongside an old Ludo board and a Ladybird book about shells. Our daughter was invited to flick through 50-year-old comic books and handle old-fashioned toys, while we enjoyed the childhood toys from the 1970s and, of course, doing Jimmy Saville impressions ('Now then, now then boys and girls, what 'ave we here? A plaid brooch left behind at the Glencoe massacre...'Ow's about that then. An old Curly Wurly wrapper.') Visitors are asked to write down old nursery rhymes they remember, while visiting Macdonalds can log their details in an ancestry register.

Open *mid-May–Sep Mon–Sat 10am–5pm.* ***Adm*** *£2, children free.*

Glencoe Visitor Centre

GREEN ALL AGES

Glencoe, 01855 811302, ***www.glencoe-nts.org.uk****. Off the A82, 1.6km south of Glencoe.*

This is a good place to stare moodily from a viewing platform out at the infamous site of the Glencoe Massacre, and to wonder sadly about the brutal slaughter of the Macdonald clan in 1692. After which you can eat a fantastic Brie and red onion panini in the visitor centre café.

At this eco-friendly centre (it sits on stilts above a birch wood, the insulation is sheep wool and there's something about the drains we forget) visitors can feel what it's like to climb on ice (cold) and discover how Glencoe was formed. Our daughter got an activity book to go with the hundreds of others we have clogging up the back of the car (unread) and there are video presentations including one about the massacre. The café sells childen's Massacre Lunchboxes (dinosaur lunchboxes really, but Massacre Lunchboxes would have been so much better).

***Open** daily Mar 10am–4pm, Apr–Aug 9.30am–5.30pm, Sep–Oct 10am–5pm, Nov–Feb 10am–4pm (Thurs–Sun). **Adm** £5, children £4. **Amenities** café (children' lunchbox £3.50).*

Ice Factor ★ AGES OVER 7

*Leven Road, Kinlochleven, Lochaber, 01855 831100, **www.ice-factor.co.uk**.*

Children as young as 7 with no mountaineering experience and

The Glencoe Visitor Centre

little sense of personal frailty can have a go here at the biggest indoor ice-climbing wall in the world. The 15m wall is inside a giant refrigerator that can drop to –10°C, so bring warm clothes. All equipment is supplied, there are instructors to coach technique and the only requirements are: a) climbers must fit into at least a size-4 ice-boot; and b) must never have watched the

The Glencoe Massacre

After the Macdonalds, seen as fanatical supporters of former Catholic King James I, failed to swear allegiance to Protestant King William III, his followers took action. On 1st February, 1692, Robert Campbell marched a company of the Earl of Argyll's regiment, many recruited from the Campbell clan, into Glencoe where for a few days they enjoyed the hospitality of the Macdonalds. Then, at 5am on 13th February, they rose and killed 38 of their hosts, many more perishing in the mountains having fled. Although acting under orders, and only a small portion being Campbells, the incident resonates through history – right up to today – as the most treacherous inter-clan betrayal of all time. In fact when the Glencoe Visitor Centre opened in 2002 under the management of a Campbell (Roddy Campbell) the appointment caused national outrage, until a Macdonald (Julie MacDonald) was appointed head of catering.

movie *Touching the Void*. There are also dry walls (15m and 8m) and climbers can do short tasters or full-day guided adventures, where the movable walls are rotated to reflect Scotland's classic mountains including Skye's Cuillins and Tower Ridge on Ben Nevis. Alternatively, if like our daughter you're scared of even modest inclines, there is a netted soft play area where you can scale the north face of a shallow slide eating a Percy Pig sweet. If even this is too much there are jigsaws, books and colouring.

After your climb/embarrassing fiasco – where your wife, who recently gave birth, climbs higher than you – you can enjoy lunch in the ski-lodge-style café where, looking out for the world's top climber Bill MacLeod, a regular here, you can try not to listen to your wife start sentences like 'I think the secret is weight distribution...'.

Open *Tues–Thurs 8.30am–10pm and Fri–Mon 8.30am–7pm.* ***Adm*** *£10 for ½ hour on either rock wall. £25 for one hour on ice wall.* ***Amenities*** *children's menu.*

INSIDER TIP

The **Aluminium Story**, over the road from Ice Factor, does exactly what it says on the tin.

Scottish Sea Life Sanctuary

ALL AGES

Barcaldine, Oban, Argyll 01631 720386, www.sealsanctuary.co.uk.

This seal sanctuary rescues abandoned pups along the west coast. Set stunningly on the banks of Loch Creran, it has an aquarium with touch-pools, a ray pool, a seal tank and an underwater observatory.

Open *daily in the summer 10am–5pm (call for winter times).* ***Adm*** *£9.50, children aged 3–14 £7.50, under-3s free.* ***Credit*** *AmEx, MC, V.* ***Amenities*** *café.*

FORT WILLIAM & AROUND

Fort William, the largest town in the west Highlands, bills itself as the outdoor capital of Scotland. With magnificent scenery and both the highest mountain in the UK, Ben Nevis, and the deepest loch, Morar, home to the Morag monster, we're not going to argue. A well-known mountain biking centre, it marks the end of the West Highland Way, which runs almost 160km across the Scottish Highlands from Glasgow.

The town, however, is centred on a dull pedestrianised high street selling virtually everything you can envisage wearing in the rain, and cut off from Loch Linnhe by an ugly dual carriageway. That said, there's plenty to do as a family.

Essentials

By Train There are two daytime services from London to Fort William (and an overnight sleeper service for the really hardy). The typical cost is £120 return. The journey takes around

9 hours 20 minutes. From Glasgow there are five services a day. The cost of the ticket is typically £40 return and the journey takes four hours. There are three trains a day from Edinburgh and one sleeper. The journey takes around five hours and costs £56. There is also the West Highland Line between Fort William and Mallaig. For more train information contact **First Scotrail** (*08457 484950*, ***www.firstgroup.com/scotrail***).

By Bus Fort William has seven daily **Scottish Citylink** (*08705 505050*, ***www.citylink.co.uk***) connections to Glasgow. The journey takes three hours and costs around £36 return. From Inverness there is a two-a-day service costing £15.60 return. Journey time is two hours. From Edinburgh the journey, costing £42.60 return, will take almost five hours. There are also limited local bus services operated by **Highland Country Buses** (*01397 702373*) based at Fort William Bus Station in Ardgour Road to and from towns in the Great Glen. A Royal Mail Post Bus (*01463 256273*) serves remoter areas.

By Car The best approach from the south is the M8 and A82 from Glasgow. The journey of around 160km takes up to 2½ hours. From Edinburgh the best way is the M9, A84, A85 and then the A82. The journey is around 190km and will take about three hours. Glencoe is around 32km away on the A82; allow 30 minutes. Inverness is around 100km away further along the A822. Journey time is just over an hour.

Visitor Information

The **Fort William Tourist Information Centre** (*01397 703781*, ***www.visithighlands.com***) is at the Cameron Centre in Cameron Square. It's open April–May Monday–Saturday 9am–5pm (Sunday 10am–4pm); June–August Monday–Saturday 9am–6pm (Sunday 10am–4pm); September Monday–Saturday 9am–5pm (Sunday 10am–4pm); October Monday–Friday 10am–5pm (Saturday 10am–4pm, Sunday 10am–2pm); November–March Monday–Friday 10am–5pm (Saturday 10am–4pm).

What to See & Do

The Jacobite Steam Train ★

ALL AGES

*Station Square, Fort William, 01524 737751 or 01524 737753, **www.steamtrain.info**.*

This 135km return trip from Fort William to Mallaig is an especially great day out for Harry Potter fans and older people who like tea and steam engines. The train, which first ran in 1901, stops at Glenfinnan, whose 21-arch viaduct is famous from the Potter movies. For children not yet bitten by the magician bug, there's the chance to have their photo taken with the train driver on the footplate at Mallaig. The scenery isbreathtaking, with views of Loch Shiel, the beaches of Morar where *Highlander* was filmed and, on summery days, you can see Eigg, Rum, Muck and even Skye. The journey (two hours each way) takes in the most westerly mainland railway station in Britain (Arisaig), passes close by the deepest freshwater loch in Britain (Loch Morar) and the shortest river in Britain (River Morar) before arriving next to the deepest seawater loch in Europe – Loch Nevis.

The steam is, of course, especially romantic (although not great for respiration if you enter a tunnel with your window open). There are gripes however. The stop in Glenfinnan gives just enough time to get off with your double buggy and comment on the length of the queues for the railway museum before you must collapse the buggy and hoof it back on to the train. An hour and a half in Mallaig is just long enough to think you'll get a comfortable lunch in but also just short enough to worry all through your lunch that if the waitress doesn't hurry up you'll miss the train back, get stranded in the town and end up as a herring fishermen. The train is a good idea if you have older children either a) better equipped at appreciating the beauty of a tree-lined loch or b) just so into Harry Potter that nothing in the world matters now they've bought a Dumbledore T-shirt from the train shop.

Open *one train a day leaving Fort William at 10.20am and returning at 4.00pm: 19th May–27th June (Mon–Fri), 28th June–31st Aug (every day), 1st Sep–10th Oct (Mon–Fri).*
Adm *return fare £29.50, children £17, under-5s (if not requiring a seat i.e. four hours on your lap) free; first class (including tea and coffee, larger seats and more leg room) £42.50, children £21.50.*

The Jacobite Steam Train, Fort William

INSIDER TIP

If you have toddlers, buy them colouring-in books and pens at the Fort William station kiosk. The four hours in a train carriage with only a small corridor full of elderly people carrying mint teas back to their companions can drag if you're just 2 and uninterested in the depths of various Scottish lochs.

MALLAIG

Mallaig is the bustling fishing port where Bonnie Prince Charlie landed from the Outer Hebrides dressed as a woman after fleeing redcoats after the defeat at Culloden in 1746. Not that you'd know this from visiting the town, which seems blissfully/charmingly/annoyingly unaware that anyone would be interested in visiting it for anything other than a bag of fat chips. As the aquarium has recently closed down, **Mallaig Heritage Centre** (*01687 462085*, ***www.mallaigheritagecentre.org.uk***) is left as the star attraction, a dry museum in Station Road full of facts about the Knoydart Clearances (disappointingly nothing to do with snooker) and photos of nets of fish. A better idea is to hire a cab (Franco's taxis: *01687 462800*, £12 return, £18 if you want them to hang around) to Loch Morar. The 300m deep loch is said to contain its own Nessie-style beast, the 3-humped 9m long Morag, which attacked two fishermen in 1969. He has been sighted 34 times since 1887, although not while we were standing on the freezing loch-side eating cheese and Marmite sandwiches looking out across the still grey water with a pair of mini-binoculars my wife liberated from the Royal Court theatre. Just as well really; each sighting is said to herald the death of a member of the Macdonald clan. And nobody wants that...except maybe the Campbells.

Glenfinnan Monument Visitor Centre ALL AGES

Glenfinnan, Lochaber, 08444 932221, ***www.nts.org.uk****.*

The main attraction here, the Glenfinnan monument, which marks where Bonnie Prince Charlie raised his standard in 1745, has been upstaged by what happens at 10.50am every morning at a fence the other end of the car park – the Jacobite steam train crosses Glenfinnan viaduct about 300m away. The image of a loco crossing this bridge was used in several Harry Potter movies; when we visited the visitor centre it was lined with camera-brandishing Potter fans one of whom was so excited he was about to ignore the Keep Out signs and trespass across National Trust land to get a closer shot – until his wife read his mind. 'There are rangers in 4x4s behind those trees just waiting for someone to make a fool of themselves. I'll be so embarrassed if you start scrambling over that field.'

The Visitor Centre contains a small exhibition on the 1745

Jacobite cause and a model of some soldiers milling about. Our daughter enjoyed a quiz where she pulled various levers to answer questions she didn't understand about Bonnie Prince Charlie. Over the road is the Monument, modelled on Nelson's. It was built in 1815 when romanticism about the Stuart cause was in full bloom. A spiral staircase leads to a viewing platform where you see the statue of the highlander at the head of Loch Shiel with the hills of Ardgour, Moidart and Lochaber rising dramatically around him. It's also where we also heard the man from earlier say: 'I can't see any 4x4s, darling.'

Open *daily 31st Mar–30th June 10am–5pm, July–Aug 9.30am–5.30pm, Sep–Oct 10am–5pm.* ***Adm*** *£3, children (6–16) £2, under-6s free.* ***Amenities*** *café (children's lunchbox £3.95).*

Seal Island Cruise ALL AGES

Crannog Cruises, Fort William Town Pier, 01397 700714, ***www.crannog.net****.*

This cruise, offering views of the Great Glen and Ben Nevis, gives you the chance to see basking seals, dolphins, porpoises and golden eagles (although 'chance' is the operative word). The 90-minute, 15km cruise on Loch Linnhe also takes in a mussel farm and a salmon farm, but the highlight is Seal Island. Alas, of a colony of more than 100 grey and common seals, not one made an appearance during our trip because of the wind-chill factor, which also put off the golden eagles, the dolphins, the porpoises and every other form of the wildlife from cormorants to grey herons, oystercatchers, guillemots, eider ducks and swans, we'd hoped to see. Basically we went out on a boat, stayed below in the sea-viewing lounge (where we couldn't see anything because of the rain lashing the windows) and ate two packets of cheese and onion crisps (all there was in the bar area), failed to hear a single word of the on-board commentary because the PA system wasn't working, and then, after an hour and half of occasionally nipping up to see if the rain had stopped, we returned to the pier. That said, the captain did lend our daughter his captain's fleece and give her a go at the wheel before we disembarked and it all started a pleasing new family game: pretending to be happy. 'Let's pretend to be happy.'

Sailings *daily Apr–Oct 10am, 12pm, 2pm, 4pm.* ***Adm*** *£8, children (5–16) £4, under-5s free.*

The Nevis Range ★ ALL AGES

Torlundy, Fort William, Inverness-shire, 01397 705815, ***www.nevisrange.co.uk****.*

Britain's only mountain-top gondola system takes you to the upper slopes of Scotland's 8th highest mountain, Aonach Mor, with incredible panoramic views all the way to the Outer Hebrides. The 12-minute ride (although it feels longer when you're swaying in the wind remembering James Bond movies) lifts you 645m. At the

FUN FACT Ben Nevis

1 Every year Ben Nevis (1,322m) is climbed by 100,000 visitors including, in 1998, my wife and I whose sole supplies if the weather turned bad consisted of one bag of Woolworth's pic 'n'mix (half eaten).

2 In 1911 a 20 horse-power Model T Ford was driven to the top.

3 In 1981 a group of students from Glasgow University pushed a bed up the summit accompanied for the first 1,000m (until he collapsed) by former newscaster Reginald Bosanquet.

top there's the coldest play-park in Scotland, a discovery centre (open in the summer, explaining the flora and fauna), and the opportunity to risk your life downhill mountain biking on a world championship course (under-12s not allowed), as well as paragliding, snow-biking, hang-gliding and, in the winter (end-December to end-April), skiing. Needless to say, with our whole family hyperventilating whenever the gondola crossed a support bar, we declined these tempting offers and instead had some shortbread in the Snowgoose restaurant where we debated just how windy it would have to be before we became stranded. How soon would staff start rationing shortbread? Would we become a cut off mini-community forced to live on mountain lichens? Would some of us try to return to ground-level in a blizzard, while others went fatefully on ahead to look for help? Who would survive? Who would perish? 'Daddy, I'm getting scared,' said our daughter. 'I want to go back to the hotel now.' So we did.

Beginners' ski packages start at £39 for a day, including two hours' instruction and a day's pass for beginner slopes with ski and pole hire (juniors aged 7–17 £30), while under-7s must have private instruction (£25 for an hour's lesson including a half-day's pass on beginner slopes with ski hire). Snowboarding packages are the same price, and for both it's best to book well in advance. Alternatively you can ride another chairlift (July and August only, £1) to Corrie Naneach, where you'll be treated to views over the Great Glen. Back on ground level, another option is cross-country mountain biking. Between May and September Off Beat bikes (9.30am–5pm) are based at the range. They provide free maps with cycle hire (£15 a day, £10 for a half-day; children £12 day, £8 a half-day). Routes range from 4km to 20km. Tag-alongs £10 per day (£6 a half-day), child bike seats £8 day, (£5 a half-day).

Open *daily subject to weather Sep–Oct 10am–5pm, 1st–11th Nov 10am–4pm, 20th Dec–Jan 10am–4pm, Feb–Apr 9.30am–5pm, May–June 10am–5pm, July–Aug 9.30am–6pm.* ***Adm*** *gondola £8.75, children (5–17) £5.25, under-5s free.* ***Amenities*** *café/restaurant.*

INVERNESS & AROUND

The capital of the Highlands, Scotland's fifth city is dominated by its livid pink castle and, across the River Ness, the Cathedral. **Inverness** is the shopping capital of the Highlands with its Eastgate Shopping Centre including a Marks and Spencer's and an ornamental clock with animated animals that mesmerised our daughter. The city, on the doorstep of Loch Ness, Culloden and the beach at Nairn, is small enough to get about on foot – which is lucky because the traffic was the worst we encountered in Scotland. Inverness is also home to one of the country's largest second-hand bookstore, **Leakeys** (☎ *01463 239947*) in the old Greyfriars Hall, and is the former home of ex-Liberal Democrat leader Charles Kennedy and thriller writer Alistair MacLean of *Guns of Navarone* and *Where Eagles Dare* fame.

Essentials

By Air Inverness Airport (☎ *01667 462445*, ***www.hial.co.uk***) is based at Dalcross 13km east of Inverness. The taxi fare is £13, or take bus 11 Monday–Saturday (40 minutes, £3). The airport has flights from London, Edinburgh and Glasgow. Operators include **British Airways** (☎ *0845 773 3377*, ***www.britishairways.com***), **Servisair** (☎ *01667 464040*, ***www.servisair.com***), **easyJet**, (☎ *0870 600 0000*, ***www.easyjet.com***), **Eastern Airways** (☎ *0870 366 9100*, ***www.easternairways.com***) and **Highland Airways** (☎ *0845 450 2245*, ***www.highlandairways.co.uk***).

By Train There are direct services from London to Inverness (including an overnight sleeper). There are also links from Glasgow and Edinburgh, although none between towns within the Great Glen, except the West Highland Line between Fort William and Mallaig (see p. 145). There are also connections between Glasgow (Queen Street) and Inverness with a stop at Aviemore. For more train information contact **First Scotrail** (☎ *0845 748 4950*, ***www.firstgroup.com/scotrail***).

By Bus **Inverness Coach Station** (☎ *01463 2333371*, off Academy Street) is well served. There are hourly services to Glasgow (£35.80 return) taking around 3¾ hours. From Edinburgh hourly services take the same time and cost £44 return. For a bargain price **Megabus** (☎ *01738 639095*, ***www.megabus.com***) has routes in from Perth, Dundee, Edinburgh, Aberdeen and Glasgow.

By Car The A9 from Glasgow or Edinburgh takes about 3½ hours. The A82 on the western shore of Loch Ness is a more pleasant alternative (add about an hour), and if you have time the B862 on the loch's eastern shore is quieter still.

Visitor Information

The **Inverness Tourist Information Centre** (*01463 234353*, ***www.inverness-scotland.com***) at Castle Wynd is open 9am–5pm Monday–Saturday March–end-May, 9am–6pm Monday–Saturday (Sunday 10am–4pm) end-May–end-August), 9am–5pm, Monday–Saturday (Sunday 10am–4pm) September–October. The **Drumnadrochit Tourist Information Centre** (*01456 459076*) is open from 9am–5pm Monday–Saturday April–June, 9am–6pm Monday–Saturday (Sunday 10am–4pm) July–August, 9am–5pm Monday to Saturday (Sunday 10am–4pm) in September, 9am–5pm Monday–Saturday in October, 10am–1.30pm Monday–Friday November– March. For **Fort Augustus Tourist Information Centre** call *013220 366779* (***www.fortaugustus.org***).

What to See & Do

Bogbain Adventure and Heritage Farm ★ ALL AGES

Bogbain of Inshes, 01463 772800, ***www.bogbainfarm.com****. Off the A9, 5km south of Inverness on the slip road B9177 for Milton of Leys.*

Children can ride quad bikes, shoot at paintball targets (guns too heavy for under-6s) and score penalties against a goal-keeping dog at this farm that also serves excellent home-made food. Opened by a couple who found there was nothing for youngsters in Inverness, there's also a play-barn of hay bails and a craft centre. Children can ride electric go-karts, operate mini diggers, see highland cattle, and there are sheep dog demonstrations by Jean, the collie, whose goalkeeping skills made him personality of the year for 2007 in the *Inverness City Advertiser* (he got a paw to both my wife's penalties, although not mine – blast them low to the right, his weak side). Our daughter's favourite was the trampoline (or bouncealine, as she called it).

Open *daily 10am–6pm except quads (Wed 3–5pm, Thurs–Sun 10am–5pm; during school holidays all activities available 10am–6pm).* ***Adm*** *barn and play area £3.50; digger (over-3s) £2.50; go-karts (over-3s) £1.00; junior quads (6–12 year-olds) £4; adult quads (15 minutes) £8, 30 minutes £14, 1 hour £24; paintball (20 balls) £3; arts and crafts £3; all-day pass £10 (adults and under-2s free).* ***Amenities*** *baby-changing, café (with highchairs and children's snack packs, £2.95).*

Caledonian Canal Heritage Centre ALL AGES

Ardchattan House, Fort Augustus, Inverness-shire, 01320 366493.

Based beside an impressive flight of seven locks, this museum in a converted lock-keeper's cottage tells the story of the Caledonian Canal. It was designed in 1803 by Thomas Telford to help mariners avoid the long and pirate-prone route around the top of Scotland. While you are mugging up on history for the inevitable later car quiz with your wife, toddlers will be kept amused by a British Waterways book of stickers about being safe around water. They get to press various buttons on interactive displays about local walks, while beside the wire Nessie model outside (if you can fight off thoughts of your little ones plummeting to the bottom of a lock with their being-safe-around-water badges still on) it's a good spot to watch the world, and boats, go by.

The Centre is now part of the Great Glen Way from Fort William to Inverness, so watch out for foot-sore walkers passing through. You can wave your car keys at them.

Open *daily Apr–Oct 9.30am–5.30pm.* ***Adm*** *free.*

Clansman Centre ★ ALL AGES

Fort Augustus, Loch Ness, Inverness-shire, 01320 366444, www.scottish-swords.com.

Here children can dress up like 17th-century clansmen and learn how to maim rivals with ancient weapons. The jolly if brutal history lesson in Highland life, based inside an old schoolhouse done up like a turf home with pans, skulls and antlers hanging from the ceilings, lasts around 45 minutes. You'll learn how to put on belted plaid and gain an insight into how the typical Braveheart ate, lived, fought and survived harsh repressions. At the end boys can try and persuade their fathers to part with £250 for a claymore sword in the Celtic craft workshop, that they now know how to sever the heads of foes with.

Open *daily(ish) 10am–6pm Apr–Oct.* ***Adm*** *£3.50 children £3, family ticket (two adults, two children) £10.* ***Amenities*** *shop.*

Highland and Rare Breeds Croft, Rowanlea

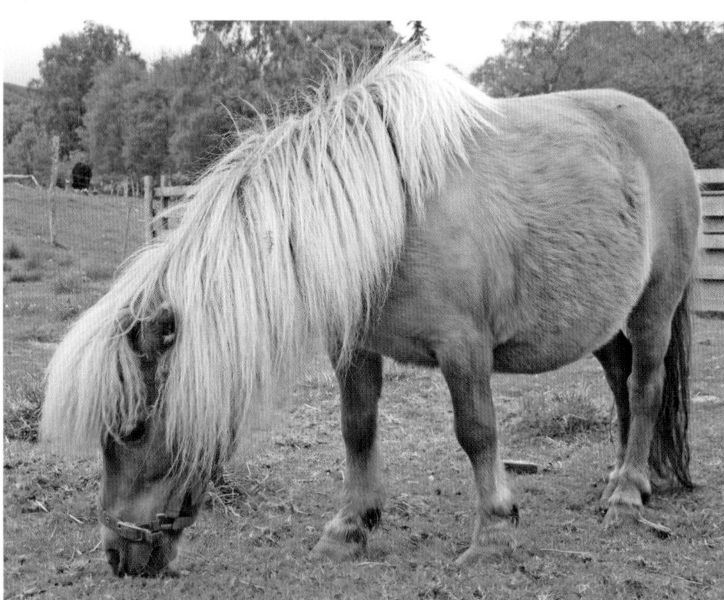

Highland and Rare Breeds Croft ALL AGES

*Rowanlea, Fort Augustus, Inverness-shire, 01320 366433, **www.highlandrarebreeds.com**.*

This park has Highland cattle, Shetland ponies, red deer, ducks, goats, Tamworth pigs, hens and other farmyard favourites. There are picnic tables, children are given a list of animals to go around like mini-admin clerks ticking off, and there's a wishing well that cost us more than the entrance fee in small change.

***Open** daily 10am–6pm from Easter weekend to 1st Oct. **Adm** family ticket (two adults and children) £5. **Amenities** picnic area.*

Loch Ness 2000 Exhibition Centre AGES OVER 5

*Next to the Drumnadrochit Hotel, Drumnadrochit, Inverness-shire, 01456 450573, **www.loch-ness-scotland.com**.*

Seven themed rooms here purport to take the visitor on a scientific discovery to uncover the truth behind the legend of the monster, from its roots in Gaelic myth to present-day sightings and the theory that it might all be an above-average-weight sturgeon. Or, as the narrator grandly states: 'You must be naturalist and detective, judge and jury.' Actually I had to be a strict father to stop our daughter clambering over a model of a sonar submersible. Interesting perhaps for 8-year-olds and above, for our toddler there was no interactivity, nothing at her own height and it was often too dark to find chocolate gems in the depths of our emergency bag to keep her quiet as pseudo-scientists with large moustaches debated thermo-climes. She did, however, enjoy the thousands of monster teddies in the gift shop,

Loch Ness

1 There is more water in Loch Ness than in all the lakes of England and Wales put together.
2 The water, never known to freeze, is drinkable (if very dark) because of the peat.
3 In 1900 occultist Aleister Crowley, dubbed 'the wickedest man in the world', moved into Boleskine House (later owned by Jimmy Page of Led Zeppelin) on the shores of Loch Ness. He'd hold black masses, orgies and summon demons, which caused him to be blamed for the death of a local butcher who accidentally severed an artery with a meat cleaver and bled to death. Crowley had written the names of demons on a bill from the man's shop.
4 In 1952 Englishman John Cobbs became the first man to travel 200mph (320kph) in a jet-propelled speedboat, 'The Crusader'. The speed attempt ended in tragedy when Cobb crashed and later died of his wounds. His remains still lie at the bottom of the loch.
5 On New Year's Eve 1940 a Wellington Bomber crashed into Loch Ness.

Urquhart Castle looking over Loch Ness

where my wife bought a Nessie beanie hat, I suspect, just to annoy me.

Open *daily Nov–Mar 10am–3.30pm, Apr–May 9.30am–5pm, June 9am–6pm, July–Aug 9am–8pm, Sep–9am–6pm, Oct 9.30am–5.30pm.* ***Adm*** *£5.95, children (over 7) £4, under-7s free.* ***Amenities*** *shop.*

Original Loch Ness Monster Visitor Centre AGES OVER 7

Drumnadrochit, Inverness, 01456 450342, ***www.lochnesscentre.com****.*

Now in competition with the Loch Ness 2000 Exhibition (see above), this place is fighting a losing battle. With none of the scientific blather and techy high-jinks, it is just a corridor of photos culminating in a nice sit down in a mini-cinema showing a boring Nessie movie on a loop. That said, we enjoyed a brief moment of hilarity when the film showed a stand-off between a Scandinavian scientist hell-bent on trawling the loch and a male white witch who felt this disrespectful. Their discussion descends into a wonderful cat-fight with the witch, as the scientist prepares his sonars, loudly using a word to describe him that rhymes with punt. Disney wouldn't approve but it made us laugh.

Open *daily 9am–5pm (till 8pm end of June–August).* ***Adm*** *£4, children (5–12) £3, under-5s free.*

Urquhart Castle ★★ ALL AGES

Drumnadrochit, Inverness-shire, 01456 450551, ***www.historic-scotland.gov.uk****. On the A82, south of Drumnadrochit.*

Once held by Edward I and Robert the Bruce, the castle was besieged in 1545 and saw its last action in 1689 when blah blah blah, forget all that...these ruins are the best location in Scotland to spot Nessie. With views restricted by trees on the A82, especially in summer, Nessie-hunters climb the old Grant

The Legend of Nessie

The first mention of the legend occurs in St Adamnan's 17th century biography of St Columba: in 565 the saint becalmed an aquatic animal that attacked one of his monks. Modern interest dates to the publication in 1934 of London surgeon R.K. Wilson's photograph (now known to be a hoax) of the neck and head of the beast. More recent encounters feature anglers seeing inexplicable ripples and the notorious 1961 incident when 30 hotel guests saw a pair of humps cruise half a mile along the loch. Despite hi-tech sonar surveys failing to produce evidence (believers say the monster hid in a cave to escape detection), the legend lives on, interest owing much to the reliance upon it of tourism, particular in Drumnadrochit. That said, no one knows where the unknown layers of silt at the bottom of the loch begin and end – best estimates measure the loch at about 225m deep, deeper than the North Sea. Others point to undiscovered channels linking the loch to the sea. What scientists have found in the depth of the loch – pure white eels and rare artic char – offers fertile grounds for speculation. Theories of what Nessie is range from a Baltic sturgeon to a plesiosaur from the dinosaur age.

Tower with their telephoto lenses hoping to see a break in the waters. Watch out for them nattering about plesiosaurs, Operation Deepscan and the Dinsdale film. You can annoy them by saying loudly to your toddler, 'Don't be silly – they proved it was a giant sturgeon years ago.' My wife, who actually half believes, brought binoculars, although after a fruitless five-minute search all it took was a suggestion of a buttered scone in the café to abandon her quest. The castle has picnic spots to gaze out at the cruisers of tourists approaching, and a giant trebuchet. The visitor centre has a short film about the history of the castle, as well as artefacts including gemstones, arrowheads and an almost complete (if exceptionally dull) ewer.

***Open** daily Apr–Oct 9.30am–6pm, Nov–Mar 9.30am–5pm (last entry 45 minutes before closing). **Adm** £6.50, children (5–16) £3.25, under-5s free. **Amenities** café (children's lunches £3.75), picnic area.*

CULLODEN

On 16th April 1746 the last battle on British soil was fought. It marked the end of a civil war for succession to the throne, under way since 1688 when King James VII of Scotland (and II of England) was deposed in favour of William of Orange. In 1744 the French planned an invasion to replace Protestant George II with Catholic James VII's son, the 'Old Pretender', but a storm wrecked their fleet. The following year the Old Pretender's son,

Charles Edward Stuart (Bonnie Prince Charlie), gathered an army and raised his standard at Glenfinnan. He reached Derby, in England, on 4th December 1745 where, despite being all for pressing on to London, he accepted the need to retreat because the French were not ready to invade. What no one knew was that Welsh Jacobites had risen in support, others in Oxfordshire were about to, and London was in panic. George II's court had packed their belongings onto ships ready to flee to the Continent. What would might happened if Bonnie Prince Charlie had gainsayed his advisers and marched on London? George II would have fled and the English and French might have avoided 70 years of conflict. The English would not have raised taxes in the colonies to pay for this, meaning the Americans would have had no cause to seek independence. And, perhaps, the French Revolution and the Napoleonic Wars would not have happened. Not to mention the invention of the Big Mac.

Culloden Battlefield and Visitor Centre ALL AGES

*Culloden Moor, Inverness, 01463 790607, **www.nts.org.uk**. 3km on from Bog Bain, follow signs off A9 north of Inverness.*

At this new visitor centre at the site of Scotland's second-most famous battlefield, war-minded boys will enjoy the 'immersion theatre' designed to replicate the experience of Culloden minus getting your head lopped off. Other interactive displays show would-be generals how the battle unfolded and each entrance ticket has a special code that, scanned at various audio machines, tells the story of one of 12 different characters associated with the battle. The battlefield itself is a boggy moor with a memorial cairn that people wandered around contemplating the silence and significance of Britain's last battlefield, until maybe they heard our daughter shouting: 'Dolly has been naughty in the shop. And she will never ever have a biscuit ever *ever* again.'

***Open** daily Nov–Mar 10am–4pm, Apr–Oct 9am–6pm. **Adm** £8, children (5–16) £6.50, under-5s free.*

NAIRN

Nairn's beaches and spectacular sea views across the Moray Firth make the town a magnet for families. It has the most hours of sunshine in Scotland, very low rainfall and a delightful and very English cricket square just off the beach. It has been popular with holidaymakers since Victorian times, and feels like the Scottish equivalent of Eastbourne, just with less pensioners eating Eccles cakes. The sandy beachfront with an outdoor children's play-pool and a play-park alongside the Links tearoom is a lovely place to spend an afternoon. Our daughter had a great game of hide-and-seek in the dunes before she

Cawdor Castle, Nairn

fell off some driftwood, got sand in her eyes, cried, remembered she'd left her Dolly, Mrs Dolly, in the Astra's roofbox, cried some more and was eventually carried under my arm like a plank of wood back to the car.

Cawdor Castle ★ ALL AGES

Nairn, Inverness-shire, ☎ 01667 404401, www.cawdorcastle.com.

Cawdor Castle has a great maze and beautiful gardens. Alas, it's also where we believe the Countess Dowager of Cawdor herself caught our daughter weeing in the moat. There's some history – an old Thane of Cawdor was mentioned in Shakespeare's *Macbeth* and, more interestingly in 1976, a hidden trap door was found in the drawing room that was used to dispatch any unwelcome visitor straight down a chute carved within the thickness of the castle wall into a dungeon with no other means of entry or exit (surely after the wet-room, the next must-have home accessory). Children get an activity sheet and there are nature trails. Alternatively, if you are small in size, you can simply hug your arms close to your chest and roll down the grass slopes of the old moat like a log shouting 'ohhh-hhh' moments before weeing in front of a minor royal.

***Open** daily 1st May–14th Oct 10am–5.30pm. **Adm** £7.90, children (5–15) £4.90, under-5s free.*

THE BLACK ISLE

The mysterious Black Isle across the North Kessock bridge from Inverness is mysterious for two reasons. It isn't an island – it's a fertile peninsula between Cromarty Firth and the Moray Firth dotted with picturesque villages – and it isn't black. In fact its rolling green hills make it look more like Sussex or Devon than the Highlands. So why the name? Some say it is named black for its associations with witchcraft. Others believe the peninsula is named after its mild climate – there's very little frost, which leaves fields 'black' in winter, rather than white with snow. Another suggestion is that the name is a translation from the Gaelic Eilean Dubh, which maybe is a shortening of Eilean Dubhtaich meaning, it is thought, St Duthus Isle, someone possibly connected with the area. OK, basically nobody knows why it is called the Black Isle.

The 18th century town of Cromarty (of shipping forecast fame) is its major attraction, along with Chanonry Point, where you can view bottle-nosed dolphins at play and where the death of Coinneach Odhar, more commonly known as the Brahan Seer, is commemorated by a memorial stone on the spot not far from where he was executed in the traditional manner of the annoying know-all: in a barrel of boiling tar. For anyone wanting more atmosphere, Chanonry Point and its surrounding area forms the backdrop for an out-of-print environmental thriller available in all good local Oxfam shops, called *The Chanonry Encounter*. Written by Scottish-American author Steve Cameron it involves...wait for it...communication between local dolphins...and wait for it a little longer...hoping to warn humans of dangers to the Earth. The novel highlights the story of the Brahan Seer (he famously predicted the building of the 1847 Caledonian Canal, but also claimed Scotland would get overrun with Giant Sheep) and other local legends. Among them, the fact we rather laboured earlier: that the Black Isle is neither black nor an island.

Essentials & Visitor Information

Car is your only real option here. From Inverness cross the North Kessock Bridge on the A9. The A832 takes you on to Cromarty. There are no local tourist information centres on the Black Isle. For information about the area try ***www.iknowscotland.co.uk***, ***www.undiscoveredscotland.co.uk/areamuir/info.html*** and ***www.black-isle.info/Cromarty/attractions.html***.

What to See & Do

Black Isle Wildlife and Country Park ★★ ALL AGES

The Croft, Drumsmittal. North Kessock, Ross-shire, ☎ 01463 731656.

We were chased around this park by two goats who launched themselves at us on their hind legs so enthusiastically to get our bag of animal feed we abandoned it at their feet before scampering off to see the rheas, one of which pecked my finger so hard I couldn't put my hand in my pocket for two days. Despite these indignities, this is a great little park where our toddler held a variety of animals in the hatchery including a baby rabbit (dropped), a duck (dropped) and a python ('no daddy, no'). Open-top incubators allow children to see how chicks develop with hatchings in spring and summer. Elsewhere you see zebras, meerkats, a mynah bird that says 'I love you', potbellied pigs, goats, raccoons and peacocks.

The park is five minutes drive from Inverness on the A9. Cross the Kessock Bridge over the Beauly Firth from Inverness and take the first turning left at the mini-roundabout. Strange signs imply you're lost. You're not.

***Open** Apr–Oct 10am–6pm, Nov–Mar 10am–4pm (reduced facilities). **Adm** £6, children £4.50, family ticket (two adults and up to three children) £22.00, under-3s free. **Amenities** café, play area.*

Cromarty Courthouse Museum ALL AGES

*Church Street, Cromarty, 📞 01381 600418, **www.cromarty-courthouse.org.uk**.*

The original old Cromarty Courthouse has animatronic models playing out an 18th century court case that so terrified our daughter she fastened herself to my leg like a shin-pad for the rest of the visit. If she hadn't been swinging from my leg she might have tried on some of the period costumes at the back of the court, or had fun with the quiz handed out on entrance. You can also visit the cells, where there is a mannequin of Sir Thomas Urquhart, a 17th century royalist who invented a universal language, translated Rabelais more bawdily than the original and died during a fit of laughter on hearing the news of the restoration of Charles II. That's what you call a full life.

***Open** Apr–Oct 10am–5pm. **Adm** £5 (plus 10% off meals at Cromarty Arms pub over the road), children (5–16) £4, under-5s free, family ticket (two adults and up to four children) £15.*

Hugh Miller Museum and Birthplace Cottage ALL AGES

*Church Street, Cromarty, 📞 01381 60045, **www.nts.org.uk**.*

Here children can view fossils through a magnifying glass and learn about the life and work of pioneering geologist Hugh Miller through touch-screen TV quizzes. Hugh Miller, the son of a captain who drowned at sea, started life as a stonemason. It was working in quarries that sparked his interest in fossils. Self-taught, he was fortunate that Cromarty was home to two important Devonian fossil deposits, from which he built up his collection now on display at the National Museum in Edinburgh. A friend of Charles Darwin, and the first man to bring the study of fossils to the wider public, he was also a celebrated journalist, author and editor. Miller, whose great grandfather John Feddes was a buccaneer who built the cottage using

The Weirdest Thing in Scotland: the Clootie Well

The best approach to Cromarty is the south side of the Black Isle on the A832 where, north of Munlochy, unmarked by the roadside, you'll see a '**clootie well**'. Reminiscent of something from a very scary episode of *Wire in the Blood*, it's a natural spring within a wood whose tree branches are draped in rotting children's clothes. (Little ones might find this a bit scary.) Dating back to pre-Christian times, superstition has it that if a sick person leaves a piece of clothing (a clootie) next to a magical spring, as the clothing decays so does the sickness. My fearful wife, crossing herself furiously like a superstitious bog-woman, refused to get out of the car and shouted at me through the passenger window as I photographed this shrine, 'For God's sake. This is wrong. Please can we go now. I want to see the dolphins. Don't leave that glove. It was just a rhea bite. Please don't leave that glove. I want to see the dolphins. The children want to see them. Oh my God, I don't believe it. I told you not to leave that glove. You don't believe in it so why are you leaving the glove. You're being ridiculous. Pick up that glove. Ben, you told me your hand was getting better. This is so stupid. Ben, go back and get that glove. I bought you those gloves from BHS. Go back and get that glove. For God's sake, they cost me £15. Now there's a car coming. Get out of there. Right, forget it we're not going to see the dolphins. Let's go back to the hotel.'

plundered Spanish gold and silver, died tragically aged 54 following a serious of terrifying nightmares that prompted him to shoot himself in the chest.

The visit includes an audio tour of Miller's birthplace followed by a trip round the museum next door, on the top floor of which is a workbench and magnifying glass where our daughter tried to steal a 15 million year-old fossilised shark tooth before we bundled her back downstairs. The museum's highlights include Miller's old stonemason's hammer while at the back there is a wild garden with a well we considered throwing our daughter down.

Open *daily 31st Mar–30th Sep 12.30pm–4.30pm, 1st Oct–31st October Sun–Wed 12.30pm–4.30pm.* ***Adm*** *£5, children (under 5–18) £2.50, under-5s free.*

AVIEMORE & AROUND

Developed fairly unsuccessfully in the 1960s as a ski resort (the snow and weather were too variable), and once a favourite of Sir Walter Scott and Queen Victoria, the town of Aviemore now resembles a sort of Milton Keynes with mountains. Housing estates, shopping centres and youths loitering about in football shirts make it aesthetically fairly vulgar

TIP Chanonry Point

This spit of land extending into the Moray Firth is the best dolphin-watching spot in Europe. The pod of 130 bottle-nosed dolphins and occasionally seals, porpoises and minke whales come for the salmon here that the unique tides throw up. They can be seen throughout the year, apart from when we visited in May, according to my wife, because I spent too long ghouling around the Clootie Well near Munlochy (see above). A beach in the shadow of Chanonry lighthouse has a patch of sand for children to build castles and is full of couples and picnicking families taking it in turns with binoculars to scan the horizon.

To find Chanonry Point drive to the end of the village of Fortrose and follow the golf club signs. The best time is two hours before low tide and at the changing of the tides. Alternatively try a boat trip with **Ecoventures** (*01381 600323*, ***www.ecoventures.co.uk***) based at the Harbour Workshop, Victoria Place, in Cromarty. Two-hour trips leave three times daily in a rigid inflatable (wet weather gear included). They cost £20, (children aged 5–12, £15).

---

after the beauty of the surrounding Highlands. Although this might soon be about to change. An attempted transformation in 2000 resulted in the demolition of many of its original eyesores, including a Santa Claus theme park, and although many of the planned new visitor attractions failed to materialise, the area is back on the up after a new private capital initiative started in 2006. Farmer's markets have moved in and although the area still has, in parts, a market-town-on-a-Friday-night feel to it, there are plenty of family-friendly activities nearby – including every imaginable outdoor pursuit from husky dog sledging to skiing. And of course, the pristine mountain air and unspoilt scenery that made the area famous is only a short drive in any direction. Add the town's close proximity to the only freely grazing reindeer herd in the UK and it's a place most youngsters including our 2-year-old daughter ('When I am older I will have a reindeer') can't help but be drawn to.

Essentials

By Rail There are hourly services from Glasgow. The journey takes 2 hours 40 minutes and costs £41.20 return. From Edinburgh it's £10 cheaper and the journey is 40 minutes shorter. Services run two-hourly. From Inverness, hourly services take around 45 minutes and cost £14.40 return. For more train information contact **First Scotrail** (*0845 748 4950*, ***www.firstgroup.com/scotrail***).

By Bus There are regular services to Aviemore from Inverness, taking about 45 minutes and costing £12. From Edinburgh services run hourly and take around four hours (£31.80 return). From Glasgow it is the same, except journey-time is half an hour quicker.

By Car Aviemore is best approached from Inverness and the north by the A9. The journey – around 40km across mountainous country – will take about 40 minutes. If you're coming from Aberdeen take the A944, A97, A939 and then A95. It's about 96km but might take a couple of hours on these roads. From Edinburgh, take the M90 then A9. About 208km, it takes about 3½ hours. From Glasgow start on the M9 before following much the same route along the A9.

Visitor Information

The **Aviemore Tourist Information Centre** (*01479 810363*, ***www.visitaviemore.co.uk***) is on Grampian Road (the main road at the south end of the village). It is open 9am–5pm Monday–Saturday (Sunday 10am–4pm) April–October, and Monday–Friday 9am–5pm (Saturday 10am–4pm) November–March.

What to See & Do

Highland Wildlife Park

ALL AGES

*Kincraig, Kingussue, Inverness-shire, 01540 651270, **www.highlandwildlifepark.org**.*

We had a small argument while staring at a hunk of meat on a stick in the wolf section here when, after I asked my wife what she would do if I fell from the viewing gallery into the enclosure, she said rather chillingly 'Shield her (our daughter's) eyes'. This half-safari, half-zoo showcases animals native to the Highlands or in danger of extinction. You drive the first section listening to a CD telling you about the animals you're passing, which include European bison, the once almost extinct Przewalski's Horse (like normal horses but more stupid looking) and the reindeer that our daughter was disappointed weren't dragging Santa. There were also polecats, wildcats, beavers, badgers and golden eagles. The walk-around section includes the (award-winning) wolf enclosure, otters, snow monkeys and at the time of going to press the park was planning to introduce Siberian tigers. In the Antler's café my wife admitted, after the initial shock, she might actually think to call the ranger to say, 'My husband's being gored. Come with a gun.' We bought each other a key-ring featuring a monkey to make up.

Open *Apr–Oct 10am–5pm (last entry 4pm), Nov–Mar 10am–4 pm.* ***Adm*** *(including audio guide and guidebook) £10, children £7.50.* ***Amenities*** *café (children's menu).*

Landmark Forest Theme Park ★ ALL AGES

*Carrbridge, Inverness-shire, 0800 7313446, **www.landmark-centre.co.uk**.*

Climbing into a small pod on the Falcon watercoaster and careering over the equivalent of a 12m waterfall makes a pretty good family bonding opportunity in anyone's book. Set in a pine forest, this fun-park has the tallest timber tower in the country (105 steps with great views of the Cairngorms), a steam-powered sawmill (our daughter thought it was a monster and cried), go-karts and a massive Clydesdale horse called Lex (our daughter thought it was a monster and cried). There's a gentle squirrel trail, the Ant City adventure playground and microworld, where you can see various already small things seem even smaller through a microscope. There is also a big slide (for over-5s) plus for older children, a rooftop woodland walk and bungee jump (minimum height requirement 1.5m). Unfortunately there was also the 10m Pinnacle climbing wall where my wife demonstrated that her Ice Factor success in Kinlochleven (see p. 141) was no fluke, shimmying to the top in a few seconds.

The restaurant, where she bragged ceaselessly, has a children's menu, a tots' area and a warm-up station for baby's bottles where I spent several minutes pretending to microwave baby formula just to get away from my wife's crowing.

Open *Apr–mid-July 10am–6pm, mid-July–mid-August 10am–7pm, Sep–Oct 10am–5pm, Nov–Mar 10am–5pm.* ***Adm*** *31st Mar–28th October £9.75, children (5–14) £7.60, under-5s free. 29th Oct–20th Mar £3.20, children £2.35.* ***Amenities*** *restaurant.*

Rothiemurchus Centre ★★

ALL AGES

Aviemore, Inverness-shire, ☎ 01479 812345, ***www.rothiemurchus.net****. On the B970.*

Everywhere you turn on this 10,100-hectare estate there are people ski-walking, mountain biking or launching themselves into Loch Morlich. The Centre forms part of the **Cairngorm National Park**, and the host of family-friendly activities also includes ranger-led walks, canoeing and pony trekking as well as offbeat pastimes such as dog-sledding. For older children there's quad-biking, clay pigeon shooting (over-12s) and skiing. The dog sledding (over-6s) lasts 2½ hours, costs £50 (children £35) and includes children giving them food and water as well as a trip around the museum dedicated to famous dog-musher Scotty Allan. Afterwards there's an exhilarating 30-minute sled ride through the forest with wonderful views, if you can bear to look as you hang on. Tours run October–April as long as the temperature is a minimum of 12°C (bring warm and waterproof clothes). You can also visit the museum and dogs outside these times (£8, children £4) but beware, children might, like our daughter, become so attached to Aladdin, a 12-year-old Siberian husky, they start to demand their own huge, semi-wild blue-eyed dog when they're back in the car.

Mountain biking is another option (a half-day's cycle hire £15, children £6, maps

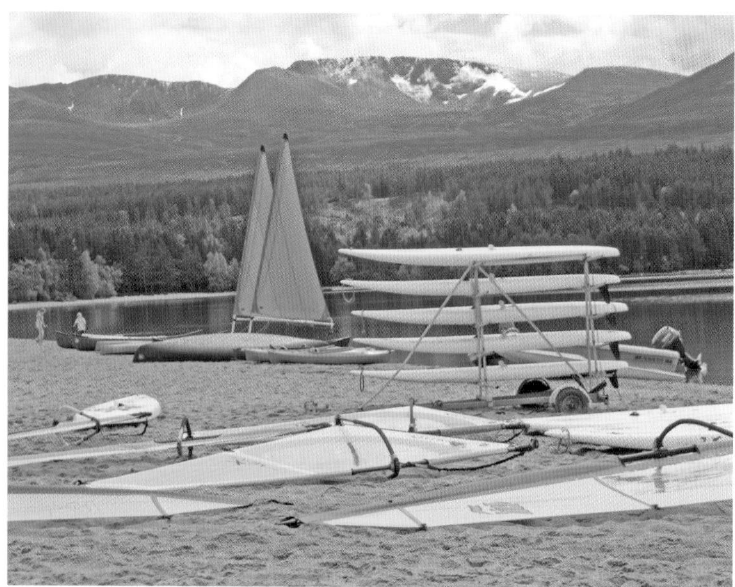

Watersports on Lake Morlich

included). Tagalongs are available as well as covered buggies, tandems and, we're not making this up, penny farthings (ask at **Bothy Bikes** ☎ *01479 810111*). There's also pony trekking (20 minutes £10, minimum age 4), canoeing on the River Spey (2½ hours £40, under-18s £30, minimum age 6), Land Rover safaris (£15 a head) and ranger-guided walks (1½ hours. £10, children £5).

***Open** daily 9.30am–5pm all year.*

The Cairngorm Reindeer Centre ★ ALL AGES

Glenmore, Aviemore, Inverness-shire, ☎ 01479 861228, www.reindeer-company-demon.co.uk.

Our daughter hand-fed a reindeer here from the only free-ranging herd in Britain, and then fell so in love with one called Ferrari (named after the speed he approaches his dinner) she made him a birthday card out of an old Wotsit packet. The reindeer were brought to Scotland in 1952; most graze on pasture in the lower reaches of the Cairngorms while the rest remain at the paddock, which has a Santa's bothy where children cuddle a soft-toy Rudolph and post their Christmas wish-lists while learning about the effect of climate change on reindeer (as it gets warmer, some of their noses go less red at Christmas).

Tours to see reindeer leave at 11am and 2.30pm daily (May–September) with an extra 3.30pm visit July–August. It's an easy 20-minute walk (leave buggies behind and hire a baby carrier, £1) to the pasture, where very docile reindeer (except when a mobile rings – they go crazy then) are petted and fed pellets by hand.

***Open** daily (except January–early February) 10am–5pm. **Adm** (paddock and tour) £8, children (6–16) £4, under-6s free. Paddock only £2.50, children £1.50.*

SKYE & TOBERMORY

Skye is the largest and most northerly island in the Inner Hebrides, and has some of the most breathtaking scenery in Scotland. It's so remote that in the 18th century Bonnie Prince Charlie fled here disguised as a maid after defeat at Culloden (p. 153). Named after the old Norse word for cloud, the butterfly-shaped island has plummeting cliffs, dramatic headlands, white coral beaches, black sandy shores and nowadays many, many gift shops selling Argyll socks. Skye's biggest draw isn't the socks (the socks are rubbish, I bought a pair and they fell apart) but the beautiful Cuillin mountain ridge, whose peaks are among the most striking in Britain. If you aren't an experienced walker, however, and Cuillin does demand it, a better way to escape the summer crowds (and sock purchase temptations) is a visit to Glendale and the cliffs of Nest Point, taking in the toy museum en route. If you have time the island's capital, Portree, has colourful houses and a traditional harbour, but some of the most changeable weather in Scotland. One word of serious warning: please don't be put off if someone suddenly addresses you in a shop near the Point of Sleat in an unintelligible language: it's not that they don't want you to buy their socks (they do), it's just Gaelic, in which a third of the population here are fluent.

The next most visited island in Scotland is probably **Mull**, in particular its capital **Tobermory**, the real-life multicoloured harbour town of the children's TV series *Balamory*. It also has another children's TV character named after it, a Womble. Tobermory is worth a visit, in our opinion, for these reasons alone, although it also has a picturesque little fishing port and in recent years has been attracting visitors for its passing Minke whales, porpoises and dolphins, as well as for some impressive eagles.

Essentials

By Bus There are regular services from Inverness to Portree that take four hours and cost £31.60 return. Glasgow is six hours: the service runs four times a day and costs £53.30 return. From Edinburgh add an hour to the journey time and £10 to the return ticket.

By Boat Tobermory is best accessed by the **CalMac** (*☎ 01475 637607*, ***www.calmac.co.uk***) car ferry from Oban (a speedy 40 minutes); they run around seven times a day. You'll come into Craignure. Tobermory is 38km north-west, the road being mostly single track. The main crossing point by ferry to Skye is from Mallaig to Armadale. The CalMac ferry costs £18.75 per car for one journey; for a five-day return, £32.50. The crossing takes 30 minutes and services operate almost hourly.

By Car To get to Skye approach via the A87, which spurs off from either the A82 or the A887. Fort William is the nearest large town; from there it's about 80km (about 1½ hours). From Aviemore add 1½ hours, and from Inverness it takes about 3½ hours. On the island itself the same main road is the same A87. To get to the ferry departure point for the Isle of Mull take the A85 to Oban, which is itself a fair hoof away from any major city. From Glasgow the M8 is best to the A82, then the A83 and finally the A816 north. Journey time is about three hours. From Inverness (2½ hours) the A82 south gets you most of the way there, until you pick up the A828.

Visitor Information

There are seasonal tourist information centres at Bettyhill and Broadford on Skye, while the **Portree Tourist Information Centre** (*01478 612137*) is open all year. The **Craignure Tourist Information Centre** (*09707 200609*) on the Isle of Mull is open all year, but the **Tobermory Tourist information Centre** (*0707 200625*) on Main Street is only open April–October and occasionally at other times; ring ahead.

What to See & Do

Armadale Castle Gardens and Museum of the Isles

ALL AGES

*Armadale, Sleat, Isle of Skye, 01471 844305/227, **www.clandonald.com**.*

When the clouds blot out the sun and there's a late afternoon chill, there's no moodier place than the gardens of these castle ruins to gaze out across the Sound of Sleat. That is, until your baby son wakes up and vomits undigested breast milk over his last clean 'I love my mummy' jumper. It really is *very* pretty here, while inside the Clan Macdonald Visitor Centre a multimedia exhibit recounts the story of the lords that ruled the Isles. It also has a 5.5m larch skiff our daughter thought was a bath-tub.

***Open** daily 2nd Apr–26th Oct 9.30am–5.30pm. **Adm** £5, children £3.80, family ticket (two adults and up to four children) £14.*

Glendale Toy Museum

ALL AGES

*Holmisdale House, Glendale, Isle of Skye, 01470 511240, **www.toy-museum.co.uk**.*

Thanks to the house rule ('anything children can reach they can play with/break') and owner Terry's idiosyncratic commentary ('This is our ugliest doll. My wife calls this one the dead one'), this is a really fun stop for adults too. He runs it from his house with his wife, Paddy. Terry's scatter-gun remarks also included: 'And this is our Fergie range of dolls. I think they had a

Princess Margaret one with gin and cigarettes.' Plus, 'Action Men [pointing to an empty box]...they've gone to Iraq.' Our daughter meanwhile loved the quintuplet dolls modelled on the first ever surviving quins of 1935. An Aladdin's cave of treasures.

***Open** Mon–Sat 10am–6pm. **Adm** £3, children (4 and over) £1, under-4s free.*

Skye Serpentarium Reptile World ★ ALL AGES

*The Old Mill, Harrapool, Broadfood, Isle of Skye, 01471 822209/ 822533, **www.skyeserpentarium.org.uk**.*

This is where my tortoise-phobic wife shamed herself, hyperventilating into her asthma inhaler after unexpectedly seeing a pancake tortoise. 'Take me back to the monitor lizards NOW. You said they were hibernating.' But don't be misled, this is a fabulous place for anyone not insane enough to fear one of the world's slowest-moving land creatures. The centre has frogs, lizards and snakes, many of which – including the royal pythons – visitors can touch. Run by husband-and-wife team Alex and Catherine Shearer, little ones feel instantly welcome with talks tailored to their age group, animals in low-level enclosures and bright lighting (not the darkness of most reptile houses) to dispel trepidation. The Watermill coffee shop sells home-made soups, cakes (£2) and ice-cream and, at the gift shop, if you intend to scare your wife in the dead of night (I did), there's lots of tortoise memorabilia.

***Open** Mon–Sat 10am–5pm mid-Mar–27th Oct, 10am–5pm Sun July–Aug. **Adm** £3, children over-2 £2, under-2s free, family ticket (two adults and up to four children) £9. **Amenities** café, shop.*

Tobermory (Balamory) ★ AGES UNDER 7

Parents of toddlers need no introduction to Main Street in

Glendale Toy Museum

Tobermory on the Isle of Mull, famously the setting of children's TV favourite *Balamory*. Although filming stopped years ago, millions of children will recognise the harbour's different coloured houses. Day-long children's tours take in the homes of Miss Hoolie, Spencer, Josie Jump and PC Plum, as well as Edie McCredie's garage plus the Pocket and Sweet's shop. Tours also include Angus Stewart's art studio to see photos of the filming, a lunch stop in town (1½ hours), a visit to a farm where children can bottle-feed goats and rabbits and finally the *Balamory Express* (Mull Rail), the miniature train that makes regular appearances on the programme. Outings start with a pick up at Craignure pier at 10.45am where Mull Rail terminates at 4.45pm, in time for the 5pm ferry return to Oban. The tours, in an eight-seater minibus, can be cut short to return at 3pm.

Tours are arranged by **About Mull Tours** (*07887 774550, www.mullion.taxi.com*), although don't expect the local tourist board to mention them (they denied to us that they existed), since they're re-branding the island as a wildlife haven. What's the Story in Balamory? Well, they've also stopped producing a map of where to find the characters' homes because they're sick of ferry-loads of children charging around shouting about Miss Hoolie's stripey jumper when they've got golden eagles nearby.

Open *all year.* ***Adm*** *£80 for a family, or £25 per head (£15 per child).*

FAMILY-FRIENDLY ACCOMMODATION

MODERATE

Best Western Palace Hotel and Spa ★

8 Ness Walk, Inverness, 01463 223243, www.bw-invernesspalace.co.uk.

If you don't mind clambering over the suitcases that mount up in reception every morning when a coach party arrives, this hotel has a great swimming pool that our daughter had virtually to herself. Walkable from town, there's also a steam room, spa bath and Starbucks in the lobby. Children receive activity packs. Ask for family room 26 on the 2nd floor with high ceilings and wonderful views across the River Ness of Inverness Castle. A baby-listening service allows you to dine in the Sovereign restaurant, serving school-dinnerish meals tailored towards its easily-satisfied tour groups, but breakfast (£9.95, children 5–10 £4.95, under-5s free) is a spectacular buffet.

Rooms Rates *£99–129 (without breakfast).* ***Credit*** *AmEx, MC, BV.* ***Amenities*** *parking, laundry, WiFi (laptops to borrow), Playstation, restaurant (£16.95 for three courses, with highchairs, children's menu), spa, pool.* ***In room*** *TV, cot, DVD players.*

INSIDER TIP

Leave double buggies in the car. The wonky lift with its old-fashioned iron-shutter is round a tricky corner and almost impossible to tackle without breaking into an uncomfortable, expletive-rich sweat.

Glen Nevis Lodges ★

*Glen Nevis, Fort William, ☎ 01397 702191, **www.glen-nevis.co.uk.***

Here in the foothills of Ben Nevis you can expect mountain tranquillity without isolation, highland cattle in nearby fields for the children to stare at/tease, and a good family-friendly restaurant (5–11pm) you can walk to. Lodges have three bedrooms, a huge lounge and kitchen area (microwave, fridge-freezer, double-oven, washer/dryer, dishwasher, coffee-maker), a bathroom and separate shower room. There's a children's play area and a shop for basics with a nearby mini-mart stocking everything from wine to baby food. On sunny days we marvelled at the 360° views; on rainy ones we thanked our lucky stars we weren't camping.

***Rates** £530–795 per week. **Credit** AmEx, MC, V. **Open** all year except 3rd Nov–21st Dec and 6th Jan–9th Feb. **Amenities** kitchen, play area.*

Isles of Glencoe Hotel ★★

*Ballachulish, Scottish Highlands, ☎ 0871 222 3415, **www.islesofglencoe.com.***

With large windows overlooking Loch Leven, this hotel's family rooms have some of the finest views in the Highlands. There are pin-drop quiet walks nearby and our daughter loved the indoor swimming pool with children's floats. Outside there's an adventure playground and family rooms come with a special children's alcove so there's no need to creep about after they're asleep. The restaurant has equally spectacular views, average food although the staff were great with our daughter, refusing to get flustered when she got through eight pats of butter making herself a slice of bread. A bonus for those with older children is the den (with TV

Glen Nevis Lodges

and DVDs to skulk off to after they've eaten). Even better is teatime hour at 6pm, when all the guests' children eat together (or not, if you are our daughter who wanted to eat/waste dairy products with us).

***Rates** standard double from £75–170. **Credit** all credit cards accepted. **Amenities** indoor swimming pool, gym, sauna, jacuzzi, restaurant and bar, kids' den. **In room** TV, cot, DVD players.*

Linnhe Lochside Holidays Caravan and Camping Park ★

*Corpach, Fort William, 01397 772376, **www.linnhe-lochside-holidays.co.uk**.*

This park on the banks on Loch Eil is stunning in May, with the rhododendrons in bloom. And you may even see seals and otters playing in the water if you don't freeze to death in your bed. It's a friendly place, with two children's playgrounds as well as an inside toddler room by the laundry block. Static caravans sleep up to six. There is a useful shop selling frozen food, fresh pastries and homemade bread and a Co-op and a Spar in nearby Corpach. Bed linen is for hire (£7.50 per person) as are towels (£1.50 each).

Most caravans have a shower, two bedrooms (one double, one twin), plus a fold-out double in the lounge where there's a dining table and a TV whose terrible reception made watching a Liverpool Champions' League football fixture resemble staring at some vibrating iron filings (the mountains affect the signal). That said, a handyman came out double quick to fix it. Also watch the fire. It's one where you have the gas on for ages before it suddenly snarls alight hoping to melt your match-hand.

Minimum stay is three days.

***Rates** Bronze (£45–60 per night), Silver type 1 (slighter bigger caravans) £50–75, Silver type 2 (three bedrooms, no foldaway bed in lounge) £53–80, Gold (newer caravans and loch views) £53–80, and Platinum (same as Gold but with double glazing) £55–84. **Credit** MC, V. **Amenities** extra blankets and electric heater available, kitchen with microwave, TV.*

INSIDER TIP

Go Platinum. It costs more but you get newer caravans with loch views plus double-glazing.

Lochanshelloch Cottage

*Cawdor Estate, Cawdor, Inverness-shire, 01667 402402, **www.cawdor.com**.*

This beautiful family cottage with three bedrooms and an open fire is the perfect base for the beach at Nairn. As well as two twins and a double room, the cottage has a well-equipped kitchen (including fridge-freezer, microwave, dishwasher and washing machine) plus a homely living room with a TV and CD and DVD players. The large garden has BBQ equipment, tables and chairs. There are games and children's books and a welcome hamper (eggs, fruit juice, bread, milk, tea and coffee, and a nice touch, we thought, wine). Ask for highchairs and cots.

MacDonald Aviemore Highland Resort

***Rates** (minimum three nights) £345–975, a week £575–1070. **Credit** AmEx, MC, V. **Amenities** TV/DVD, kitchen, garden.*

Macdonald Aviemore Highland Resort ★

*Aviemore, Inverness-shire, ☎ 0845 608 3734, **www.aviemorehighlandresort.com**.*

With four hotels and 18 lodges, this child-friendly resort in the centre of Aviemore has accommodation for every wallet. The 3-star Academy, ideal for families on a lower budget, has a team of *Hi-de-Hi*-style entertainers staging shows and overseeing children's activities across the resort, while its Spey Bar with table tennis and pool tables is an unofficial youth club. With our children too young to chat about TV shows such as *X-factor* and *Britain's Got Talent*, we went for a lodge with a brooding mountainous backdrop. It had three bedrooms to hide from the children in, two bathrooms and a play-park next door; the cosy living room had a wood burner. The small kitchen was stocked with jams, milk and butter and a bread-bin outside was refilled each morning with fresh pastries.

The resort's Highland Leisure Arena (daily 8am–8pm) has a swimming pool with slides and wave machine and the E Zone computer video games room. For adults there's a gym and spa area with spa bath and sauna. Dining-wise, our advice is to use the pizza take-away or eat outside the resort.

***Rates** three-bed Highland Lodge – three days £600–800; four days £750–1100; seven days £1100–1680. **Credit** AmEx, MC, V. No Diners Card or Solo. **Amenities** four restaurants,* *softplay area, outdoor swing park, leisure arena with indoor pool, flumes and wave machine, spa, golf course, shopping area.*

Polmaily House Hotel

*Drumnadrochit, Loch Ness, Inverness-shire, 01456 450343, **www.polmaily.co.uk**.*

This renowned country house hotel with loads of children activities, including a trampoline, bunny park and tennis courts, has, we think, been resting on its laurels a bit. Service levels were of the *Fawlty Towers* variety: we were snapped at for ringing ahead for directions and staff all seemed to have started 'the day before' so knew next to nothing. On the upside, some family rooms have garden views and children's beds are thoughtfully separated by a curtain.

We were also told we could leave our daughter in her room and eat downstairs, as a nanny would pop in regularly. However, we never saw any evidence of said nanny, who was never mentioned again. And The Monster Club toy room at the back of the hotel, supposedly supervised, wasn't. Our funniest moment was ringing down to get milk heated for our daughter and someone in the kitchen telling us they couldn't work the microwave.

Check they don't have a big wedding the next day. Our stay co-incided with one and resulting service was poor.

Rates *£55–72 per night B&B, children aged 12–16 45% of full rate, 6–12s, 35%, under-5s free.* ***Credit*** *MC, V.* ***Amenities*** *restaurant, children's club.*

Spean Bridge Hotel

*Spean Bridge, by Fort William, Inverness-shire, 0800 619 9462, **www.speanbridgehotel.co.uk**.*

Uniquely, this place has its own commando museum in a room on the ground floor; it's full of bullets, combat knives, small arms training pamphlets, citations for Victoria crosses and ration books (did you know Rolo chocolates were standard military issue?). That may seem odd until you know the hotel is down the road from the Spean Bridge Commando Memorial, which commemorates special forces who have trained here since World War II. It also has a family room (with bath and shower) with a double and two twins on the 1st floor. Their restaurant has highchairs plus its own fish-and-chip takeaway.

The Commando Bar (camouflage curtains) has a coal fire. When we visited it was empty (or was it...maybe they were just too well hidden), apart from one large tattooed man I had a conversation with about the merits of the Challenger tank.

Rates *£70–92 per night (breakfast not included).* ***Credit*** *MC, V.* ***Amenities*** *bar, restaurant (children's menu £3.99)* ***In room*** *Sat TV.*

INEXPENSIVE

Sheena's Backpacking Lodge

*Harbour View, Mallaig, Inverness-shire, 01687 462764, **www.mallaigbackpackers.co.uk**.*

This small hostel with views of Mallaig harbour is ideal for parents who run their families like a boot camp. Efficient service from boss Sheena is combined with a family room with three no-nonsense bunk-beds behind to stand rigid in a vest and shout, 'Yes, Sergeant major Sir', after your wife suggests it's your turn to unpack the children's clothes.

Their Tea Garden café serves evening meals 6–9pm. Try the hot chocolate served with whipped cream and chocolate flakes (£2.40).

Rates *£13 per bed per night.* ***Credit*** *MC, V.* ***Amenities*** *TV lounge, café (children's menu and highchairs), shared kitchen, laundry.*

FAMILY-FRIENDLY DINING

The Glennfinnan Dining Car

Station Museum, Glenfinnan, 01397 722295.

This restaurant based at Glenfinnan Station trades off both the Harry Potter associations of the nearby Glenfinnan Viaduct and its steam train heritage. That explains the broomstick parking signs and engine shunting sounds piped inside the dinning car. Serving mainly light snacks (such as toasties), and speciality ice-creams, there's a children's menu, highchairs and waiter service with views over Loch Shiel. Buggy access is what you'd expect on an old train.

Open *daily Jun–Sep 9am–5pm and 6.30–9.30pm. Outside these dates ring ahead.* ***Menu*** *toasties £2.50.* ***Credit*** *AmEx, MC, V.* ***Amenities*** *parking, children's menu, highchairs.*

The Grog and Gruel Pub ★

66 High Street, Fort William, Inverness-shire, 01397 705078, ***www.grogandgruel.co.uk****.*

A real ale pub without a bearded walker in sight. Children are given Horace the Hog menus that double as masks: our daughter wore hers, embarrassingly, a few days later in the commando remembrance garden at Spean Bridge. They eat from a pasta and chicken nugget-style menu, while adult food is of the quality burger kind. Try the raspberry cranachan then consume several speciality ales before handing the car keys to your wife with a yeasty belch to announce, 'Your turn tonight – I feel a bit wobbly.'

Open *noon–10pm.* ***Main courses*** ***Credit*** *MC, V.* ***Amenities*** *children's menu, highchairs.*

Loch Ness Clansman Hotel ★

Brackla, Loch Ness-side, Inverness-shire, 01456 450326, ***www.lochnessview.com****.*

We had an enjoyable family lunch in the observation lounge bar tucking into steak burgers and beer-battered haddock, unable to take our eyes from the Nessie hunters pretending to listen to wives or husbands but really watching for a glimpse of the monster. The hotel has great views over Loch Ness and some observers spend all day here spinning out salads at their ringside seats.

The more formal Cobbs restaurant serves adult lunches (£7–12, dinner more) and has a mirrored wall allowing loch-views from every table. The hotel is also handy for a loch cruise: the Jacobite Cruise departs from the other side of the road.

Open *6.30–9pm and 12–3pm.* ***Main courses*** *lunch (£7–12, dinner more* ***Credit*** *AmEx, MC, V.* ***Amenities*** *children's menu (£4.25), highchairs.*

Cromarty Arms

Church St, Cromarty, 01381 600230.

This pub is handy for the Cromarty Courthouse Museum and Hugh Miller cottage. It doubles as the village newsagent (papers are laid out on the pool table) and has a local atmosphere pitched somewhere between Royston Vasey and Postman Pat's delivery round. The children's menu features great chicken teddies with beans and chips, and there's a scrappy garden, freshly caught local lobster (£12.95) and villagers who are friendly in a guarded way that occasionally involves staring. Bar staff were great, if evasive about what exactly happened to the local newsagent.

Open *Mon–Sat 11am–10pm, Sun 12.30–10pm.* ***Main courses Credit*** *MC, V.* ***Amenities*** *children's menu (£3.95), highchairs.*

The Braeval Hotel ★

Crescent Road, Nairn, Inverness-shire, 01667 452341, ***www.braevalhotel.co.uk****.*

With great views to the Moray Firth over Nairn's Central Beach, you might just spot frolicking dolphins from this family-friendly conservatory restaurant, All we saw, however, were a few overs on Nairn's cricket ground that even my wife ('Cricket, is that the one like rounders?') enjoyed (although I had bought her a sticky toffee pudding beforehand).

The relaxed restaurant serves bar meals and seafood options like langoustine and catch of the day. There is a good children's menu and colouring books and crayons if your daughter begins to say over and over again, 'You're a Boo-boo. I said you're a boo-boo. No, you're a boo boo. Daddy, I said you're a boo boo.'

Open *May–Sep noon–9pm, Oct–Apr 6–8.30pm.* ***Menu*** *two course lunch £10, dinner £15.* ***Credit*** *MC, V.* ***Amenities*** *children's menu (£2.99), highchairs.*

Girvans ★

2–4 Stephen's Brae, Inverness, 01463 711900, ***www.girvansrestaurant.co.uk****.*

One of the busiest restaurants in Inverness, Girvans has modern art on the walls, a relaxed atmosphere, children's menus and staff who made our daughter laugh by pulling faces (not sure if deliberately) when she wouldn't eat her picky lunch (£3.80 for fresh fruit, cheese, pitta bread and crisps). Because it's right next to the East Gate Centre, there's a lunchtime rush 12.30–1.30pm, when you'll queue to sit down. The menu features light bites such as baguettes, toasties, salads, pastas and burgers, with more elaborate evening meals.

Open Mon–Sat 9am–9pm (Sun 10am–9pm), dinner served 6.30–9.30pm. ***Main courses*** from £7. ***Credit*** AmEx, MC, V. ***Amenities*** baby-changing, highchairs.

La Taverna Ristorante Pizzeria and Café Bar

Grampian Road, Aviemore, 01479 810683, ***www.highrange.co.uk****.*

This family-friendly Italian has an excellent all-you-can-eat all-day buffet served in an Alpine Lodge-style setting (big fireplace, wooden tables) with mountain views. Lunch (12–4pm) is good value with children aged 4–10 eating at the buffet (pizza, pasta, etc.) for £4.95, under-3s free. At dinner more food options are added. Staff are friendly, used to children and have all the kit you'll need.

Open *daily noon–9.30pm.* ***Buffet*** *£7.95 lunch, £11.95 dinner.* ***Credit*** *AmEx, MC, V.* ***Amenities*** *baby-changing, highchairs, children's menu £4.95.*

INSIDER TIP ›

Ask for a bottom section seat (tables 1–12) for probably the best Cairngorms views in Aviemore.

The Bistro at Bosville Hotel

Bosville Terrace, Portree, Isle of Skye, 0871 961 0752, ***www.bosvillehotel.co.uk****.*

Our daughter enjoyed yet another large bowl of mussels here (a starter from the adult menu, £5.25) at a table overlooking the boats in the harbour, where earlier that afternoon she had dropped/thrown and lost her favourite dolly during a tantrum. The nautically-themed restaurant has a children's menu (fish and chips £2.50) and great desserts. Try the iced Belgian dark chocolate parfait.

Open *daily 5–9pm.* ***Main courses Credit*** *AmEx, MC, V.* ***Amenities*** *children's menu £2.50.*

Castle Restaurant

41 Castle St, Inverness, 01463 230925.

This busy café has views of the castle, and is generally full of workmen coming in for take-aways, old ladies sipping soup and families flinging chips around. Their children's menu offers egg and chips (£2.85), burger and chips and sausage and chips – actually almost anything with chips – as well as options such as spaghetti bolognaise (£2.75). Adults meals range in complexity and price from sausage and chips to steak and (you guessed it) chips. Expect large portions, noise and old ladies upsetting your wife by commenting on your baby son: 'he's a bit of a bruiser. He looks like his mum'.

Between 2pm and 5.30pm it's quieter. The old ladies are home watching *The Weakest Link*.

Open *Mon–Sat 9am–8.30pm.* ***Main courses*** *£4.50–10.95.* ***Amenities*** *children's menu.*

7 Aberdeenshire & the North East Coast

ABERDEENSHIRE

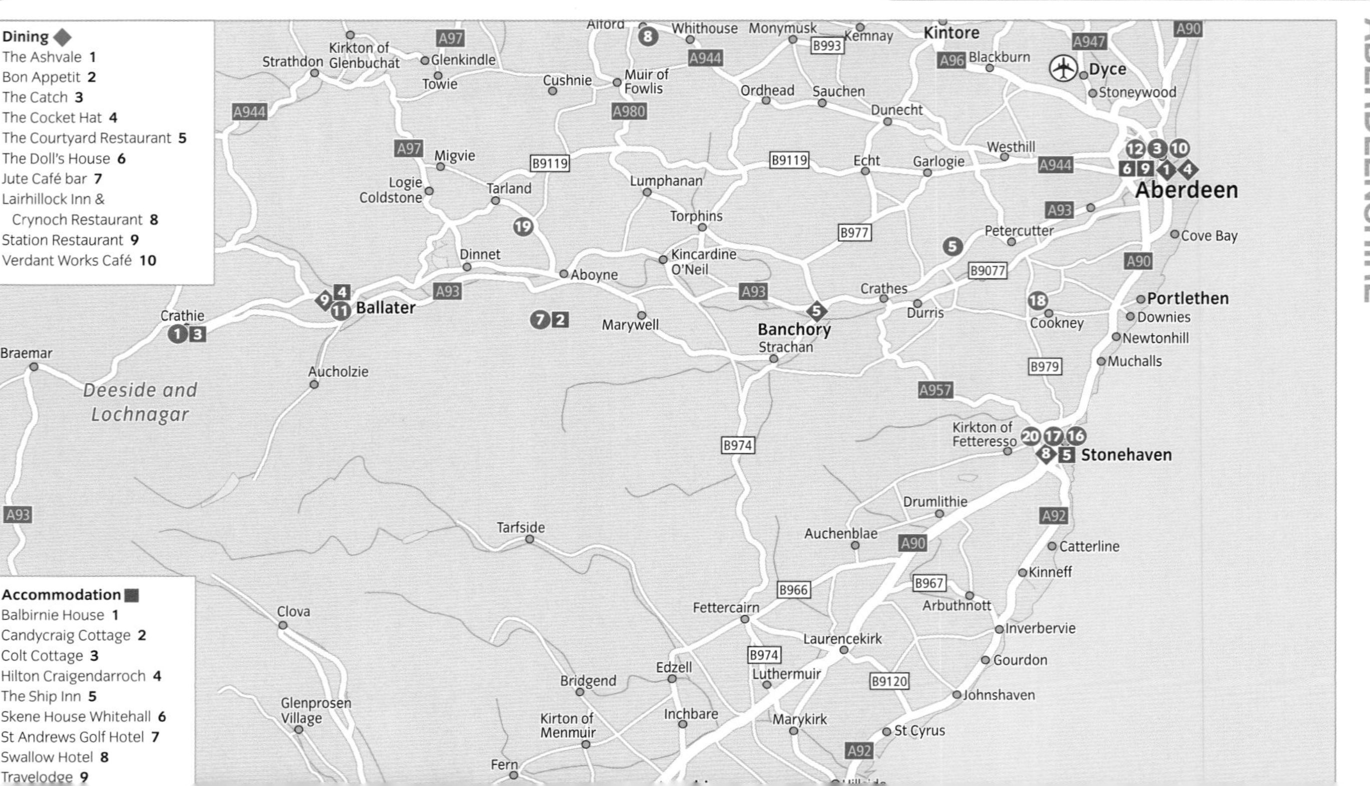

NORTH SEA
Attractions
Balmoral Castle 1
British Golf Museum 2
Codonas Amusement Park 3
Discovery Point 4
Drum Castle 5
Glamis Castle 6
Glen Tanar Estate 7
Grampian Transport Museum 8
J M Barrie's Birthplace 9
Maritime Museum 10
The Old Royal Station 11
Satrosphere 12
Scotland's Secret Bunker 13
Sensation 14
St Andrews Cathedral 15
Stonehaven Harbour 16
Stonehaven Open-Air Swimming Pool 17
Storybook Glen 18
Tomnaverie Stone Circle 19
The Tolbooth Museum 20
0 5 mi
0 5 km
Kingoldrum
Kirriemuir
Oathlaw
Lunanhead
Farnell
Ferryden
Forfar
Guthrie
Friockheim
Letham
Lunan Bay
Inverkeilor
Marywell
St Vigeans
Arbroath
Bridgend of Lintrathen
Bridge of Cally
Kirton of Airlie
Graigton of Airlie
Alyth
Glamis
Rattray
Blairgowrie
Kinloch
Meigle
Eassie
Inverarity
Carmyllie
Arbirlot
Coupar Angus
Newtyle
Tealing
Monikie
Craigton
Muirdrum
East Haven
Guildtown
Burrelton
Lundie
Muirhead
Newbigging
Barry
Carnoustie
Collace
Liff
Monifieth
Abernyte
Dundee
Broughty-Ferry
Balbeggie
Invergowrie
Tayport
Inchture
Newport-on-Tay
Rait
Wormit
Firth of Tay
Balmerino
Perth
Kinfauns
Errol
Kilmany
Leuchars
St Andrews Bay
Glencarse
Luthrie
Dairsie or Osnaburgh
St Andrews
Bridge of Earn
Newburgh
Abernethy
Aberargie
Monimail
Cupar
Strathkinness
Boarhills
Pitscottie
Springfield
Auchtermuchty
Kingsbarns
Dunino
Glenfarg
Ceres
Peat Inn
Strathmiglo
Ladybank
Gateside
Largoward
Craigrothie
Carnbee
Falkland
Crail
Milnathort
Kirkton of Largo or Upper Largo
Kilrenny
Kinross
Kinneswood
Lower Largo
Anstruther
Leslie
Markinch
Kennoway
Kilconquhar
Pittenweem
Loch Leven
Leven
St Monans
A93
B951
B957
A933
A926
A932
A92
B9128
A94
B961
A923
A928
A933
B978
A984
A923
B954
A90
A93
A92
B953
A94
A90
A92
A91
M90
A913
A915
A917
A912
A916
A91
B940
A92
A917
A911

This area used to be called Grampian until someone realised it sounded a bit too much like the mass plural for 100,000 Scottish people feeling grumpy about the five-day weather forecast. Now it is known either rather snappily (by us) as 'Aberdeenshire and the North East Coast', or more colloquially in other guidebooks as 'the Shoulder of Scotland' (though please don't ask for directions to the 'shoulder of Scotland': you will be laughed and pointed at). The area is characterised by forest and fertile land veined with rivers backed by majestic mountains. Around its edges the coastline is a succession of long (and freezing) sandy beaches with quaint fishing villages rich in pirate lore and genuine sausage-fingered fishermen, some of whom probably do point tobacco pipes out to sea beyond the quay and say, 'saw a whale out by Alderman's Point this mornin'. Forty feet she was and black as a gypsy's curse.' The countryside boasts the greatest preponderance of baronial castles in Scotland and a host of distilleries. Royal obsessives like my wife (she drinks a toast to her Majesty from her 1977 Silver Jubilee mug on the Queen's Birthday) will even get to nose around the Queen's summer residence, Balmoral, and the birthplace of Princess Margaret, Glamis Castle.

The region also contains three of Scotland's major cities. Dundee is the city of jam, journalism and something we suspect might be quite boring called jute. (Take our advice just nod when it's mentioned and walk out backwards from the room smiling). Dundee is also home to some of Britain's favourite comic-book creations as well as Captain Scott's Antarctic research ship, the *Discovery*, and lots of other sciencey things involving some very hard words, two of which are pharmacogenomics and proteomics. And while it wouldn't win any awards for raw beauty, its centre is easily walkable, and with the only statue in Scotland dedicated to Desperate Dan, certainly worth an outing.

Aberdeen is Dundee's more prosperous neighbour. It is the engine room of the region and a city famous for being made almost entirely of granite. Everything is made of granite. Roads, buildings, bridges – even their food, which depending on your point of view, sparkles on a sunny day like precious jewels or makes the whole place look grey, a touch boring or a bit like watching a bad film on a black and white television.

St Andrews, meanwhile, nestled in a sweeping bay north of the Firth of Forth, is a small posh enclave unlike anywhere else in Scotland. Prepare your eyes to be besieged with the rainbow colours of Pringle jumpers. Your ears will be assaulted by the deafening clank of golf club bags being hoofed hither and thither on the way to the city's famous courses. And in St Andrews there is the added bonus for the visitor – it's almost always Pimm's o'clock. The ancient university attracts well-heeled students from all over the world. Although it's home to golf's governing body, the Royal and Ancient, the city has a studied dignity broken only by the occasional bread-roll fight in fresher's week. My forelock tugging 'yes M'am' wife, however, just liked it because Prince William studied here (he apparently liked the fishcakes at the Doll's House restaurant).

CHILDREN'S TOP 10 ATTRACTIONS

❶ **Spot** one of the rarest UK birds, the capercaille, and learn about nature in the back of a bouncy jeep on the Glen Tanar estate. See p. 186.

❷ **Put** your hand inside a mini-tornado at the Satrosphere science centre in Aberdeen. See p. 182.

❸ **Climb** aboard Captain Scott's *Discovery* at Dundee Harbour. See p. 194.

❹ **Tremble** in the presence of the Grey Lady at Princess Margaret's childhood home, Glamis Castle. See p. 195.

❺ **Find** out what you'll look like in 20 years time, at the Sensation science centre in Dundee. See p. 194.

❻ **Try** to consume an £8.15 Ashvale Whale (an enormous ½ kg cod fillet and chips) at Aberdeen's most famous fish and chip shop. See p. 206.

❼ **Scare/thrill** your children by perching them a metre above the ground on a precarious penny farthing at the Grampian Transport Museum. See p. 187.

❽ **Lie** on a raised podium dressed as your favourite Peter Pan character and pretend you're flying to Neverland. See p. 196.

❾ **Stay** at Colt Cottage on the Balmoral Estate and hope the Queen, out riding, pops in for tea and cakes. See p. 203.

❿ **Sit** by a bay window and look out to sea across the beach where *Chariots of Fire* was filmed, at the St Andrews Golf Hotel. See p. 202.

ABERDEEN

Scotland's third city sprung to prominence in 1970 after oil was discovered in the North Sea. Overnight Aberdeen became a mini-Dallas. Home to wealthy oil companies, its airport was one of the busiest in the UK. House prices leapt, everyone started singing Country and Western songs and wearing 10-gallon hats (they didn't), and then in the 1980s the price of oil collapsed to $10 a barrel (from its height of $80) and Aberdonians came out of the shower like Bobby Ewing. It was all just a dream.

On a more even footing now, its city centre focuses on the grand, mile-long Union Street. The imposing harbour has a long sandy beach stretching between the mouths of the River Don and the River Dee, but forget the swimming costume: Aberdeen is further north than Moscow. Around Aberdeen, along the River Dee, you'll also find the Queen's summer residence at Balmoral and some spectacular scenery.

Essentials

By Air Aberdeen's **Dyce Airport** (***www.aberdeenairport.com***), 11km northwest of the city, is served by flights from all over the UK. Carriers include **British Airways** (☎ *0844 493 0787, www.baa.com*), **British Midland** (☎ *0870 607 0555, www.flybmi.com*), **EasyJet** (☎ *0871 244 2366, www.easyjet.com*) and **KLM** (☎ *0870 243 0541, www.klm.com*). Buses run to the city centre (single £1.30) and taxis are available from both the terminal forecourt (**Rainbow Airport Taxis**, ☎ *01224 725 500, www.rainbow87.com*) and from a booking office (**ComCab Taxis**, ☎ *01224 353 535*) at the Broomfield Terminal end of the forecourt.

By Train The main train station is on Guild Street in the city centre, with services operated by **First ScotRail** (☎ *0845 748 4950, www.nationalrail.co.uk*) and going hourly to Edinburgh (2½ hours, from £42 return), to Glasgow hourly (2½ hours, from £42 return), and to Leuchars near St Andrews (hourly, £28 return) with a journey-time of 1½ hours. To London it is almost 18 hours (from £117 return) and Inverness is just over two hours (from £25 return).

By Bus Long distance **National Express** coaches (☎ *0870 580 8080, www.nationalexpress.com*) from London (Victoria) arrive in Guild Street, at a terminal beside the train station. The journey takes a cool 12 hours 20 minutes direct (and three hours longer if indirect). The two direct buses are at 9am and 10.50pm travelling overnight. Six buses travel indirect between these times. The cost of the journey varies depending on the day of the week of travel (cheaper mid-week) and how much in advance the ticket is booked (seven days notice normally lops off £10). Basically you're looking at between £43.40 and £52.50.

Aberdeen Harbour

There are Scottish Citylink (📞 *0870 550 5050*, ***www.citylink.co.uk***) hourly connections to Dundee costing £20.30 for a standard return though much less on saver returns between Monday to Thursday (as low as £6). They also have hourly services to Edinburgh and Glasgow (both journey-times: 3 hours and 10 minutes) and each costing £36.90 for a standard return.

By Car You can travel from Edinburgh and Glasgow to Aberdeen on the A90/M90 while the A92 coastal route is more leisurely. Most scenic – and worth the extra time – is the A93 from Perth, north to Blairgowwrie and into Glen Shee, then over the Cairnwell Pass, the highest main road in the UK. Snow can make it difficult in winter but in summer it's an amazing trip, with its lonely farmhouses in the middle of nowhere, disused bothies and dry-stone walls that seem to go on forever. Expect to see paranoid makeshift signs put out by farmers warning of sheep crossing. At one point we passed a sequence of signs that grew in insistence over a few miles from a simple 'caution sheep crossing' to the more emotive 'caution lambs crossing', becoming 'caution *young* lambs crossing', until they finally pleaded 'please, sheep do not know the green cross code'. The detour is over 160km and will take double the time it normally takes on major road. You're looking at four hours or so.

Visitor Information

Aberdeen's tourist office (📞 *01224 288828*, ***www.visitscotland.com***) is at 23 Union Street and open July–August, Monday–Saturday 9am–6.30pm and Sunday 10am–4pm. April–June and September–October hours are Monday–Saturday 9am–5.30pm, and the rest of the year Monday–Saturday 9am–4.30pm. Ask for a copy of *Go Wild With Your Child In And Around Aberdeen* produced by Scottish Natural Heritage (📞 *01738 444180*, ***www.snh.org.uk***). The booklet gives info on some little-known activities in the area.

What to See & Do

Codonas Amusement Park

ALL AGES

Beach Boulevard, Aberdeen,
📞 *01224 595910*, ***www.codonas.com****.*

If you're after a bit of traditional British seaside entertainment and you don't mind the wind off the Atlantic giving you a headache as you bite into frozen-solid Mister Whippy ice-cream, Codonas Amusement Park is an option. There are rides galore – ghost train, big wheel, haunted house, log flume, rollercoasters, and of course (our favourite) the catchily named Shockwave chair-o-planes. There's a stage here for live music and entertainment acts (peak season only) while Sunset Boulevard is geared towards younger children with a Treasure Island Kiddie Area (remote-controlled pirate ships, etc.) and Rambo's Kids Adventureland (slides, ropes). There's plenty to fill an afternoon but pick a day when the Aberdeen haar (mist) doesn't roll in off the sea – you can feel cheated on the Grampian Eye big wheel when you can't see further than the safety bar. Also beware of the toddlers' safari train. Our daughter rode it approximately 578 times only agreeing to dismount when we promised a doughnut during Cheeko The Clown's free show.

Also part of Codonas is the Miami Beach complex offering the Ocean Diner (ribs, steaks, barbecue chicken and ice-cream) plus coffee shop, juice bar and pool areas as well as a choice of simulator games.

Open *Apr–Sep Sat and Sun 11am–6pm (as well on school holidays) and Oct 12–5pm, closed Nov–Mar.* ***Adm*** *£10.99 (including a meal at Miami beach.)* ***Amenities*** *restaurant.*

Maritime Museum ALL AGES

Shiprow, Aberdeen, 01224 337700, ***www.aagm.co.uk****.*

Someone somewhere got fed up with trying to explain what daddy did when he went off to the rigs for months in a boiler suit and the result is the Aberdeen Maritime Museum. The museum tells the story of the city's relationship with the sea, incorporating exhibits on shipbuilding, port history, whaling and the oil industry. Don't be surprised to see a giant whale's ear bone getting equal billing with a remote-controlled underwater robot used to fix inaccessible parts of ships. Although not magnificent for youngsters, our daughter did get a kick out of the ear bone, as well as the giant replica (the biggest in the world) of an oil platform in the lobby towering towards the roof and revealing, on the top floor, model men going about their business on the rig. The museum's other highlights include a replica of oil worker living quarters, the 'newt suit' for underwater diving and model ships (the cannon-festooned gunship was attracting war-minded young boys on our visit). There are plenty of buttons to press to reveal disappointingly dull (if you're only 2) information about Aberdeen harbour. There are also quizzes for children of different age ranges, with rewards on completion, or if you ask/demand a badge before the end because your daughter is fed up and wants to get to Codonas as she's heard there's a clown called Cheeko.

Open *Mon–Sat 10am–5pm, Sun noon–3pm).* ***Adm*** *free.* ***Amenities*** *café (children's lunch £3).*

Satrosphere ★ ALL AGES

179 Constitution St, Aberdeen, 01224 640340, ***www.satrosphere.net****.*

This science museum based at the city's old tramsheds gives children the chance to put their hand inside a mini-tornado and work out what a pot of paint would weigh on Jupiter. It also gave my wife and I a renewed opportunity (see p. 68) to argue over reaction times and thus who's been the best driver in Scotland (me). Fun for all children, though best for primary schoolers, the museum has 50 interactive exhibits including puzzles, a plasma ball, a harp with laser-light strings and a water vortex. The highlight is a mini-tornado created out of water vapour and a fan. That's 90cm tall and 5cm in diameter, and which I kept expecting to gather strength from the sweat on my forehead (from my go on the floor piano) and rise to the sky, thickening crazily into an unstoppable tempest and going on to flatten the city. There are handy stools for younger ones to reach higher-up displays.

Open *daily 10am–5pm.* ***Adm*** *£5.75, children £4.50, family ticket (two adults two children, or three adults one child) £17.* ***Amenities*** *baby-changing, café (with children's menu and highchairs), free parking.*

Storybook Glen ★ AGES UNDER 7

Maryculter, Off Deeside Rd, Aberdeen, ☎ 01224 732941, ***www.storybookglenaberdeen.co.uk****.*

This children's theme park in 11 hectares of flower-bedecked gardens includes models of more than 100 nursery rhyme and fairytale characters, which our daughter was able to clamber all over and on occasions have interesting chats with ('Noddy, I got my holiday glove on'). Sold as a fairytale world for all ages it is mainly for pre-schoolers. We had a fun morning listening to our daughter recognising children's TV characters represented in flaking fibreglass, although it was irritating we weren't allowed to eat our picnic inside the Glen. Refusing to cough up at the (we must admit) quite reasonably priced self-service restaurant (children's portions half price), we dug in and consumed our sandwiches on the grassy area outside the entrance taking bitter swipes at the representation of Postman Pat: 'His nose was never that big...his glasses have narrower

Storybook Glen, Maryculter

Balmoral Castle, Ballater

frames… the scale's all wrong', while thinking of characters they'd sloppily overlooked: 'No Piggly-wiggly. That's incompetence.'

***Open** Mar–Oct 10am–6pm (last entry 4pm), Nov–Feb 10am–4pm. **Adm** £5.75, children £4. **Amenities** restaurant.*

AROUND ABERDEEN

Escaping Aberdeen into castle country you'll learn about ghosts from Scotland's turbulent past, while in Royal Deeside you can explore the grounds of the Queen's summer residence and buy a royal approved newspaper in Ballater. Along the coast you'll find quiet sandy beaches and the picturesque fishing town of Stonehaven. Inland the Grampian highlands are home to ancient stone circles, great remote drives where you'll come across phone boxes in the middle of nowhere, ruined crofter's cottages over-run with sheep, drystone walls that stretch endlessly, and some of the country's greatest scenery.

Balmoral Castle ★ ALL AGES

*Balmoral Estate, Ballater, Aberdeenshire, ☎ 01339 742534, **www.balmoralcastle.com**.*

TIP Local Information

There are useful tourist offices at the Old Royal Station Ballater (☎ *01339 755306*) and 66 Allardice Street, Stonehaven (☎ *01569 762806*). Both are open April–June and September–October, Monday–Saturday, 10am–1pm and 2pm–5pm; July–August, Monday–Saturday, 10am–7pm and Sunday 1pm–5.30pm.

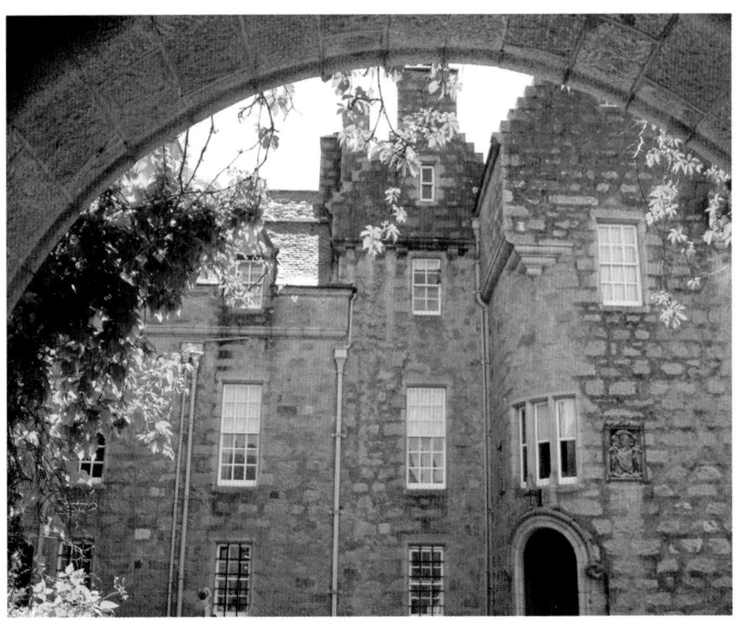

Drum Castle, near Banchory

A visit here starts with a tractor-pulled carriage ride through the estate entrance that our daughter loved almost as much as where we were deposited – the estate stables, full of ponies, two of which she named Nickleboo. This official summer residence of the Queen is a lived-in castle, so only one room (the Ballroom) is open to the public. It contains Edwin Landseer (1802–1873) paintings of Royal pets (no budgies for M'am), but the 20,200-hectare grounds are the main draw. During the guided tour (£1 extra) you'll learn about Queen Victoria's relationship with manservant John Brown, and also how she was so mean with her electricity that Liberal Prime Minister William Gladstone considered the castle purgatory it was that cold. There is a sunken rose garden designed to be in bloom when the Queen is in residence between August and October and a bronze statue of a wild boar our daughter rode while shouting 'Giddy-up, piggy'.

If you have time, a three-hour safari in a Land Rover Discovery (9am–noon or 2–5pm) with a ranger (£45 a head) takes in great views of Lochnagar mountain, red squirrels, falcons and maybe even a poisonous adder. Yes – there are adders here, although don't worry, they are more frightened of you than you are of them (unless you're me).

***Open** daily 29th Mar–31st July 10am–5pm. **Adm** £7 (with audio tour) or (£8 with a guide), children (5–16) £3), under-5s free, family ticket (two adults and up to four children) £15.*

***Amenities** baby-changing, café (with highchairs), children's entertainment.*

Drum Castle ALL AGES

*Drumoak, 01330 811204, **www.nts.org.uk**.16km west of Aberdeen off A93.*

The battlements of the 13th century keep were being used when we visited by pre-teen boys re-enacting a sword-fight from Robin Hood, while for older children grown out of belting each other with baguette sticks there are grisly tales. For instance, the dungeons – closed to protect hibernating bats – played witness to the torture and grisly murder of a priest who'd become over-familiar with the wife of the 7th laird, while the 17th laird himself spent two years hidden in a gap above a ceiling and beneath the floor of what's now the manager's bathroom after fleeing the Scots' defeat at Culloden in 1746 (see p. 153). You can see a portrait of him in more upright times in the dining room, and in the drawing room one of Mary Irvine, who hid him, sliding presumably very thin slices of venison between the floorboards to keep him alive. Elsewhere there is a lock of King Malcolm's hair (he's believed to be the inspiration for Shakespeare's *Macbeth*).

Owned for 500 years by the Clan Irvine until it passed to the National Trust for Scotland, the castle is full of 16th century furniture and so lived-in looking (no roped off areas) you half think you might be in a very posh Four Seasons. There are separate children's quizzes for under-5s, 5–8s and over-9s, and walks including a mile's woodland stroll through the Old Wood of Drum, where there are no poisonous snakes at all.

***Open** daily except Tues and Fri 31st Mar–30th Jun 12.30–5pm, 1st Jul–31st Aug daily 11am–5pm, 1st Sep–31st Oct daily 12.30pm–5pm (but closed Tue and Fri). **Adm** £8, children £5. **Amenities** café.*

Glen Tanar Estate ★★★

FIND ALL AGES

*Brooks House, Glen Tanar, Aboyne, Aberdeenshire, 01339 886451, **www.glentanar.co.uk**.*

If you've always been distrustful of nature because of the amount of walking its appreciation involves, then we suggest a Land Rover Safari, ideally in the best place in Scotland to take one. The Glen Tanar Estate is home to 10,100 hectares of what remains of Scotland's Caledonian pine forest, with stunning views of Mount Keane. On our 16km safari we saw every form of wildlife that ranger Mike Martin told us we had a chance of spotting, including a golden eagle, an osprey, grey and red squirrels,

FUN FACT Regal Camouflage

During the war the Royal train was repainted the same colours as ordinary trains so it was not such an obvious target for enemy bombers.

FUN FACT Ballater

While you're in Ballater check out all the 'by royal appointment' businesses supporting enormous royal crescents above their doorways. It can to be a great comfort to buy and make your lunch from a sandwich loaf made by the royal approved Ballater bakers. It was for my wife, anyway. You can also have a royal appointed windscreen washer replaced at the Ballater garage and read *Now!* magazine by Royal Appointment from the local paper shop.

crossbills, bull finches, rabbits, not to mention the biggest coup of all (spotted by me!) a capercaille. OK, so I didn't know it was a capercaille (one of only 20 on the estate and 1,000 left in the UK) when I said, 'Mike, what's that brown thing?' but who cares. After lunch (bring your own) we learnt how the estate was managed with biodiversity in mind as well as the glacial geology of Scotland, and became so enthused by Mike's passion for the outdoors I actually found myself asking a question about larch while my wife wanted to know the type of cover grouse preferred. When our daughter woke up, Mike managed to pass his enthusiasm on to her (and she normally walks in a huge arc around anything on the ground she cannot identify as either a stick or a crisp packet). By the end she was bending over a wood ants' nests, touching cuckoo spit and trying to pronounce the word braeberry with a dozen pine cones in her Dora The Explorer bag. Superb.

***Tour price** £45 per head, £22 (or so) for children depending on age, under-5s free. Bring your own car seat and book a couple of days in advance.*

Grampian Transport Museum

★ ALL AGES

Alford, Aberdeenshire, ☎ 01975 522292, ***www.gtm.org.uk****.*

At this hands-on museum in the middle of nowhere youngsters can climb into the driver's seat of a huge Mack snowplough, jump on the old Aberdeen Tram and perch on the saddle of a precarious penny farthing ('Too high. Get me off, Daddy.'). If you can, time your visit to coincide with one of the museum's special ride-on fun-days (usually in the school holidays). Children get to drive round the museum's old race circuit in Ferrari super-cars or old steam lorries. Elsewhere boys will love the Hornby model train sets, the collection of motorbikes and the Jaguar XKR used as a stunt car in the James Bond movie *Die Another Day*. When we were here there was a Dalek display upstairs (no lift) with an explanation of how the Tardis worked, and featuring some scary *Dr Who* music that startled our daughter almost as much as *God Save The Queen* suddenly playing at full kilter on the giant Mortier dancehall organ downstairs. Elsewhere there is a car shaped like a massive sauce bottle and a Sinclair

Grampion Transport Museum, Alford

C5 competing to be the most ridiculous forms of transport in the last 100 years.

***Open** daily 1st Apr–30th Sep10am–5pm, Oct 10–4pm. **Adm** £5.40, children £2.70, under-5s free), family ticket (two adults and up to three children under 16) £13.50. **Amenities** café, children's quizzes.*

Old Royal Station ALL AGES

*Station Square, Ballater 013397 55306, **www.visitscotland.com.***

Children can put on a Queen Victoria mask and stroke an unlifelike model of her pet collie, Sharp, at this old rail station where royalty disembarked for 100 years for their summer retreat at Balmoral Castle. The station platform has been recreated with waxworks of Queen Victoria and her daughter Louise alighting from the Royal Saloon, once one of 15 carriages on the enormous 600-foot Royal train. After disembarkation the Queen would be greeted by a Guard of Honour from the Black Watch as well as thousands of well-wishers in Station Square before being escorted by a cavalcade of

FUN FACT Haute Cuisine

Stonehaven's Haven Fish Bar was the likely origin of the deep-fried Mars bar, a snack now culturally associated with Scotland and its health record. The premises are now the award-winning Carron fish and chip shop on Allardice Street.

Scottish Greys along the beacon-lit Deeside road to Balmoral, every church bell for miles ringing (exactly how I'd love to start the Hatch family's annual two-weeks in Longleat Center Parcs). The tradition (getting on a train to come to Scotland) began to wane with George VI, who preferred driving, and was killed off by the Beeching cuts when the line closed. The museum didn't over-excite our toddler even when we tried to explain that Queens are the mothers of princesses (her favourite human form), although my wife was quietly pleased with a pair of gold-handled scissors encased in glass once used by a member of the Royal family to cut an unspecified ribbon opening an unknown object, instantly a contender in our competition to find the most boring thing behind glass in Scotland.

***Open** daily July–7th Sept 9am–6pm, and 10–5pm the rest of the time.*
***Adm** free.*

Stonehaven Harbour ALL AGES

One of the prettiest in North East Scotland, this was once a favourite port for marauding pirates and also where James 'the Old Pretender' landed during the First Jacobite Rising of 1715. The harbour's heyday came more prosaically in the 19th century when it grew into an important herring fishing port. Nowadays mainly leisure cruisers moor here, although we did find an old sea salt down by the lobster pots.

The best way here is via a 20-minute buggy-friendly board-walk stroll along the white sands of Stonehaven Bay connecting the harbour with the open-air pool. On the way you can try to spot bottle-nosed dolphins, porpoises and minke whales in the summer, although my own particular walk was spoiled by my wife's insistence that a 'dodgy-looking man' (he had a beanie hat on) loitering (simply standing) near our parked car planned to break in the moment we were

The Old Royal Station, Ballater

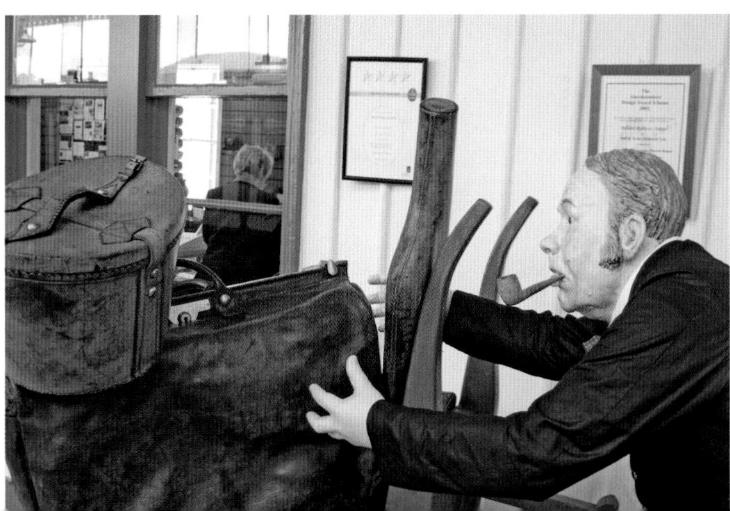

FUN FACT **Hmm, Fishy**

Herring fishermen used to string piano wire around their boats. When the wire hummed it meant a shoal of silver darlings was nearby.

out of sight to steal our portable DVD player, our iPod stereo syncher and, who knows, maybe our daughter's *Thomas The Tank Engine* jigsaw puzzle as well. Needless to say the car was fine. The bay is also a base for many seabirds although, unable to tell the difference between a razorbill and a seagull or indeed any other whitish bird and a seagull, we can't say what we saw, only that there were lots of them.

Stonehaven Open-Air Swimming Pool ALL AGES

*Queen Elizabeth Park, Beach Rd, Cowie, Stonehaven, ☎ 01569 762134, **www.stonehavenopenairpool.co.uk**.*

The only one of its kind in Britain, this saltwater, Art Deco *Hi-de-Hi*-style swimming pool perched on the seafront at Stonehaven is heated to an impressive 28°C (think of the bath just before you top it up with more hot water). The pool is packed with locals and tourists here for the slides and water chutes, and chance to shout 'Ted can't hear you', in hilarious northern accents until told to shut up by their wives from Lancashire who actually quite liked the holiday camp sit-com because they

Stonehaven Harbour

had an aunty Beryl who looked a bit like 'that thick maid Peggy'.

There are plenty of shady places for gingers to sit on sun-loungers and complain about their freckles merging, and if you have older children and are here on Wednesday nights in July and August, midnight under-the-stars swims are available (£4, children £3). Bing bong campers.

***Open** June 1–7.30pm (weekends 10am–1pm), July–mid-Aug 10am–7.30pm (weekends 11am–6pm), mid-Aug–9th September 1pm–7pm (weekends 10am–6pm). **Adm** £3.50, children £2, family ticket (two adults, two children) £9. **Amenities** café, free parking.*

The Tolbooth Museum ALL AGES

The Harbour, Stonehaven, Kincardineshire, 01771 622807.

The town's oldest building was originally a quayside shed used to store landed provisions when Earl Marischal renovated Dunnottar Castle in the 1600s. It was later used as a court and a prison, whose most famous detainees were three Episcopalian ministers John Troup, John Petrie and Alexander Greig who, outlawed by the Hanoverians, continued to preach to their congregations who waded through the sea and scrambled over rocks to hear their sermons issued through jail windows. There is a quiz for children, who will love the stocks. Also here is a cast replica of the world's oldest creature known to have lived on land. The fossil found in Cowie by an Aberdeen bus driver is a 1cm millipede around 428 million years old.

***Open** Apr–Oct Wed–Mon 1.30–4.30pm. **Adm** free.*

Tomnaverie Stone Circle

ALL AGES

6.5km northwest of Aboyne, off the B9094 Aboyne/Tarland road.

This ancient stone circle, around 4,500 years old, was overrun with teenagers when we visited, saying some quite alarming things about 'the 11-year solar flare cycle'. Up a relatively steep 250m path from the car park below, the circle's altar stone might have been used to sacrifice animals (or possibly humans), although nowadays brave the wind and the teenage Goths (we also heard one say 'neuro-resonant field systems') and you're treated to great views over Tarland, and Lochnagar 32km away. Our daughter had fun playing hide-and-seek among the stones characteristic of this part of Scotland before we sacrificed her to a fertility god for refusing to climb back into the buggy.

***Open** all year. **Adm** free. **Amenities** parking.*

DUNDEE

Scotland's fourth city, a whaling and textile hub on the banks of the River Tay, became famous in the 1800s for its three Js: jute, journalism and jam, which was invented after James Keiller bought a cargo of Seville oranges for his wife Janet, who, in a typically frugal way, discovering they were sour, invented marmalade so they wouldn't go to waste. It's also where Robert Bruce was declared King of the Scots in 1309. The city's radical past is reflected in its harbouring of religious reformer John Knox (see p. 36) and the fact that, instead of statutes honouring kings, generals and statesmen in its city centre, it simply has Desperate Dan and Mini the Minx (comic book publisher D.C. Thomson is based here). Dundee is small enough to walk around and notable for having the most hours of sunshine of any Scottish city, its purest air, the greenest spaces, and because singer K.T. Tunstall studied at the High School of Dundee. Though on the flipside, Ricky Ross from Deacon Blue did, too.

Essentials

By Air Dundee Airport (*01382 643242*, **www.dundeecity.gov.uk/airport**) off the A85 on Riverside Drive is 5km west of the city centre (10 minutes in a cab, £5). The main operator is Air France (*0870 144343*, **www.airfrance.co.uk**), with four flights a day to London (City Airport) during the week, one on Saturday and two on Sunday. The journey is roughly 80 minutes and costs from £142 return. Flybe (*0871 700 2000*, **www.flybe.com**) also have flights from Belfast (one a day except Saturday) taking 50 minutes, starting at £80, and also to Birmingham (three a day, one on Sunday) costing from £80 and taking an hour and 75 minutes, respectively.

The airport has free parking. Look out for the great views of the Tay estuary and its bridges during take-off and landing.

By Train If arriving by train you'll pitch up at Taybridge Station on South Union Street about 1km south of the centre. Services operated by First ScotRail (*0845 748 4950*, **www.nationalrail.co.uk**) run three times a day to Edinburgh (£22.20 return, 1 hour, 20 minutes). There are hourly connections to Glasgow (£30.40 return, 1½ hours) and twice-hourly services to Aberdeen (£24.20 return, 1¼ hours).

By Bus Long-distance buses arrive at the Seagate Bus Station, 200m east of the centre. **National Express** (*0870 580 8080*, **www.nationalexpress.com**) has eight daily services from London (Victoria). Of these only two are direct (at 10.30am and 10.30pm). Travelling outside these times adds a sapping three hours to a journey already standing at 11 hours. Ticket prices range from £40 to £51.50 for return depending on day of travel and how early the seat is reserved. **Scottish Citylink** (*0870 550 5050*, **www.citylink.co.uk**) has an hourly service to Glasgow costing £20.30 for a standard return and taking an hour and 40 minutes. There are half-hourly services to Edinburgh for £19.30 standard return (1¾ hours). Connections

Robert Falcon Scott

Scott returned to Antarctica after a previous research trip in 1910 wanting to be the first to the Pole, but was beaten by Norwegian Roald Amundsen after a series of setbacks involving dogs, the weather and his equipment. The bodies of Scott and his two colleagues were discovered eight months after the failed expedition, at Cape Evans still in their sleeping bags inside their tents. The bodies, undisturbed, were left entombed in a cairn of ice under the cross of two skis, where, under the Ross Ice Shelf, they remain to this day.

to Aberdeen are hourly costing £20.30 standard return (though as low as £6 if travelling between Monday and Thursday). The journey will take an hour and twenty minutes.

By Car The M90 from Edinburgh takes you within a few kilometres of Dundee. If you're arriving from Fife, take the A91 and the A914 crossing the spectacular Tay Bridge into Dundee, although the M90/A90 is faster. It's about an hour from Edinburgh.

Visitor information

Dundee's tourist office (☎ *01382 527527, www.angusanddundee.co.uk*) is at 21 Castle Street and open June–September Monday–Saturday 9am–6pm (Sunday 12pm–4pm); October–May Monday–Saturday 9am–5pm.

What to See & Do

Discovery Point ★★ ALL AGES

Discovery Quay, Riverside Drive, Dundee, ☎ 01382 201245, www.Rrsdiscovery.com.

Captain Scott sailed the *RRS Discovery* to the Antarctic where it became trapped in ice for two winters a few years before his doomed mission to the South Pole. The modern, family-friendly museum beside the restored three-masted ship tells the story of Scott and the continent he fell in love with, that later claimed his life. Good for older children, who will enjoy running up and down the deck shouting 'iceberg', it's also great for youngsters who can experience the difficulty of loading a floating boat using a dummy crane and seeing what it's like to be a sperm whale trying to look for squid with your eyes too far apart on your head. Exhibits include an under-mitten used on an Antarctic mission and a very cold room (about the temperature of a supermarket's diary aisle) called the Polorama full of dummies of explorers doing scientific-looking things in coats. There's also a film about how the boat became locked in ice and a mocked-up boiler demonstrating how hungry for coal the ship was (each lump moved it 40m, about the distance our daughter travels

Discovery Point, Dundee

per motivationally offered chocolate finger). Afterwards you can make jokes about the death of Captain Oates ('I'm going to the gift shop. I might be some time').

Open Apr–Oct Mon–Sat 10am–6pm (Sun 11am–6pm), Nov–Mar Mon–Sat 10am–5pm (Sun 11am–5pm). ***Adm*** *£6.95, children (5–16) £4.25, under-5s free, family ticket (two adults, two children) £20.* ***Amenities*** *café (with highchairs), WiFi.*

Sensation ★ ALL AGES

Greenmarket, Dundee, 01382 228800, ***www.sensation.org.uk****.*

If you ever want to find out what you'd look like as a monkey, wander through a nasal passage, have a look at your own brain or try your hand at keyhole surgery, Sensation is for you. Set up as a millennium 'live science centre' about how the senses work, Sensation has evolved into an all-singing, all dancing explosion of touchy feely experiences (80 in all) explaining how the body works. A giant head invites you to climb through the mouth, up the throat and out of a human nose, while a wall of tiny mirrors shows how you'd look if you had half the face of someone else. Other technology presents your face 20 years on and shows how it would look

FUN FACT The Last Witness

The birth of HRH The Princess Margaret Rose in 1930 was attended by then Home Secretary, John Robert Clynes. He was there to verify the identity of the Royal child – the last time that this ancient practice, to prevent the illegitimate substitution of a potential heir to the throne, was practised.

JM Barrie

James Matthew Barrie was born to a family of Scottish weavers, the 9th child of 10. Aged 6, his brother David, his mother's favourite, died in a skating accident on the eve of his 14th birthday. His mother never recovered, ignored the young Barrie, and found comfort in the fact her dead son would remain a boy forever, never to leave her. Many believe *Peter Pan* was inspired by these traumatic events, with Wendy a version of his mother and Peter Pan a portrayal of his lost brother. At the age of 13, Barrie was sent away to boarding school at the Dumfries Academy. Here he spent much time in the garden of Moat Brae house, playing pirates, and perhaps dreaming up Captain Hook.

on a monkey (much the same in my case). There are memory experiments and optical illusions, while keyhole surgery (pioneered at Dundee University) is practised on Headless Harry. On-the-spot demos happen throughout the day with staff, many with teacher-training experience, performing simple experiments as children sit on the floor and watch (or, like our daughter, demand the Percy Pig sweet we said she could have after her wee wee).

***Open** daily 10am–5pm **Adm** £6.95, children (4–15) £4.95, under-4s free, family ticket (two adults, two children) £20. **Amenities** café (children's meals £2.99), Internet (free).*

AROUND DUNDEE

The two highlights for children on the northern outskirts of the Dundee are close by: Glamis Castle and Kirriemuir, where JM Barrie was born. Take the A90 out of the city then the A928.

Glamis Castle ★★ ALL AGES

*Glamis, ☎ 01307 840393, **www.glamis-castle.co.uk**. 10km west of Forfar.*

The Disneyesque castle where Princess Margaret was born helped inspire our daughter's confusing fascination with princesses that saw her for almost a week go to bed with her Mickey Mouse slippers on in case 'I turn into a puntkin (pumpkin)'. This turreted five-storey pile, approached by a mile-long avenue of trees, is owned and lived in by the 18th Earl of Strathmore and Kinghorn, a second cousin to the queen. In his family for over 600 years, its legends mostly concern ghosts. The chink of money heard through a stone wall in the crypt near a Victorian replica of a jousting suit of armour is said to be the ghost of the Earl of Crawford, who lost his soul to the devil in a game of cards played on the Sabbath. Another ghost story on the guided tour concerns a Grey Lady, said to be Janet Douglas,

Glamis Castle

wife of the 6th Lord Glamis and burnt in Edinburgh as a witch, who haunts the family chapel. The story goes that her ghost enters the chapel, kneels in prayer before the altar and then sits quietly in the back row, where a cooling in the air temperature gives her presence away.

Children are given an activity sheet, a guidebook and a prize if they complete the Glamis Quest. There's a play area outside, Highland cattle in surrounding fields as well as plenty of interest in the castle including the outfit of the last jester in Scotland, and the Queen Mum's old dolls' house. You can also see a bedspread the Queen Mother embroidered with the names of all her 10 children, possibly so she wouldn't forget them, the robes worn by Edward II during his coronation and a watch belonging to James 'the Old Pretender'.

Ninety steps mean leaving buggies in the ticket office. Try the Forfar Bridies in the kitchen restaurant.

Open *Mar–Oct 10am–6pm, Nov–Dec 11am–5pm.* ***Adm*** *£7.50 (grounds-only £3.70), children up to 16 £4.30 (grounds only £2.70), under-5s free.* ***Amenities*** *café/restaurant, guided tour (50 minutes, every 15 minutes), play area.*

JM Barrie's Birthplace ★

ALL AGES

9 Brechin Rd, Kirriemuir, ☎ 0844 493 2142, ***www.nts.org.uk****.*

In an annexe here, against the rhythmic ticking of Captain Hook's swallowed clock, children can lie on a raised podium dressed as their favourite *Peter Pan* character (Wendy for our daughter, Peter

FUN FACT Golf

1 Early shepherds used their curved staffs to hit stones in a simple game of 'golf' as early as 2,000 years ago.
2 The first golf balls were made of leather stuffed with feathers.
3 Golf is the only sport to be played in outer space. On 6th February 1971, Alan Shepard hit a golf ball on the moon.
4 Golf was originally a man's game and this is how it may have got its name: Gentlemen Only Ladies Forbidden. Alternatively it may be derived from the old Scots verb 'to gowff' meaning to 'strike hard'.
5 Golf balls reach speeds of 270kph.
6 The chances of making two holes-in-one in a round of golf are one in 67 million.
7 Golf was invented in Japan, though whisper it quietly here.

for my wife; I read *Victor* magazine as a boy so took no active part) and pretend they're flying to Neverland. There's even a wind machine to blow their hair realistically. Also in this magical room are a puppet theatre and a bedroom mocked up like Peter Pan's. The rest of the whitewashed cottage is a little like your gran's. Rooms are arranged as they would have been in JM Barrie's time and you can see the bedroom where Barrie was born, the kitchen, a small office containing Barrie's writing desk from his London flat in Adelphi Terrace (check out the scuff marks from his shirt cuffs), while in the garden there is a statue of Peter Pan and a large living willow hedge crocodile whose open jaws our daughter had great fun running into. Also here is a copy of Barrie's jokey contract of payment made with Princess Margaret, who

JM Barrie's Birthplace, Kirriemuir

Barrie met at her 3rd birthday at Glamis castle. For allowing him to use a few words she uttered at her birthday in his play, *Boy David*, she was to receive a penny per performance. After the play closed King George VI, Margaret's father, sent Barrie a letter threatening legal action if the debt were not paid. Barrie started collecting pennies in a bag (only 55 of them, as the play was a flop!), intending to deliver them to Buckingham Palace in person. However, Barrie died on 21st June, 1937, his pennies undelivered.

Open *31st Mar–30th June Sat–Wed noon–5pm (Sun 1–5pm), 1st July–31st Aug daily 11am–5pm (Sun 1–5pm), 1st Sep–31st Oct Sat–Wed noon–5pm (Sun 1–5pm).* ***Adm*** *£5, children £4.*

ST ANDREWS & AROUND

St Andrews is a pilgrimage for golfers from all over the world, with a university often compared to Oxford and Cambridge, and boasting Prince William as an alma mater. He spent four years here studying and wooing former waitress Kate Middleton. Not a large place with just three main streets full of brightly coloured souls clanking clubs about, the city is surrounded by green space and two magnificent beaches. West Sands is famous as the location for the slow-motion running scene at the beginning of 1981 Oscar-winning *Chariots of Fire*, while a little further round the shore there are rockpools full of youngsters ferreting for starfish. East Sands, overlooked by St Andrews cathedral, has lifeguards and an adjacent park with a children's play area. Surfers use this beach when its windy.

Essentials

By Train The nearest station is Leuchars on the Edinburgh–Dundee line 8km away; regular buses make the 15-minute journey. There are hourly services to Aberdeen (1½ hours) costing £22 return. Also hourly connections to Glasgow (£22 return, two hours), and Edinburgh (£16, one hour).

By Bus Stagecoach (*☎ 01334 474238*, ***www.stagecoachbus.com***) has four hourly services to Dundee (30 minutes) costing £6.70 return. They have hourly connections to Edinburgh and Glasgow for around £10, taking 1¾ hours and 2½ hours respectively.

By Car If arriving from the south, the city is best approached via the A9/M90 followed briefly by a stint on the A91.From the north, it's the A90 and then the A914, A919 and A91.

Visitor Information

The tourist office (*☎ 01334 472021*) is on 70 Market Street and is open from April–June Monday–Saturday 9.30am–5.30pm, Sunday 11am–4pm; July–August Monday–Saturday 9.30am–7pm, Sunday 10am–5pm; September–October Monday–Saturday 9.30am–6pm, Sunday 11am–4pm; and

November–March Monday–Saturday 9.30am–5pm.

What to See & Do

British Golf Museum ★

ALL AGES

*Bruce Embankment, St Andrews, Fife, 01334 460046, **www.britishgolfmuseum.co.uk**.*

Here you can see the oldest set of clubs in the world, learn why a birdie is so named (because bird meant great shot in 19th century American slang), while at the special 18th hole toddlers get a chance to dress up like old fashioned players and try their hand at golf/hitting their dad's legs repeatedly with a putter. There are also jigsaw puzzles, a colouring-in station, quizzes and computer golf. Based over the road from the Royal and Ancient Clubhouse, the museum tells the story of golf from the Middle Ages, when James II banned the sport because its popularity was putting people off archery, through to the present day triumphs of Tiger Woods. Adults can watch old Open Championships on television, refresh their memories on rules, or if they're my wife – who took 10 shots on the 15th at the Cadonas amusement park Treasure Island course because 'My hands were too cold' – study (for putting tips) the bronzed grip of Nick Faldo. You can also see a statue of the father of golf, Old Tom Morris, who standardised the number of holes on a course to 18 (there used to be 23 on St Andrews' Old Course), managed hazards such as bunkers for the first time, designed many famous courses (such as Muirfield and Carnoustie) and still holds the record as the oldest winner of the Open Championship (46) in 1867.

***Open** daily Mar–Oct Mon–Sat 9.30am–5.30pm (Sun 10am–5pm), Nov–Mar Mon–Sun 10am–4pm. **Adm** £5.25, children (under 15) £2.90, under-5s free.*

St Andrews Cathedral **ALL AGES**

The Pends, St Andrews, 01334 472563.

Once the largest building in Scotland, the cathedral is worth a visit for the views of the town from the top of St Rule's Tower. It's 157 steps, so park your buggy at the visitor centre and take a papoose; the top is blustery but safe. Consecrated in 1318 in the presence of Robert the Bruce, it was sacked during the Reformation by supporters of John Knox. Golfing

St Andrews Cathedral

enthusuaists will find Old Tom Morris buried here, as well as Robert Chambers (of dictionary fame). There are no baby-changing facilities or toilets.

***Open** Apr–Sep 9.30am–6.30pm, Oct–Mar 9.30am–4.30pm. **Adm** £4, children £2, under-5s free.*

Scotland's Secret Bunker ★

AGES OVER 7

*Scotcrown Ltd, Crown Buildings, Troywood, Fife, ☎ 01333 310301, **www.secretbunker.co.uk**.*

Hidden under an unassuming Scottish farmhouse (locals never knew it was here until it was declassified in the 1990s), this fortified bunker was originally built as an early warning radar base. When advances in technology made it defunct, a new use was found: it became an emergency base for the British government in the event of a Soviet nuclear strike. Although it doesn't exactly sound like a day at the zoo, older children especially will have fun exploring it.

The bunker, constructed here because of the proximity of the Royal Navy Rosyth docks and nearby RAF Leuchars, is accessed via an eerie 150m tunnel (our daughter loved the echo) under several metres of reinforced concrete, which opens up into an enormous, multi-level labyrinth where up to 300 servicemen and women and public figures would have lived, organised regional government and hopefully felt a little guilty that the rest of us had died up top hiding under our kitchen tables with our baked bean tins and *Protect and Survive* manuals. The base had its own BBC station, emergency power and an annexe for the Home Secretary and his wife. Despite all the weaponry (there is a room full of missiles that older boys will drool over) the bunker strikes anti-war notes with a CND Room as well as a powerful film (not for children of any age) about the firestorm following a nuclear attack.

There are some inadvertently funny touches, too. The manikins, especially the German ones, are strangely camp – with their chiselled jaws and luxuriant hair they were possibly ex-window models from Burtons clothes shop. Also check out the strange RAF Ops room full of iron crosses, jerry helmets and a copy of *Mein Kampf* open (inappropriately?) at a page showing Hitler's author photo. To complicate the message, the gift shop is crammed with plastic machine guns, real bullet casings and T-shirts with radioactive symbols on them. Our daughter's highlight was skipping down the corridors 'playing horsey', and having a go on the 'puters' in the free Internet-equipped, 1950s-style restaurant (macaroni and chips £4.50, ice-cream £2). Unsettling for those who remember the nuclear documentaries from their childhoods, it's a relief on the surface to hear birds singing...even if we could also hear two youngsters fresh from the gift shop shouting 'You have entered a restricted zone. You have not shown your code 2 accesses privilege pass' before

Tank outside Scotland's Secret Bunker, Troywood

opening fire with their new toy machine guns.

***Open** daily 23rd Mar–Oct 10am–6pm (last entry 5pm). **Adm** £8, children £5, under-5s free, family ticket £23 (two adults, two children). **Amenities** Internet (free), restaurant.*

INSIDER TIP

Even if it's a sunny day, take a jumper and a coat as it gets cold down there.

FAMILY-FRIENDLY ACCOMMODATION

EXPENSIVE

Balbirnie House ★

*Balbirnie Park, Markinch by Glenrothes, Fife, ☎ 01592 610066, **www.balbirnie.co.uk**.*

The sort of home-from-home country house where the friendly staff make you feel more like you've rolled up at a very rich mate's place; the duty manager even nipped home to borrow the Internet cable we needed to connect our laptop. The 18th century building, set in the 5½ hectares of Balbirnie Park, was full of sweet smelling lilies when we visited, while the grounds are packed with great walks, mostly buggy friendly. The informal Bistro restaurant has a children's menu and crayons and paper for when our daughter decided 'I want to go back to the room. Dolly's tired' and needed to be resisted. Cairney Farm (open May–October) with a maze and mini-tractors for youngsters is a few kilometres away.

Candycraig Cottage, Aboyne

***Rates** family room (two bedrooms) £250 per night, children £20 extra (under-2s free). **Credit Amenities** golf course, parking, craft shop, restaurant (children's menu £7.50, and highchairs), WiFi. **In room** flat-screen TV (with children's TV channel), DVD player, broadband.*

St Andrews Golf Hotel

*40 The Scores, St Andrews, Fife, 01334 472611, **www.standrews-golf.co.uk**.*

With dramatic bay window views over the sea across the western sands beach where *Chariots of Fire* was filmed, this family-run boutique hotel is just a hooked 10 iron away from the first tee on St Andrews' famous Old Course. The location makes it pricey, although a good way to recoup your outlay is at breakfast where it's possible (although foolish) to have both a continental and a full Scottish one after the other for no extra charge. You can also have fun walking everywhere in slow motion to the *Chariots of Fire* theme tune. The Bobby Jones suite includes a double-bed with a fold-down sofa-bed and enough space for a z-bed and a cot (provided free). For youngsters there's a large grassy garden at the back of the hotel and a children's menu with colouring-in and crayons at its Number 40 restaurant (main courses £17, children's £8.50). Buggy pushers avoid the front steps by entering via the back. Check website for offers.

***Rates** Family room (double or twin room with sofa bed, cots available) £250. Children (aged 5–15) £15 extra, under-5s free. **Amenities** bar. **In room** TV (with children's TV channel), Molton Brown accessories.*

MODERATE

Candycraig Cottage ★★

*Glen Tanar estate, Brooks House, Glen Tanar, Aboyne, Aberdeenshire, 01339 886451, **www.glentanar.co.uk**.*

Up a bouncy farm track in the middle of nowhere with great views of Ben Avon, this cottage made my wife and I feel part of an episode of nostalgic TV series *District Nurse* especially when Liz, the housekeeper, and would-be Nerys Hughes, dropped round home-cooked meals like they were emergency food parcels. The beautiful cottage has two bathrooms (one up, one down), three bedrooms (two with twin beds, one double), a large living room with a wood-burning fire, a games compendium for children to scatter the tiddly-winks from all around the house and a great kitchen breakfast room. The TV, when we worked out its various remotes, had more channels than I've had birthdays, although we preferred to switch it off and spend the night pretending to be 1920s miners stricken with emphysema as we ate our chicken breast stuffed with haggis followed by fruit compote, fed the fire and talked in pretend Welsh murmurs. On the estate there is also West Lodge, which has one less bedroom and bathroom.

Rates *£300–900 per week.* ***Amenities*** *kitchen, parking, sat TV.*

Colt Cottage ★

Balmoral Estate, Ballater, Aberdeenshire, ☎ 013397 42534, ***www.balmoralcastle.com****.*

The idea that you can stay in a cottage on the Balmoral Estate, within the security gate, and not have to be cleared by MI5 is almost as appealing as the prospect of giving your holiday address to friends in this flippant manner: 'Oh just send it to the castle.' And of course there is the outside chance the Queen might stop by and offer you a knighthood and a slice of her 20,100 hectare estate. Colt cottage itself has two bedrooms accommodating a double and a single bed plus a sofa-bed. The lounge has a widescreen TV and a DVD player while the kitchen has a microwave and fridge-freezer. Travel cots can be provided and there are games and puzzles for children.

There are other cottages available on the estate – one sleeping up to 13 – but book well in advance.

Rates *£600 per week.* ***Amenities*** *cots, parking (free), kitchen, TV/DVD player.*

Skene House Whitehall

2 Whitehall Place, Aberdeen, ☎ 01224 635971, ***www.skene-house.co.uk****.*

Two and three-bed serviced apartments have their own garden with play equipment for children, while a continental breakfast (cooked alternative £8) and a free drink at the honesty bar come with the rate. 10 minutes outside the city centre but close to Codonas Amusement Park, parking is free, reception is manned 24 hours and all apartments (with separate kitchens and lounges) have Tellies (including children's TV channel), a microwave, fridge-freezer and cooker. Best are the ground floor flats (as there's no lift) and if you book early ask for an apartment with a dishwasher and washing machine (no extra charge). DVD players and cots are available.

FUN FACT The One That Didn't Get Away 

The world's longest worm was found on a beach at St Andrews. It was a whopping 54m ribbon worm.

There's a Morrisons supermarket for supplies or a closer Co-op for bread, milk and the Kinder Egg my wife demanded after dinner because 'I've got to breast feed him in a minute and need something to look forward to.' Check website for offers.

Rates *two bedroom apartment (double and a single) £117–163 per night. Three bed apartment (double and two singles) £164–188, (double and two twins) £216–267.* ***Amenities*** *kitchen, DVD player.*

Swallow Hotel

Kingsway West, Dundee, 01382 641122, ***www.swallow-hotels.com****.*

Set in 2 hectares of grounds with a heated indoor swimming pool (armbands and floats for youngsters) the hotel also has a pleasant garden restaurant (3 courses for £20) in its beautiful conservatory. Rooms at the Swallow are tartan themed, as are many in Scotland – perhaps not so odd until you imagine an English hotel with St George Cross carpets.

Rates *£122 for interconnecting rooms.* ***Amenities*** *parking, pool, restaurant (with children's menu £8), spa (sauna, steam room), gym.* ***In room*** *TV.*

INEXPENSIVE

The Ship Inn

5 Shoreland, Stonehaven, 01569 762617, ***www.shipinnstonehaven.com****.*

This 18th century pub has a family room (double bed, a single with z-bed if needed) on the 2nd floor overlooking the quaint harbour and sea beyond. There's no lift so leave buggies in your car. Travel cots are provided and the breakfast is substantial.

This is also a great place for lunch or dinner. It serves fresh, homemade meals focusing on locally-caught fish. There's a children's menu (£4.25 for a main, home-made burgers and macaroni cheese etc.) The restaurant opens daily July–August noon–9.30pm and in the rest of the year noon–2.15pm and 5.30–9.30pm. The room can be noisy on warm summer nights as drinkers spill outside the pub below.

Rates *family room £100 (if sleeping three or four), £85 (if sleeping two) under-1s free.* ***Amenities*** *restaurant (main courses from £7.25)* ***In room*** *TV.*

Travelodge

9 Bridge Street, Aberdeen, 01224 584555, ***www.travelodge.co.uk****.*

A no-frills option for families on a budget, this central hotel at £65 for a family room sleeping four (one double bed and a sofa bed) is clean and only noisy when drunks occasionally fight in the street after midnight. Breakfast (£7.50) is buffet-style, although children under 15 eat free. Lunch and dinner are available between 5pm–10pm (main meals around £7).

***Rates** £65 per night. **Amenities** car parking (beneath the hotel although only 25 places for 97 rooms). **In room** TV.*

University of St Andrews

GREEN

*David Rothwell Apartments, Buchanan Gardens, St Andrews, 01334 462000, **www.discover standrews.com.***

A great budget alternative for families, the university offers s pacious five-bed flats full of mod-cons for half the cost of most one-room hotel options. All bedrooms have TVs, double beds and en suite showers, but no baths. There's a small kitchen-diner with green-conscious Bosch appliances including a dishwasher, microwave, fridge-freezer and cooker. There are more than 70 five-bed flats that have won environmental awards for the grass roof. There is a brasserie here selling cooked breakfasts and panini-style lunches and dinners, and children's games are available from the James Bond villain-sounding 'Central Complex'.

Rooms are only bookable for a minimum of three nights in the summer (2nd June–8th September). The complex is 2½ km from the city centre.

***Rates** three nights £280, seven nights £540. Although you can negotiate a slightly lower rate if don't take all five bedrooms (which are each separately lockable). **Amenities** kitchen, parking (free), reception (24 hr), restaurant (7am–8pm). **In room** shower only, TV.*

FAMILY-FRIENDLY DINING

MODERATE

Bon Appetit ★

*22–26 Exchange St, Dundee, 01382 809000, **www.bonappetit-dundee.com.***

A French restaurant where our daughter was allowed to stir a pot of hot sauce on the oven while wearing a chef's hat before she settled down to her favourite new past-time – washing her fingers every five seconds in the finger bowl that came with her moule marinere ('Cos otherwise I will get a tummyache and I will die'). The restaurant doesn't have a children's menu (although they have paper and pens for drawing) but will cook pretty much anything requested. All mains also come as starters, the perfect size for toddlers. The restaurant (white linen tables but relaxed) was opened three years ago by a lovely Scottish couple who spent 16 years learning their business in France. This is reflected not just in the dishes, but in the framed French newspapers on the walls that my wife annoyingly understood ('It's actually very interesting – they're talking about CAP talks').

***Open** Mon–Sat noon–2pm and 5.30–9.30pm. **Main courses** from £11.95. **Credit** MC, V. **Amenities** children's menu (£6.95), highchairs.*

Lairhillock Inn & Crynoch Restaurant

*Netherley, Nr Stonehaven, 01569 730001, **www.lairhillock.co.uk.***

This 200-year-old coaching inn has a good children's menu and offers child-sized portions of adult choices. Dishes are freshly prepared and use local produce. Décor is Harvester-style so expect incongruous farm implements hanging on the wall.

Open *Mon–Thurs and Sun 11am–11pm, Fri–Sat 11am–midnight.* ***Main courses*** *from £9.* ***Amenities*** *baby-changing, children's menu (£4.50), highchairs.*

Station Restaurant

Station Square, Ballater, ☎ 01339 755050.

Next to the old Royal Station Museum (see p. 188), this genteel restaurant with its glass ceiling and large ferns makes for a convenient family lunch stop, especially if your wife loves the Royal family and wants to hang around near where they once got on and off a particular train. The restaurant fails admirably (or disappointingly in my wife's case) to cash in on its royal connections, relying instead on simple home cooking to bring in trade. Our daughter loved the buttered pasta, although not as much as her vanilla ice-cream with chocolate buttons (£1.50), while my wife was quiet throughout her fresh haddock and homemade chips (£8) lost no doubt in a reverie about some embroidery by the Queen Mum we'd seen at Glamis Castle the day before. ('I just think it's amazing someone so elevated likes needlework.')

Open *daily 10am–5pm and 6.30–8.30pm.* ***Amenities*** *children's menu (around £5).*

The Doll's House ★

*3 Church Square, St Andrews, ☎ 01334 477422, **www.dolls-house.co.uk**.*

Children have a play cubby-hole under the stairs full of toys and books at this restaurant where my wife became pathetically obsessed with Prince William, wooer of Kate Middleton, a former waitress here. Themed around an old child's nursery, our daughter loved the pictures of Alice in Wonderland on the walls and the covers of old children's books, while my wife annoyingly kept asking different members of staff if he (Prince William) ever came back 'for old time's sake'. We left before dessert and had a squabble on the street after she said: 'I just said he was very handsome. He is very handsome in a boyish way. And his little red cheeks when he's embarrassed.' If eating at the weekend book well in advance. If eating with a royal-obsessed wife bring earplugs.

Open *noon–3pm and 5–9.30pm daily (last orders half an hour before).* ***Menu*** *£6.95 two-course lunch, £12.95 dinner.* ***Amenities*** *children's menu (£4.95).*

INEXPENSIVE

The Ashvale ★

*42–48 Great Western Road, Aberdeen, ☎ 01224 596981, **www.theashvale.co.uk**.*

After much goading from my wife I took the Ashvale Challenge here and attempted to consume an £8.15 Ashvale Whale (a huge ½ kg cod fillet and chips) at Aberdeen's most famous fish and chip shop. If you complete the task on the premises (that fittingly overlook a cemetery) you are treated (if you are mad or have a deathwish) to a second one free, or else to a sweet of your choice. Plus you get a certificate to impress your greediest friends. We came on a Saturday when there was a children's entertainer, and I blame the way he savagely twisted his balloon sausage dogs for my failure to complete the challenge (it reminded me what I was doing to my large intestine) although admittedly learning ex-Liverpool football legend Graeme Souness (coronary bypass aged 38) likes it here didn't help either.

There is an under-12s Harry Haddock Menu (£3.75 for sausage, burger or haddock and chips, with free drink) while under-5s eat free.

Open *daily 11.45am–11pm.* ***Main courses*** *from £7.*

The Catch ★

St Andrews Aquarium, The Scores, St Andrews, ☎ 01334 474786, ***www.standrewsaquarium.co.uk****.*

This simple restaurant serving freshly caught haddock is popular with passing celebrities (Sir Sean Connery and Boris Becker have eaten here). They come mainly for the great sea views. To eat here you don't have to pay to enter the aquarium (£6.50, children 3–15 £4.60, under-3s free) although as a bonus you do get a sneaky free peak from several tables at the two resident seals, Laurel and Hardy, in their pool. If you do visit, seal feeding is at noon and 3pm, there are children's quizzes kand you get to handle starfish, anemones, sea urchins and crabs at various touch-pools. There is also a British fish area that includes haddock, but you can't, disappointingly, select your own to eat at the restaurant with your fat chips.

Open *11am–4pm daily Feb–Nov.* ***Main courses*** *from £7* ***Credit*** *MC, V.* ***Amenities*** *baby-changing, children's menu (from £3), highchairs.*

The Cocket Hat

North Anderson Drive, Aberdeen, ☎ 01224 695684.

Do a clever deal. In exchange for an hour in the pub restaurant (burger and chips £7) offer your children a go in the Whacky Warehouse soft-play area (£2.50 per hour, additional half-hours 50p). The cleverness? When your child is in the warehouse clambering over play bridges, through squidgy rollers with up to another 59 youngsters shrieking at the tops of their voices like some crazy scene from *Planet of the Apes*, you can sit overlooking the netting quietly sipping one (or more) of the 12 different single malt whiskies on offer.

Open *Fri 5–9pm, Sat 11am–9pm, Sun 11am–7pm; restaurant daily noon–9.30pm.* ***Amenities*** *baby-changing, children's menu (£2.95 main), highchairs.*

The Courtyard Restaurant ★

Crathes Castle, Banchory, Aberdeen & Grampian, ☎ 0844 4932166, ***www.nts.org.uk****.*

This is a great place for a quick lunch before or after a visit to Crathes Castle (admission: adult £10, children £5, under-5s free). The self-service, sandwich-style food (children's lunchboxes available for £3.75) is home-made (try the excellent soup) and you can eat inside or out. After your meal you can relax with a cup of tea while your children have a go at the 7½ m-high Sky Climbing Wall (£5, 5-year-olds and up only) visible from the restaurant. Alternatively and more formal, the Horsemill restaurant has waitress-served hot lunches. You don't need to pay the castle entrance fee to eat.

The castle highlight is the Green Lady ghost said to haunt the nursery on the 4th floor where hundreds of years ago a baby's skeleton was discovered beneath the hearthstone. Children's quizzes are available and there is a buggy-friendly almost 1km walk (The Viewpoint) through woodland full of deer and beavers that leads to a spot with great views of Scolty Hill. There's also an adventure playground, where our daughter, who had recently learned the phrase from my wife, called four people, including one skin-headed father with a tattoo on his shoulder of HMS Sheffield 'my cute little darlin'.

***Open** daily 10.30–5.30pm May–Sep, 10.30am–4.30pm Oct–Apr. **Main courses** (restaurant) from £6. **Amenities** baby-changing, children's lunchboxes (£3.75), highchairs.*

Jute Café Bar

*Dundee Contemporary Arts, 152 Nethergate, Dundee, 01382 909246, **www.dca.org.uk***

This sophisticated but friendly restaurant attached to the famous cinema and gallery complex serves delicious Brie panini and more formal main meals to the chatter of a trendy arts crowd discussing 'Bertolucci's finest achievement'. Our toddler enjoyed pointing at the modern art on the walls and saying: 'And what's THAT?' The contemporary art gallery in this Richard Murphy designed building (what you'd expect inside) is free.

***Open** Mon–Sat 10.30am–midnight (children until 8pm), Sun 12pm–midnight (children until 8pm). **Main courses** from £10.95 (lunch). **Credit** MC, V. **Amenities** baby-changing, children's menu (from £3.50), highchairs.*

Verdant Works Café

*West Henderson's Wynd, Dundee, 01382 226659, **www.verdantworks.com**.*

A handy refuelling stop after a visit to this child-friendly museum about jute. Your children can dress up, sail mini cargo ships and still fail to learn what jute actually is. You don't, however, have to pay for the museum (£5.95, children 5 and over £4, under-5s free) to get into the basement café serving toasties (£3.50, cheese, ham, etc.) and sandwiches (£2.75), as well as baked potatoes and cakes. There's a lift for buggy pushers. The museum has workshops during school holidays featuring activities such as paper-making and weaving.

***Open** daily 11am–4pm (closed Mon and Tues 1st Nov–mid-March). **Credit** MC, V. **Amenities** baby-changing, highchairs.*

8 South West Scotland & the Borders

SOUTH WEST SCOTLAND

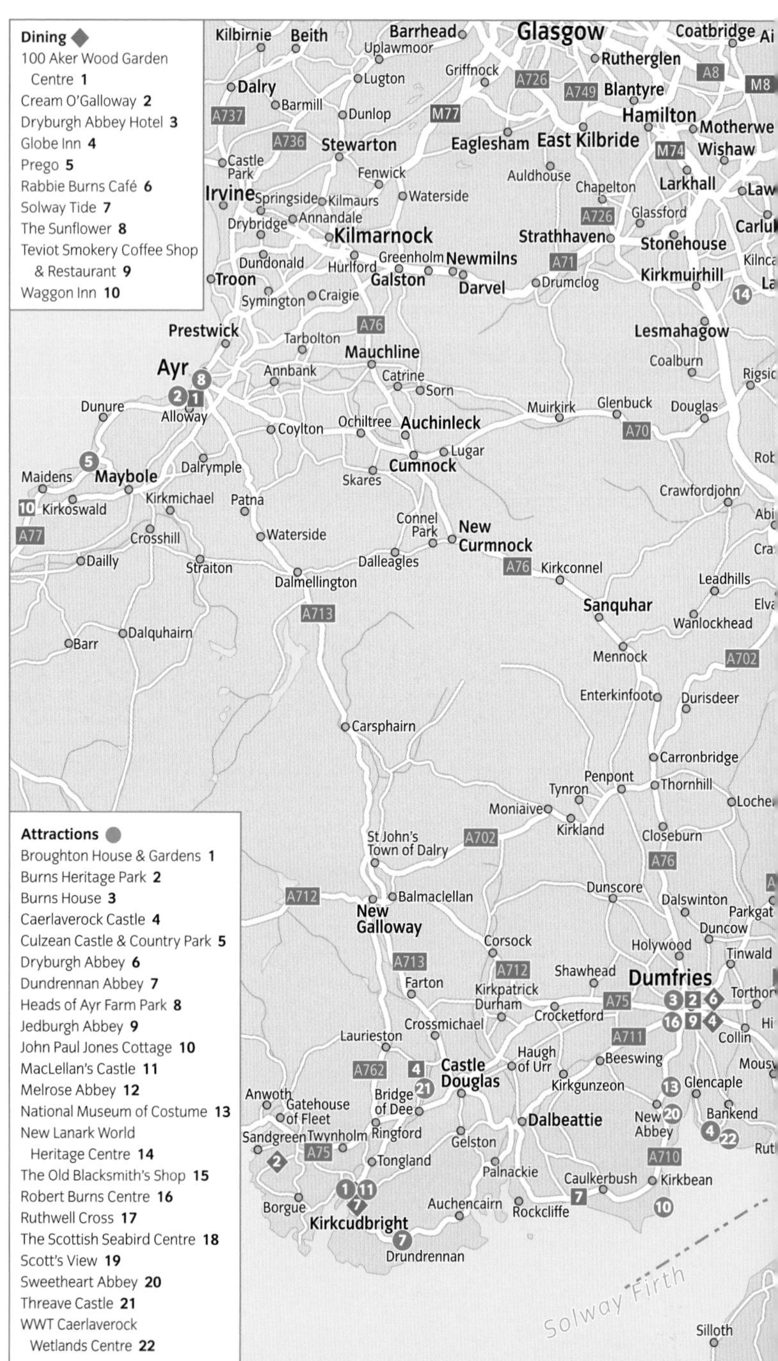

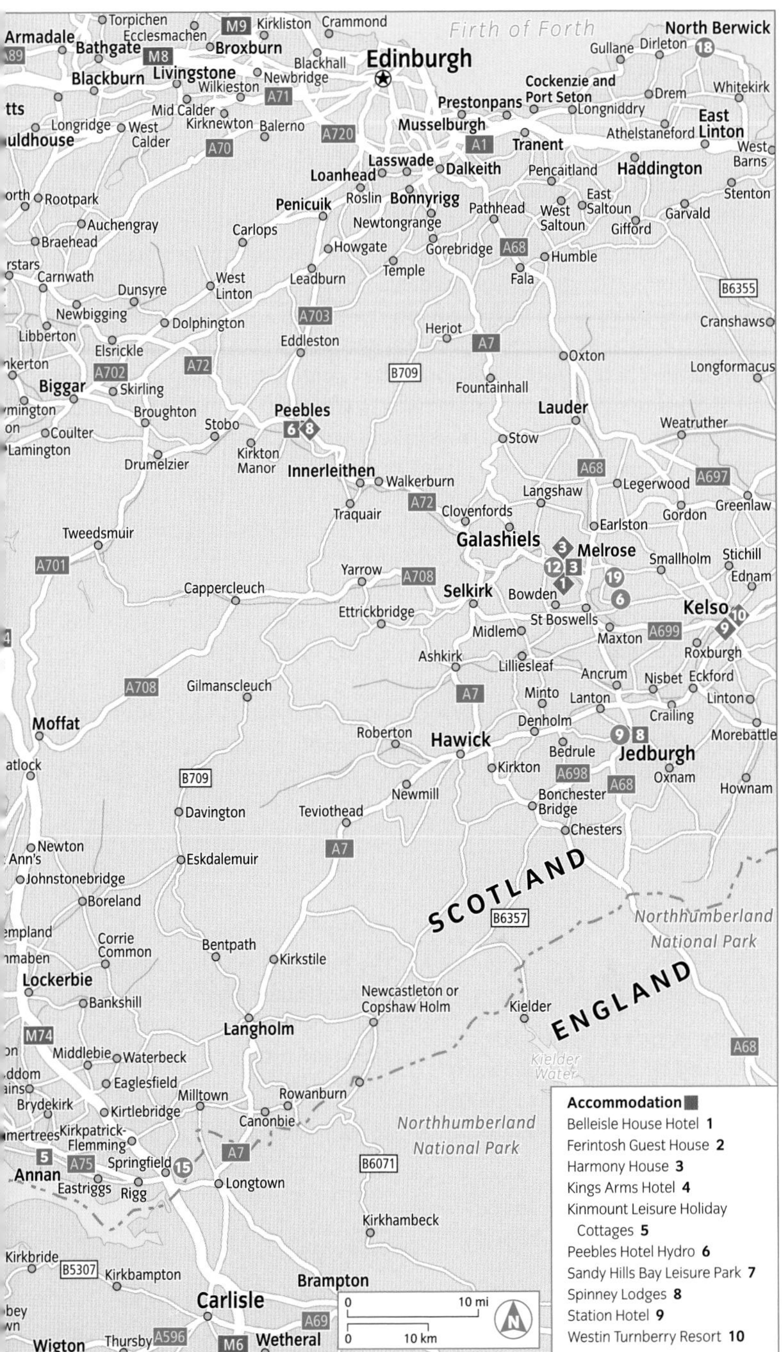

Accommodation

- Belleisle House Hotel **1**
- Ferintosh Guest House **2**
- Harmony House **3**
- Kings Arms Hotel **4**
- Kinmount Leisure Holiday Cottages **5**
- Peebles Hotel Hydro **6**
- Sandy Hills Bay Leisure Park **7**
- Spinney Lodges **8**
- Station Hotel **9**
- Westin Turnberry Resort **10**

Short of actually forcing you off the road and compelling you to listen to a pipe band while eating shortbread from a plaid tin, there isn't a lot more the Scots could do to let you know that you've crossed the border from England. Road signs reminded us 'You Are Now in Scotland' or 'Welcome to Scotland' so many times we actually felt like we had won some sort of a driving competition in getting here. It is a shame, though, that most people continue north through an area of the country so evidently pleased to see its visitors, without stopping to see what it offers.

The **Borders** encompasses the whole 144km course of one of Scotland's longest rivers, the Tweed. Its fast-flowing torrents pass ruined abbeys, stately homes, medieval keeps and luxuriant woodland, confirming there is more to Scotland than lochs and brooding glens. Sparsely populated (sheep outnumber people 14 to 1), they invented rugby sevens here, probably because they couldn't make up a full team of 15. Summer crowds are unlikely to trouble you in a region that has borne the brunt of centuries of conflict between Scotland and its Auld Enemy, England. That's ancient history now, provided you don't allude to a lack of attendance at the last two football World Cups.

North of here, tucked beneath Glasgow and Edinburgh, lies **South Lanarkshire**, where New Lanark faithfully preserves a 19th century window to Scotland's industrial past. To the west on the shores of the Solway Firth is **Dumfries**, a must for Rabbie Burns fans (he lived here towards the end of his life). Washed by the North Atlantic Drift (Scotland's low-rent answer to the Gulf Stream), the Solway Firth is also famous for its rare wildlife, including natterjack toads, remote bays and the sandstone ruins of Caerlaverock Castle. Further along the coast lies **Kirkcudbright**, once a thriving port, then an artist's retreat and now a gentle, well-preserved early 19th century town that's also home to a giant wooden rabbit that our daughter still mentions to this day.

CHILDREN'S TOP 10 ATTRACTIONS

❶ **Play** farmer on a tiny tractor, make and fly kites on the beach and pony trek during at a stay at the Westin Turnberry Hotel. See p. 230.

❷ **Call** in at the ice-cream factory at the Cream O'Galloway for a taste of one of their 30 flavours. See p. 236.

❸ **Visit** the guinea pig village at the Heads of Ayr Farm Park where (unless I had an ear infection) the creatures all whistle at the same time in the same way. See p. 219.

❹ **Take** a boat ride to Threave Castle, buy a plastic knight's helmet from the shop and then re-enact the famous 1455 siege. See p. 223.

❺ **Make** sandcastles at the smugglers' cove of Port Carrick during a visit to Culzean Castle. See p. 218.

6 **Dress** up as princesses and monks at Jedburgh Abbey. See p. 225.

7 **Hunt** for Britain's rarest amphibian, the natterjack toad, in the grounds of the UK's only triangular castle. See p. 217.

8 **Search** for starfish in rock-pools off the shoreline of the Solway Firth, while staying at the Sandy Hills Bay Leisure Park. See p. 233.

9 **Gawp** at couples getting married in a forge to a backdrop of Celine Dion tracks at Gretna Green's Old Blacksmith. See p. 238.

10 **Make** your own pizza and then gorge yourself on sticks of caramelised sauce at Prego's in Lanark. See p. 234.

SOUTHWEST SCOTLAND

Dumfries is Scotland's warmest and southern-most major town, so don't be surprised to find palm trees, exotic plants in gardens and parks along the shores of Solway Firth, and actual sunbathing in Scotland. The town where Scotland's Bard **Robert Burns** died, like Alloway in Ayrshire where he was born, has become a sort of theme park for tourists. The Dumfries claim to Burns (he lived here for six years) is stronger than Alloway's, only in so far as you can't choose where you're born, but you can where you live. Dumfries is also linked with Royal Jacobite rebel Bonnie Prince Charlie. In 1745, in room 6 of the County Hotel (demolished in the 1980s and opposite the current Marks & Spencer store), he punished the town for not supporting his rebellion by demanding £2,000 and 1,000 pairs of shoes (for his army).

Also worth visiting is **Kirkcudbright** (pronounced *kir-coo-bree*), a laid-back little town with a beautiful harbour and best-kept-village-style gardens that are still as popular with artists as they were when the Glasgow Boys centred their painting activities here in the 19th century.

Essentials

By Air The closest Scottish airport is **Glasgow Prestwick Airport** (✆ *0871 223 0700*, ***www.gpia.co.uk***) near Ayr. Its main carrier is **Ryanair** (***www.ryanair.com***).

By Train Rail is only really useful for getting to Dumfries. There are direct trains from Carlisle to Dumfries (35 minutes), also stopping at Gretna Green and Annan. There's also a seven-a-day service (1½ hours) from Glasgow Central to Dumfries. For more information call **National Rail Enquiries** (✆ *0845 748 4950*).

By Bus **National Express** (✆ *0807 580 8080*, ***www.nationalexpress.com***) has seven daily

Burns

Robert Burns (1759–1796), usually known as Rabbie Burns, is Scotland's Favourite Son, the Ploughman Poet (he once had a job on a farm), the Bard of Ayrshire and That Bloke Who Wrote *Auld Lang Syne*. He is the National Poet of Scotland and celebrated worldwide, on Burns Night (25th January), as a cultural icon among Scots, especially those who have relocated to other parts of the world. His life (knocking about with barmaids mainly) and work (a light tone) propelled him to a sort of charismatic cult hero in the 19th and 20th centuries. Burns is also remembered on Hogmonay (New Year's Eve), when the first few lines of his *Auld Lang Syne* are sung by drunken revellers the world over at midnight. Other famous Burns works include *Scots Wha Hae*, which served for a long time as Scotland's unofficial national anthem, *Tam O'Shanter*, *Address to a Haggis* and *A Letter to a Sausage* (okay, that last one's a lie).

connections to Dumfries from London Victoria. The cost is around £39 return; the journey takes about eight hours. There are also two services a day from Carlisle. **Scottish Citylink** (*0807 550 5050*, ***www.citylink.co.uk***) and **First Bus** (*0131 663 9233*, ***www.firstbus.co.uk***) as well as **Stagecoach Western** (*01387 253496*) also operate domestic services to Dumfries.

By Car The M6, becoming the **A74(M)**, is the main route into Dumfries from the south, connecting to the A75 at Gretna. If you have time, use the **B725**: you'll pass wildfowl nature trails on the mud and merse grasslands along the Solway Firth, and be treated to views of the amazingly rapid tides that divide Scotland from Cumbria. If you're coming in from Glasgow take the M74, A74(M) and A76. It's about 112km (around 1½ hours).

Visitor Information

The **Dumfries and Galloway Tourist Board** (*01387 253862*, ***www.dumfriesandgalloway.co.uk***) is at 64 Whitesands, Dumfries. There are also seasonal offices at Gatehouse of Fleet, Galashiels, Gretna Green, Selkirk, Castle Douglas and Kirkcudbright.

What to See & Do

Broughton House and Gardens ALL AGES

12 High Street, Kirkcudbright, Dumfries and Galloway, 01557 330437, ***www.nts.org.uk****.*

The former home of influential Glasgow Boy artist **E.A Hornel** contains much of his work, has a beautiful Japanese-influenced garden, and more importantly if you are aged 2, the largest sculpture of a rabbit in Scotland. There are many examples of Hornel's work including his

post-Impressionist phase. At the height of his fame he moved here, inspiring many other artists to do the same, and creating the town's reputation (that still exists today) as a painters' haven. The house is popular with arty folk in berets studying his thick brush strokes, but not a bad family outing provided you leave the buggy at reception. (There is a lift, but you miss the final floor and the garden is narrow).
As well as the 3m pagan rabbit sculpture, children are given a quiz and can follow a **garden trail** to find items among the shrubbery including (slightly gruesomely) a stone child's coffin, as well as more fun things such as the garden's illusive tabby cat, one-eyed Oscar. On completion of the quiz children get to rummage for a sweet in a lucky dip jar and enter an annual draw to win £50 in book tokens.

Open *22nd Mar–30th June Thurs–Mon 12–5pm, daily July–Aug 12–5pm and 1st Sep–31st Oct Thurs–Mon 12–5pm. Gardens additionally open 1st Feb–21st Mar Monday–Fri 11am–4pm.* ***Adm*** *£8, children (5–18) £5, under-5s free.*

Burns Heritage Park ALL AGES

*Murdoch's Lone, Alloway, Ayr, 01292 443700, **www.burnsheritagepark.com**.*

A sort of Graceland for Robbie Burns fans, except with slightly better taste and a lot more quilted jackets with Burns' crests for sale. The park is spread over several sites, all within walking distance. The **Tam O'Shanter Experience**, the natural starting point, features a 12-minute reading of one of Burns's most famous works set against the backdrop of a film of the events he's describing. It involved too many cackling witches for our daughter, who burst into tears and had to be led from the auditorium pointing accusingly at the screen. However, there is a great outside play area behind the glass-walled café enabling my wife and I to eat two cakes before it rained and our daughter came inside and lodged herself in the Wendy House, where she served several children pretend cups of tea, proudly announcing: 'I seen a witch'.

Burns Cottage, built in the 18th century, is where the poet was born and lived until the age of 7. Our daughter seemed mildly interested in the fact that as a small boy Burns lived, slept and ate all in the same room, next to where the family animals lived, although she asked to leave during a short film about his life and work because 'I have

FUN FACT

With Friends Like These...

Burns died a few days before the birth of his son Maxwell, who was ironically named after his friend, the physician Dr Maxwell, who unwittingly hastened the poet's death of rheumatic heart disease. He wrongly diagnosed gout and advised Burns on cold, possibly fatal dunks in the Solway Firth.

Burns Cottage

a poorly rash, and I need medicent?' (She hadn't got a rash and received no medicine.)

The **Burns Monument** was erected in 1823 and is set in flower gardens full of wistful looking middle-aged women, who all looked like Hattie Jacques. **The Brig a' Doon,** at the bottom of the hill, is the scene of the famous ending of Burns' Tam O'Shanter. It's where Scottish couples like to pose kissing, although in our daughter's case slightly less romantically she went for a sneaky al fresco wee because the Burns Monument toilets were bolted shut. The **Kirk of Alloway** and its crumbling ruins is where the witches were first seen in Tam O'Shanter. It is also the site of Burns' father William's grave.

Open *Apr–Oct 9.30am–5.30pm, Nov–Mar 10am–5pm.* ***Adm*** *(to all attractions) £5, children (5–16) £3, under-5s free. Tam O'Shanter only £2/1.25. Burns Cottage only £4/2.50.* ***Amenities*** *baby-changing, highchairs, café (children's' lunchboxes £3.50), play area.*

Burns House ALL AGES

Burns Street, Dumfries, 01387 255297, ***www.dumfriesmuseum.demon.co.uk****.*

Dominated by 1960s flats and in front of a small garden where teenage smokers gather, this is the house where Burns died on 21st July 1796, aged just 37. Burns (or Robert, as he is mateily known by staff) lived with his long-suffering wife, Jean Armour, and the house contains the usual assortment of memorabilia – manuscripts, letters, his nutmeg grater and an old walking stick. In the larger bedroom one of the windows bears Burns' signature scratched on the glass with his diamond ring. Children are given activity packs including word search puzzles and colouring books.

In the summer there are accompanied visits to the hideously ugly Burns mausoleum at St Michael's Church (shut in the winter), which looks like a fancy portaloo. It's over the dual carriageway opposite the statue of Jean Armour at the back of the fairly creepy Gothic graveyard. Maps are available from Burns House outlining where you can find all the blue plaque gravestones of the 45 or so Burns contemporaries also buried here, including Jesse Lewers, who nursed him at the end of his life.

***Open** Apr–Sep 10am–5pm Mon–Sat (Sun 2–5pm), Oct–Mar 10am–1pm and 2–5pm Tues–Sat. **Adm** free.*

Caerlaverock Castle ★

AGES 3 AND OVER

*By Glencaple, Dumfries, ☎ 01387 770244, **www.historic-scotland.gov.uk**.*

It's very easy to lose your bearings inside the only triangular castle in the UK: we spent several panic-stricken minutes wondering if our daughter had fallen into the moat before we found her safe in the towered gatehouse singing *Wind the Bobbin In* to fresh air. The 13th century castle is famous for the siege in 1300, when 60 men led by William Wallace held a force of 3,000 of English King Edward I's men for three days. It has many peepholes and crevices, making it a great place for hide-and-seek, and there are walks around its grounds including one where you're asked to listen and watch out for the extremely rare natterjack toad (although it might have helped if we'd asked what they sounded and looked like before we took off). There's also a children's adventure park with rope bridges for older ones and a Wendy House from which our daughter sold pretend pie. There is a trebuchet near the castle shop and an exhibition room where

Caerlaverock Castle by Glencaple

youngsters can dress in feudal tunics, plus a show presented by an over-excited Tony Robinson on the 'incredible' siege.

***Open** 1st Apr–30th Sep Mon–Sun 9.30am–5.30pm, 1st Oct–31st Mar 9.30am–4.30pm. **Adm** £5, children (5–16) £2.50, under-5s free. **Amenities** play area, café, shop.*

Culzean Castle and Country Park ★★ ALL AGES

*Near Maybole, Ayrshire, 01655 884455, **www.culzeanexperience.org**.*

Culzean Castle (pronounced *col-lane*), built into a cliff over the Firth of Clyde, has a children's trail where youngsters find Lego characters in each of the 13 rooms. Robert Adam's famous oval staircase is the highlight, along with the Eisenhower exhibition on the 1st floor; he was given an apartment here in 1945 by the 5th Marquess as a thank you for his efforts as supreme allied commander in World War II. Note buggies are banned and instead you're (embarrassingly) given a toddler hip-seat, which when strapped around your waist makes it look like you have the largest bum-bag in the world.

More interesting for families are the **grounds**, especially the famous five-hectare swan pond (not fenced off), 1½ km from the castle, where the birds were bred to become the main course at castle banquets. Nowadays it is home to waterfowl, mallards and a few swan pairs. There's a picnic area and an adventure playground with zip wires, climbing frames and a toddler area. There is also a distinctive pagoda, where a monkey lived in the late 1800s (of his own free will/under house arrest/alone and sad/with his beautiful monkey bride – staff had no more information about this intriguing monkey). From here there's also a path leading to Port Carrick (five minutes' walk), a cove where you can imagine smugglers landing barrels of whisky, and ideal for sandcastles. (But too many steps for buggy pushers to get there.)

There is also a walled garden, a good second-hand bookshop, a deer park and stunning views across the Firth of Clyde.

***Open** 21st Mar–31st Oct 10am–5pm (last Adm 4pm). The visitor centre, restaurant and gift shop are also open in winter 11am–4pm. **Adm** (castle and gardens) £12, children (5–17) £8, under-5s free. Gardens only £8, children (5–17) £5, under-5s free. Family ticket (castle and gardens, two adults and up to four children) £30. **Amenities** play area, café, restaurant (with highchairs and children's lunchboxes), picnic area.*

Dundrennan Abbey ALL AGES

*Dundrennan, Kirkcudbright, Dumfries and Galloway, 01557 50026, **www.historic-scotland.gov.uk**.*

On 15th May 1568 Mary, Queen of Scots spent her last night on Scottish soil here before boarding a fishing boat for England, where she was imprisoned and eventually executed. At this enormous ruined Cistercian abbey we had a picnic, after which it rained, we got bored and we left. Frankly if I were Mary, Queen of Scots I'd give it one night and then leave early for my execution as well.

***Open** 1st Apr–30th Sep Mon–Sat 9.30am–5.30pm, Oct Sat–Wed 9.30am–4.30pm, Nov–Mar Sat–Sun 9.30am–4.30pm. **Adm** £3, children (5–16) £1.50, under-5s free. **Amenities** picnic area.*

Heads of Ayr Farm Park ★

AGES 3 TO 12

*Alloway, by Ayr, 01292 441210, **www.headsofayrfarmpack.co.uk**.*

This former Butlins camp is half petting zoo and half adventure park. Highlights include chipmunks, rats, chinchillas, wallabies, alpacas, horses and rabbits, while the **guinea pig village** alone is worth the visit. This village has its own hospital, park, houses and a church for pious guinea pigs to pray in for forgiveness and extra dandelion leaves. Also, unless I was hearing things, the guinea pigs all appear to whistle at the same time in the same way as they go about their guinea pig business in an eerie imitation of some 1940s documentary about the chirpy British worker. Elsewhere, Buster, the blue and gold macaw, says 'hello' and 'goodbye', there are two rat snakes (Zig and Zag), Ralph the camel, and Monty the Python. Our daughter also loved the combine harvester slide, the super diggers (£1 extra), the play barn and the trampoline. It was too wet and cold for the quad bikes (£4 for 12 year-olds, £3.50 for 7–11-year-olds) on the rainy day we came in June. Please see those guinea pigs.

***Open** daily Easter–28th Oct 10am–pm. **Adm** £7, children (over 2) £5.50, under-2s free. **Amenities** baby-changing, café.*

John Paul Jones Cottage

ALL AGES

*Arbigland Estate, nr. Kirkbean, Dumfriesshire, 01387 880613, **www.dumfriesmuseum.demon.co.uk**.*

The 'father of the US navy,' who was laid to rest in 1913 on the orders of US President Teddy Roosevelt in a magnificent marble sarcophagus in Annapolis in the US, was born in this small cottage overlooking the Solway Firth. In a story to captivate any adventurous young mind, Jones, a sea captain at 21, defected to the US during the American War of Independence and was considered such a fearsome pirate in Britain that, according to his biographer Benjamin Disraeli, nurses hushed the crying of their charges with the whisper of his name. Jones, who had run away to sea aged 13, led one of the most rambunctious lives of the 19th century. He sunk countless British ships, attempted to kidnap an earl, forced the French to salute the American flag, overran two forts on a near suicide mission and also found time to organise the US Navy, flog a man almost to death with a cat o' nine tails and grope a young butter-seller from St Petersburg (case never proved). All accomplished before he died, aged 45, in 1792. Scottish and US flags stand side by side in salute, but apart from an old cart or two and a few

John Paul Jones Cottage, Arbigland Estate

exhibits, there isn't a lot to look at. Fortunately the cottage's setting against the backdrop of the Solway Firth is spectacular.

***Open** 1st Apr–30th June, 1st Sep–30th Sep, 10am–5pm, Tues–Sun. Daily 1st July–31st Aug. **Adm** £2.50, children (5–16) £1, under-5s free.*

MacLellan's Castle ALL AGES

*Castle Street, Kirkcudbright, Dumfries and Galloway, 01557 331856, **www.historic-scotland.gov.uk**.*

This ruin opposite the town's tourist office isn't really a castle but a DIY project that went badly wrong. It was built in 1750 by the provost of Kirkcudbright, Thomas MacLellan of Bombire, who wanted to live in the ultimate townhouse. Making my recent effort to tile the bathroom look good, MacLellan's build stalled disastrously before he got to the fairly important business of a roof, quickly leading to his castle's dereliction. There is a small display in the kitchen of food consumed in the 18th century (a lot of rolls), and children are given an activity sheet. Park outside the tourist office over the road.

***Open** 1st Apr–30th Sep 9.30am–5.30pm. **Adm** £3.50, children (5–16) £1.75, under-5s free.*

INSIDER TIP

The best thing to do in Kirkcudbright is to wander around the relaxed and picturesque (minus the power station on the other side of the Dee estuary) town. It's full of small galleries and multicoloured houses with immaculate gardens.

National Museum of Costume ALL AGES

*Shambellie House, New Abbey, Dumfriesshire, 01387 850375, **www.nms.ac.uk**.*

Here our daughter dressed up as a Victorian schoolgirl, my wife tried on a corset and I became fascinated with a stuffed hummingbird that ladies wore as a chic accessory in the 19th century. Hands-on and friendly, Shambellie House, surrounded by wooded grounds, shows fashion changes between 1850 and 1950 using a series of roped-off, mocked up rooms. Children can try on clothes and (in the nursery) play with old-fashioned toys. There are tree trails in the garden, a quiz and a small tearoom giving onto the gardens serving snacks. In the summer the house stages a Victorian Day where staff dress up and visitors take part in traditional 19th pastimes such as hat-making.

***Open** daily 21st Mar–31st Oct 10am–5pm. **Adm** £3, children (13–18) £2, under-12s free. **Amenities** café, free parking.*

Robert Burns Centre ALL AGES

*Mill Road, Dumfries 01387 264808, **www.dumfriesmuseum.demon.co.uk**.*

Across the 15th century Devorgilla Bridge over the River Nith, this attraction based at an old watermill tells the unlikely story of Burns' rise from man of the soil to national icon. This is explained by the general literacy of Scots in the 17th century, as well the country's traditions of music, verse and dancing into which his poetry fed. The fact that Burns died young and had affairs gave him, of course, an added glamour. Or as my wife (not a fan of the revered man) put it: 'He'd be in *Closer* magazine today getting snapped outside the Met Bar.' I apologise for my wife.

For children there are jigsaw puzzles of Burns' face to complete, as well as colouring sheets on the back of copies of Burns' famous works.

***Open** Apr–Sep 10am–8pm Mon–Sat (Sun 2–5pm), Oct–Mar 10am–1pm and 2–5pm Tues–Sat. **Adm** free (film £1.60, children 80p).*

Ruthwell Cross AGES 4 AND OVER

*Ruthwell Kirk, Ruthwell Village, Dumfriesshire, 01387 870249, **www.historic-scotland.gov.uk**.*

This 7th century cross, a kind of Scottish Rosetta Stone carved in Anglo Saxon times and not translated properly until the 19th century, is worth a brief visit if you're in the area and can be bothered to get the children out of the car for a 5-minute stare at some unintelligible old masonry scratchings. The stone is fairly impressive. Its runic inscriptions contain fragments of the oldest known piece of English literature, not *Jigsaw* by Barbara Cartland but *The Dream*

TIP And If That's Not Enough Burns...

Other Burns places in Dumfries include the 18th century Midsteeple (now minus its steeple) in the High Street, where Burns lay in state before his funeral, the **Burns Statue** overlooking a floral roundabout at the start of High Street, the **Rabbie Burns Café** (see p. 236) and two of his drinking haunts – both on the High Street – the **Globe Inn** (see p. 236) and the **Hole I' the Wa'**.

of the Rood (meaning cross), telling the story of the Crucifixion from the cross's perspective. The stone was broken up in 1640 on the instructions of the General Assembly of the Church of Scotland and scattered around the churchyard. When its significance was realised following the cracking of its runic engravings some 200 years later, it was put back together by Dr Henry Duncan, a task that took him 24 years. The Church of Scotland's instruction to smash up the cross has never been repealed, which made us feel better when our daughter threw a jelly baby at it.

***Open** church door is usually left open; otherwise a notice explains where to pick up the keys. **Adm** free.*

Sweetheart Abbey ALL AGES

*New Abbey, Dumfriesshire, ☎ 01387 850397, **www.historic-scotland.gov.uk**.*

This is worth visiting to hear the romantic, if slightly gruesome, story of Lady Devorgilla of Galloway. She founded the abbey in 1275; it is now named after her in recognition of the 22 years she carried the embalmed heart of her husband, John Balliol, with her in an ivory box. There is a children's quiz and the bowling-green-flat lawns between the arches of the ruins are a serene place for a picnic, a game of hide-and-seek and a ludicrous debate about what body part of your dead partner you'd carry around in a small box if you had to. (Me: finger. Her: ear.)

Afterwards wander to the New Abbey cemetery to kneel and ask for guidance on whether to take out a fixed or tracker mortgage over a plaque telling you Sir William Paterson was buried here. He founded the Bank of England.

***Open** daily Apr–Sep 9.30am–5.30pm, Oct–Mar Sat–Wed 9.30am–4.30pm. **Adm** £3, children (5–16) £1.50, under-5s free. **Amenities** picnic area.*

FUN FACT Scotland's Electric Slope

Don't miss the 'Electric Brae' (brae means slope) on the A719 between Dunure and Croy Bay. It fascinated American GIs stationed at Prestwick Airport during the War, and even General Eisenhower when he visited Scotland. Running 400m from the bend overlooking Croy railway viaduct in the west, to the wooded Craigencroy Glen to the east, park anywhere, put your car in neutral, release the brake and announce to your children you are about to perform a magic trick worthy of David Blaine. Then step out with them and watch as your car appears to roll slowly *up*hill. The optical illusion, unfortunately lost on our daughter who doesn't yet understand gravity, is created by the surrounding topography. The term 'Electric Brae' dates from a time when it was incorrectly thought to be a phenomenon caused by electric or magnetic attraction. The spot is marked by a stone cairn inscribed with an explanation with which you needn't trouble your awestruck wife.

Threave Castle ★★ ALL AGES

*Castle Douglas, Dumfries and Galloway, 07711 223101, **www.historic-scotland.gov.uk**. 5km west of Castle Douglas on A75.*

Built by Archibald the Grim on an island in the River Dee, half the fun of this 14th century castle is getting there: it is accessed via a buggy-friendly 1km walk along a wide path through fields from a car park beside Kelton Mains Open Farm. Reaching a jetty at the River Dee you ring a brass bell to summon the boatman from the island to collect you. After the short crossing, the castle consists of a few winding spiral staircases and a gloomy basement, although at a small shed-style shop beside the castle there are activity sheets for youngsters and medieval knights' helmets on sale. We used them to re-enact the famous siege of 1455, when the hand of Margaret Douglas (my wife) was blown off by the first ever cannonball (me) fired from the Mons Meg canon by the armies of James II (our daughter with her helmet on). Even though there isn't much here, the place has great charm, bolstered by the friendly custodians, who on the way back asked our daughter to close her eyes and ring the bell and make a wish (a chocolate) that would come true if she kept it secret (she didn't). The tea-room in an outhouse of the Kelton Mains Farm makes a good ice-cream stop.

***Open** 1st Apr–30th Sep Mon–Sun 9.30am–4.30pm, Oct Sat–Wed 9.30am–3.30pm. **Adm** £4, children (5–16) £2, under-5s free. **Amenities** shop.*

WWT Caerlaverock Wetlands Centre ★ ALL AGES

*Eastpark Farm, Caerlaverock, Dumfriesshire, 01387 770200, **www.wwt.org.uk**.*

Here children get to dip nets into ponds to learn about tadpoles and waterboatmen, and can view thousands of barnacle geese darkening the skies on their return from Arctic climes. This wildlife centre based on protected salt marshes and mud flats edging the Solway Firth even has the largest set of binoculars in Scotland inside one of its observation towers. Our daughter particularly enjoyed the wild whooper swan feed at 11am (there's another at 2pm, every day October–April) that we watched from the top of the Peter Scott observatory. There are children's trails around the 600 hectare site and there's a good chance to see or hear the rarest amphibian in Britain (the natterjack toad – yellow stripe, sounds eerily tropical); at the Visitor Centre you can view, through CCTV cameras, osprey and barn owl nests, where chicks are liable to hatch in May and June. The largest binoculars in Scotland at the Farmhouse Tower take two people to lift, were used by Japanese sea admirals in World War II and enable visitors to see more than 19km across the Solway Firth, although (take it from me) shouting 'Tora, Tora, Tora' when you see a mallard is ill-advised. Other birdwatching highlights include hen harriers, merlins, short-eared owls and pink-footed geese. Look out too for otters and in the evenings there are occasional badger spotting outings.

***Open** daily 10am–5pm. **Adm** £5.50, children (4–16) £2.75, under-4s free. **Amenities** café.*

BORDERS

Scotland's marches are dotted with hamlets, undulating pastures, woodland and sheep. Cosy, scenic market towns worth a visit include Peebles, Jedburgh and Melrose, the birthplace of rugby sevens and also where King Arthur is supposedly buried, in the Eildon Hills above the town. The Borders area is even more famous for its ruined **abbeys**, founded during the reign of King David (1124–1153), who was eager to bolster his authority in these unruly areas with demonstrations of his wealth and power. Before the 1707 Act of Union, when England and Scotland were united, the Borders regularly experienced turbulent times. Consequently, the area is littered with old keeps.

Old town rivalries haven't softened with time, and each Borders town is fiercely proud. Each celebrates its independence in the Common Ridings, when locals, especially young men ('Callants'), dress in period costume and ride out to check the burgh boundaries. It's a macho business performed with an unironic pride matched only by the area's love of rugby union, which reaches a crescendo with the Melrose Sevens tournament in April.

Essentials

By Train Apart from the Edinburgh–London King's Cross line (see p. 26) which stops at Berwick-Upon-Tweed, just south of the border, there is no train service in the Borders.

By Bus National Express (*✆ 0807 580 8080, **www.nationalexpress.com***) operate a four-a-day service to both Jedburgh and Melrose. The journey takes roughly 12 hours and costs £61 return.

By Car Your own wheels are the best way to get around the Borders. From the south the main route leaves the M6 at Carlisle, taking the A7 and then the A68 south for Jedburgh, north for Melrose. For Peebles follow the A7 to Selkirk and then take the A72.

Visitor Information

The **Scottish Borders Tourist Board** has offices in **Jedburgh** (*✆ 0870 608 0404, **www.visitscotttishborders.com***) at Murray's Green, open Monday–Saturday 9.30am–4.30pm; **Peebles** (*✆ 0870 608 0404*) in the High Street, open Monday–Saturday 9.30am–5pm and Sunday 11am–3pm; **Melrose** (*✆ 0870 6080404*) at Abbey House, Abbey Street, open Friday–Saturday and Monday 10am–2pm; and **Kelso** (*✆ 0870 608 0404*) at the Town House, The Square, open Friday–Saturday and Monday 10am–2pm.

Useful websites covering sights and accommodation in the area include ***www.scot-borders.co.uk*** and ***www.discovertheborders.co.uk***.

In June each year Melrose hosts the **Borders Book Festival** (*07929 435575, **www.bordersbookfestival.org***) that always includes a host of children's authors. Former guests have included Michael Palin, impressionist Rory Bremner, novelist Ian Rankin, and Mairi Hedderwick, author of the *Katie Morag* stories.

The Abbeys

Dryburgh Abbey ALL AGES

*St Boswells, Melrose, 01835 822381, **www.historic-scotland.gov.uk**. 13km south-east of Melrose on B6404.*

Amidst the sound of chirping birds, we watched a crow feeding her chick a worm on the grassy area near the north transept close to where Sir Walter Scott and Field Marshall Earl Haig, 'the butcher of the Somme', are buried. The 800-year-old abbey is set back from the road in a secluded wood of 200-year-old trees, a peaceful place for a picnic and a dispute about our in-car DVD player. An extra bonus was watching some daredevil of the *Jackass* generation risking his life running around the precarious walls of the ruin.

***Open** 1st Apr–30th Sep Mon–Sat 9.30am–5.30pm, 1st Oct–31st Mar Mon–Sun 9.30am–4.30pm. **Adm** £4.50, children (5–16) £2.25, under-5s free.*

Melrose Abbey ALL AGES

*Abbey Street, Melrose, 01896 822562, **www.historic-scotland.gov.uk**.*

Our toddler isn't that interested in lower niche-corbels, licerne vaulting or delicate foliate tracery, yet for some reason we keep taking her to ruined abbeys. I'm not that interested in abbeys either, and neither is my wife (she thinks a niche-corbel is a type of ice-cream with nuts in it), yet for some reason we see one, hear an historical fact (in this case that the embalmed heart of Robert the Bruce was buried here) and then we simply must take a look. We can't stop ourselves.

At this abbey a commemorative stone marks the heart's resting place in the chapter house north of the sacristy, while there is also a children's quiz, a tower to climb and some great views of the mountains through the glass-less windows. And other than that it's another ruined abbey, burned down, rebuilt, burned down again like all the others.

After it we made a vow: no more abbeys. Then guess what happened.

'Oh God, no, there's another one in Jedburgh,' my wife said in the car.

'We're not going to Jedburgh,' I said. 'We're going to the deer park.'

'I know,' she said. 'I know. The deer park will be good. It will balance the chapter. It will make up for all the abbeys. Although it does say here...'.

'Please don't tell me what it says there.'

'OK. I won't say.'

'Tell me what it says there.'

'It's where Alexander III married Yolande de Dreux in 1285.'

'You fool, you should never have told me that.'

Open *daily Apr–Sep 9.30am–5.30pm, Oct–Mar 9.30am–4.30pm.* ***Adm*** *£5, children (5–16) £2.50, under-5s free.*

Jedburgh Abbey ALL AGES

Abbey Bridge End, Jedburgh, 01835 863925, ***www.historic-scotland.gov.uk****.*

Here our daughter dressed up like Yolande De Dreux and flunked the children's quiz by failing to recognise a house-martin. I walked the ruins in a monk's tunic and annoyed my wife by smiling beatifically when our buggy rolled down a steep grassy slope towards the visitor centre. The abbey, founded in 1138, is one of the best preserved in the Borders, despite its sacking by Henry VIII's men in 1544. As well as the dressing-up station, there's a quiz and a wildlife trail. Staff were helpful, finding a key to open a clanking gate to get our monster double buggy into the building, as well as pointing out a 900-year-old priceless walrus beard comb in the visitor centre we might otherwise not have been able to add to our list of most boring things behind glass in Scotland. Buggy access isn't great but it is a good **picnic spot**.

Jedburgh Abbey

Open *1st Apr–30th Sep Mon–Sun 9.30am–5pm, 1st Oct–31st Mar Mon–Sun 9.30am–4pm.* ***Adm*** *£5, children (5–16) £2.50, under-5s free.* ***Amenities*** *audioguide (free), picnic area.*

What Else to See & Do

The Scottish Seabird Centre

★ ALL AGES

The Harbour, North Berwick, 01620 890202, ***www.seabird.org****.*

Here our daughter used a remote camera to zoom in on a gannet feeding her chicks, saw a puffin, learnt to smell the difference between oil and seabird pooh and developed a rash petting a scruffy dog on the way back to the car. The building, its roof modelled on the wings of a gannet, is one of the best places to view seabirds in their natural habitats, thanks to CCTV cameras placed on islands in the Firth of Forth, including Bass

Rock, which has the largest single-rock colony of gannets in the world. As well as the gannets and puffins on Fidra, visitors (depending on the time of year, their eyesight, persistence and ability to elbow pensioners out of the way to get to the joysticks) get to view kittiwakes, seals, guillemots, bottle-nosed dolphins, whales, fulmars and Peregrine falcons. There are displays on conservation, a soft-play centre and outside sundeck tables, plus a wildlife cinema, a small aquarium, and a scratch and guess (scratch and wretch?) station where our daughter smelt various unpleasant substances, and also did a brass rubbing of a gannet.

The best time to visit is June and July, after chicks have hatched. School holidays and weekends (2–3pm) see the Puffin Club, where children are supervised in crafts such as making seal masks or puffin finger puppets.

Open *Apr–Sep Mon–Sun 10am–6pm, Feb, Mar and Oct Mon–Fri 10am–5pm (Sat–Sun 10am–5.30pm), Nov–Jan Mon–Fri 10am–4pm (Sat–Sunday 10am–5.30pm).* ***Adm*** *£6.95, children (4–15)£4.50, under-4s free.* ***Amenities*** *café (children's menu £3.25), play area.*

INSIDER TIP

The Centre is confusingly signposted. Park in the town and walk down Quality Street (like the chocolates). The centre is next to the Kirk of St Andrews. If you see a small cute Terrier here with a patch of fur missing on his left flank, don't stroke it.

New Lanark World Heritage Site ★★ ALL AGES

South Lanarkshire, 01555 661345, www.newlanark.org.

This Unesco World Heritage Site is a 200-year-old Scottish industrialist's realised dream of a model community, where workers and managers lived and worked side by side in perfect harmony (and nobody felt the need to steal stationery). In an age of 'dark Satanic Mills', forward-thinking Scot David Dale and his son-in-law Robert Owen's village provided decent homes, better wages, healthcare, a new education system for cotton workers as well as the world's first ever nursery. Surrounded by a wildlife reserve, the old sandstone mills we strolled around with a double-buggy contained a time-travel experience courtesy of Harmony, a hologram girl from the 23rd century; an activity room for toddlers; and a working, and extremely loud, textile machine. Other highlights include the story of young cotton-mill worker Annie Mcleod, a working watermill, and Robert Owen's school where our daughter dressed up as a pupil and drew on a slate a picture of the rash on her face she had acquired petting a scruffy dog in North Berwick the day before.

Open *daily Sep–May 11am–5pm, June–Aug 10.30am–5pm .* ***Adm*** *£5.95, children (3–16) £4.95, under-3s free.* ***Amenities*** *baby-changing, café (children's lunchbox £3).*

The Old Blacksmith's Shop ★

ALL AGES

*Gretna Green, ☎ 01461 338224, **www.gretnagreen.co.uk**.*

Gretna Green was famous in its day as a haven for young couples who fled England to take advantage of Scotland's lenient **marriage** laws. For around 200 years, up to 1940, they'd often end up at this forge, where an 'Anvil Priest' would do the honours. (Anyone, including a blacksmith in this case, could perform a marriage in Scotland.) Here you can see the old anvil over which weddings were conducted, and then loiter around the cowshed-like area where ceremonies are still performed today (around 1,000 last year). Sometimes against the dignified backdrop of Highland piping, other times to the music of Celine Dion.

There is also a native breeds cattle farm for children, and afterwards you can buy your wife a 'Sexy Hamper', a basket of goods containing bath and body products, a votive candle plus a few choccies for, I kid you not, £65.

Do you, Ben Hatch, now want to return to England and have a bath in your own house? I do. Do you, Dinah Hatch, now want to return home to pad around your kitchen in your loose-fitting pajamas? I do. I now pronounce your guidebook finished save for the area's accommodation and places to eat sections and an index that someone else has to compile.

***Open** Nov–Easter 9am–5pm, Easter–May 9am–6pm, June–Aug 9am–7pm, Sep–Oct 9am–6pm. **Adm** £3.75, children (12–16) £2.50, under-12s free. **Amenities** shop.*

Scott's View ★★

From the B6404, St Boswells–Kelso road, turn off along the B6356, signposted 'Dryburgh Abbey'. About 1½ km along there is a signpost for Scott's View to the right. This vantage point was the novelist's (see p. 108) favourite view in all Scotland. From the top of Bemersyde Hill above the River Tweed, it takes in the three peaks of the Eildon Hills and the Tweed Valley, whose slopes are covered in yellow broom in the spring. It was so loved by Sir Walter Scott that prior to his funeral and burial in Dryburgh Abbey (p. 235), his hearse pulled up here one final time. Our toddler especially enjoyed rolling part way down the slope, but was disappointed that, bucking what she had come to see as the custom at beauty spots, there wasn't an ice-cream van selling chocolate mini-milks. That's the tax she levies on every Scottish attraction not involving furry animals. Car parking is available.

FAMILY-FRIENDLY ACCOMMODATION

EXPENSIVE

Harmony House

Melrose, 01312 439331, **www.ntsholidays.com**.

If you want to pretend to be very rich, and perhaps fancy the idea of staring disdainfully through the curtains at the *hoi polloi* picking through your rosebushes, this seven-bed 19th century townhouse with views of Melrose Abbey and its own 1.2 hectare National Trust Garden makes a great snooty family stay. The house, whose visitors have included novelists Ian Rankin and Jeanette Winterson as well as Sir Walter Scott who lived nearby in Abbotsford, is a sumptuous Regency pile with a drawing room with working fire, four doubles, two singles, a twin room and ample parking. It has two bathrooms and a further en suite, plus a basement laundry area and its own library. The walled gardens, beautiful in the spring, are open to the public, who will stare questioningly as you unload bags of cheap supermarket shopping from the boot of your Astra in the middle of the afternoon.

Rates *short break (Mon–Fri) £750–850* ***Credit*** *MC, V.* ***Amenities*** *cook (fee), parking, garden, kitchen, TV/DVD player, cot, highchairs.*

Kinmount Leisure Holiday Cottages ★

Annan, Dumfriesshire, 01461 700486, **wwwwkinmountleisure.co.uk**.

These cottages are set in the grounds of Kinmount Castle, beside a spectacular, lily-filled lake lined with giant rhubarb plants. There are two three-bed cottages and four two-bedders for families after affordable luxury. There is a lovely mile's walk around the lake suitable for buggy-pushers and a play-park a

Harmony House, Melrose

minute from the courtyard. We stayed in the two-bed Annan House (one double with a four-poster bed and en suite, and one twin) that had a well-equipped kitchen with fridge-freezer, cooker and microwave. There was a further bathroom with an over-the-bath shower and a large open-plan kitchen–dining area off the lounge with a TV. The only drawback was the charmless manager, who kept us hanging around for an hour before we checked out because he wanted to meet us, presumably so he could then chastise us a) for not knowing the difference between a salmon loch and a lake and b) because we asked who owned the castle: 'I will not tell you who owns the castle.' The hotel is owned, we now guess, by a publicity-shy vampire.

Rates *per week (2-bed) £400–1010, (3-bed) £435–1100.* ***Amenities*** *kitchen, TV.*

Peebles Hotel Hydro ★★★

Innerleithen Road, 01721 720602, ***www.peebleshydro.co.uk.***

With spectacular views over the Tweed Valley and an unlimited-hours children's club with baby-listening free in the evenings, this is a great place for parents to relax. Family rooms (double or twin with separated bunkbeds) come with a toy box and gifts (our daughter was left a bag of hard gums we used as treats for the next three days). Activities in the children's club for the 3–7-year-olds include nature walks, puppet-making, face-painting, baking and story-time sessions, while for older ones it's swimming, assault courses, tennis and table tennis. The monkey-chaos of mealtimes is avoided with under-12s sitting down together at 5pm for supervised High Tea (6pm for older ones in the Lazels dining room). Our only gripe: finding the putting equipment was a real mission, so we played Kerplunk instead with a set we found near the reception desk and inadvertently spread some rather dangerous marbles everywhere, before we checked out and left.

Rates *double with twin bunk-beds (including dinner, bed and breakfast, per night, per adult) £110–120. Children stay free but pay for High Tea and breakfast (under-3s free, 3–6 £8, 7–12 £16, 13–16 £21.* ***Credit*** *AmEx, MC, V.* ***Amenities*** *baby-sitting (£5.50/hour), free parking, putting green, croquet, beauty salon, hairdressers.* ***In room*** *TV.*

Westin Turnberry Resort ★★★

Turnberry, Ayrshire 01655 331000, ***www.turnberry.co.uk.***

Renowned for its golf – including hosting the Open in 2009 – this scenic hotel overlooking the Irish Sea also has inventive children's activities including a £50-day-out playing farmer on a tiny tractor (actually a mini-quad bike) with the resort collie Merc. Other highlights include boats trips to Ailsa Craig (£20, two hours) and there's kite-making and flying on the beach (£25, one hour), a teddy bear woodland walk, and the Wee Owl Experience (£35, one hour) where youngsters get to learn, hold and watch resident owl, Moby. Pony-time sees those aged 8–16 grooming, saddling up and riding ponies around the estate (£50, 2½ hours) while for budding golfers (under-14s) a 30-minute lesson with a resident pro costs £30, or £149 for a whole family's 60-minute instruction, including swing analysis.

The hotel's private cottages are a walk away from the main building (it has a shuttle service), and include Glasgow Gailes – a two-bedroom house with a double room upstairs and downstairs children's room sleeping two. We had a kitchenette with a fridge and dining table but no cooker (you are expected to eat at one of the hotel's restaurants – the Tapppie Toorie has a children's menu and youngsters under 12 eat free April–September). The cottage, which has a much needed living room gas fire (although ours was impossible to light and required the concierge's help), was cosy but a slight drawback was the incredible slowness of room service.

Rates *cottage per night £229–390 (check online for better three-night packages).* ***Credit*** *AmEx, MC, V.* ***Amenities*** *baby-sitting, restaurants, parking, children's activities.* ***In room*** *TV.*

MODERATE

Ferintosh Guest House ★

30 Lovers Walk, Dumfries, ☎ 01387 252262, ***www.Ferintosh.net****.*

A fabulous B&B with friendly hosts, clean rooms, and something free – a dram of single-malt before bed and After Eights chocolates for the children. The guesthouse is run by Emma and Scottish-fied Robertson Wellen, who says 'aye' more than any native Scot you will meet here (if you don't believe me, ask if it's him who serves the best vegetarian sausages in the Borders). Children will love the two friendly collie dogs, Tesse and Ceilahd, and there are games behind reception. There's one family suite – two rooms (a twin and a double) separated by a common bathroom. The guesthouse is five minutes walk from the town centre and over the road from good family-friendly places to eat (the Station Hotel and Aberdour Hotel). They have no travel cots, but they'll store buggies, and the breakfast includes veggie options plus organic mushrooms and tomatoes.

Rates *£75–90 per room per night.* ***Amenities*** *parking (on street).* ***In room*** *TV.*

Spinney Lodges

Langlee, Jedburgh, ☎ 01835 863525, ***www.thespinney-jedburgh.co.uk****.*

In a rural setting with plenty of green space for children, the two-bedroom self-catering wooden lodge here is ideal for families. The kitchen has a dining area, a microwave, cooker and fridge, and there's a TV, DVD and electric fire in the lounge. Convector heaters on thermostats heat the rest of the lodge; bed linen and towels are provided. The Co-op supermarket in Jedburgh (3km away) stays open until 10pm (except

Ferintosh Guest House, Dumfries

Sunday, 6pm), and a basket of continental breakfast can be supplied for £3 per person if you order in advance.

Bring your own travel cot.

Rates *£60–75 per night (per week £350–480).* ***Credit*** *MC, V.* ***Amenities*** *patio furniture, parking, TV/DVD player, kitchen.*

Station Hotel

49 Lovers Walk, Dumfries, ☏ 01387 254316, ***www.stationhotel.co.uk****.*

The only down-side here is the enormous buffet breakfast, which although helping you create (steal) a great packed lunch for later also might mean you have to drive to Kirkcudbright with the top button of your trousers undone. This spacious, grand 19th century hotel has large family rooms that can accommodate extra z-beds (for free) as well as interconnecting rooms. There is a separate TV lounge and a baby-listening service enabling guests to eat at their excellent courtyard restaurant. Their two-course children's menu serves only fresh meat bought from an award-wining local butcher as well as delicious home-made fish fingers. Suggest your children try the Cowboy Special (baked beans, sausages and mash) after which they shouldn't need much encouragement to say 'yeee-haah'.

Rates *large family room £90, adjoining rooms £110.* ***Credit*** *AmEx, MC, V.* ***Amenities*** *baby-changing, bar with 27 single-malts, baby-listening, parking, laundry, garden, restaurant (highchairs, 2 courses £14.50, children's menu £5.50).* ***In room*** *Sat TV.*

INSIDER TIP

Ask for adjoining rooms 16 and 17. They've been Feng Shui'ed by an expert consultant to improve your chi through lighting and atmosphere.

INEXPENSIVE

Belleisle House Hotel

Doonfoot Road, Alloway, Ayrshire, ☎ 01292 442331.

This Georgian manor house set in large grounds, and beautiful on the outside, is disappointingly 1970s inside, although it does have a petting corner with deer, ducks and rabbits. The family room has a large double with two single beds. Burns' attractions are just a few kilometres away.

Rates *£49–89 per night.* ***Credit*** *AmEx, V.* ***Amenities*** *parking (11pm–10am), laundry, restaurant (two courses £13.50, children's menu £5.95).* ***In room*** *TV.*

Kings Arms Hotel

31–33 St Andrews Street, Castle Douglas, ☎ 01556 502626, ***www.galloway-golf.co.uk****.*

There are three sleeping options here for families: a large double with bunk-beds round a corner, a room with three single beds, and two twin rooms opposite each other at the end of a corridor separated by a fire door. The restaurant offers discounts for two nights' dinner, bed and breakfast, meaning adults can eat three courses with coffee for £11 a head. If that is not enough, the full Scottish breakfast includes kippers, haddock, haggis and black pudding. Baby monitors work throughout, and there's a drying room where bikes and buggies can be stored, or you can lie down in the dark as another huge dinner approaches.

The Kings Arms is close to Threave Castle and within walking distance of Lochside Park with boating, putting and two children's play-parks.

Rates *B&B £37.50 per person per night (under-2s free, children 2–5 £10 extra, 6–14 £14 extra).* ***Credit*** *MC, V.* ***Amenities*** *bar, lounge, parking, restaurant (highchairs, children's menu £3.50) fishing and golf can be arranged.* ***In room*** *TV.*

Sandy Hills Bay Leisure Park

Sandy Hills, Dalbeattie, ☎ 01387 780257, ***www.gillespie-lesiure.co.uk****.*

On the shoreline of the Solway Firth – the 'Scottish Riviera' – with great views of the sea and a long sandy beach with rock pools, this is a good place for a family break. Three-bed static homes (one double, two twin rooms) all have double-glazing and some have gas-fired central heating (the rest have panel heaters). The kitchen has a microwave, and everything is supplied except bed-sheets and towels. There is a laundry room, children's play-park, a snack bar (hot pies, sandwiches, etc.), and a shop selling basics from bread and alcohol through to beach equipment and newspapers.

The nearby **Barend Riding Centre** (☎ *01387 780533*) offers pony-trekking (4–6-year-olds: 10-minute weenie rides £5; 6–10-year-olds: half-hour walk-out £14; 10 and over: treks £22) and the area is rich in wildlife, especially deer and rabbits. The tide in the Solway Firth is notoriously fast-moving, and leaves

8km of sandy rock pools to hunt for crabs and starfish.

Book months in advance.

Open *1st Apr–31st October.* ***Rates*** *£92–192 (for two nights). Per week £240–480. (Minimum stay one week between June–August and Bank Holiday weeks.)* ***Amenities*** *kitchen, play area, café, children's entertainment, shop.*

FAMILY-FRIENDLY DINING

EXPENSIVE

Dryburgh Abbey Hotel

St Boswells, Melrose, 01835 822261, ***www.drybrugh.co.uk****.*

At this splendid 19th century baronial mansion on the banks of the River Tweed youngsters can play boules in a grit-pit, have a go at putting on a 9-hole green or borrow bikes to cycle around the four hectare estate – all for free after their lunch. There is also a heated indoor swimming pool with floats and armbands (£4.50). The hotel, beside Dryburgh Abbey, has two dining areas, the best is the more relaxed bar lounge; adult mains include excellent wild sea-bass. More formal dining (four courses for £32) in the Hotel Tweed Restaurant (children welcome) is available 7–9pm and Sunday lunch between noon and 2pm.

Bar lounge open *12.30–2.15pm and 7–9.15pm.* ***Main courses*** *from £12.* ***Credit*** *AmEx, MC, V.* ***Amenities*** *children's menu (£3.50), pool, highchairs, baby-changing.*

MODERATE

Prego ★

3 High Street, Lanark, 01555 666300.

At this family-run Italian your children can make their own pizzas and are given a lucky bag. The restaurant's speciality, which our daughter smeared all over her face, are Prego's Sticks (a sweet dough-stick to dip in hot caramel sauce). Staff are unfazed by any flying caramel sauce, and their good children's menu includes a make-your own pizza, or a pasta dish, plus Prego Stick or ice-cream. A good place to watch the world go by, Prego is made even homelier by the hundred-year-old pictures on the walls of the Faccenda family back home in Cassino. Adult mains are pizza or pasta, as you'd expect.

Open *Tues–Sat noon–2pm and 5–10pm, Sun noon–10pm.* ***Main courses*** *from £7.* ***Credit*** *AmEx, MC, V.* ***Amenities*** *baby-changing, highchairs, children's menu (£4.95).*

100 Aker Wood Garden Centre ★

Annay Road, Melrose, 01896 823717, ***www.100akerwood.co.uk****.*

This bistro in the middle of a garden centre has a woodland walk where children can see rabbits, chickens and guinea pigs. It serves excellent mussels (£6.95), steak burgers and children's lunchboxes (£3.75 for a sandwich, drink, cheese, fruit, a toy and a lolly). There is a separate coffee shop selling sandwiches, where parents can watch their children in a play area. There's also a bouncy castle, a gift shop selling toys and the owner is prone to don a huge Tigger costume and roam the centre to entertain youngsters with his bouncing.

Open *daily 9am–5pm (June–Aug Fri–Sat until 7pm).* ***Menu*** *two courses around £13.* ***Credit*** *MC, V.* ***Amenities*** *shop, children's menu (mains £2.50).*

Teviot Smokery Coffee Shop and Restaurant ★

*Teviot Water Gardens, Kirkbank House, Kelso, Roxburghshire, 01835 850253, **www.teviotgamefaresmokery.co.uk**.*

This conservatory restaurant serves its own smoked meat, fish and cheese next to some beautiful landscaped water gardens with a children's nature challenge and an aquatic centre. The restaurant, with great countryside views, has a children's menu that always includes homemade healthy options, colouring books and pens, and friendly staff who won't mind your children drooling Homer Simpson-style over their sweet table of scones and cakes. My wife had the double open sandwich of smoked salmon, smoked house pate, Orkney herrings and mixed salad (£7.95) and loved it almost as much as listening to country folk at a nearby table discussing grouse shooting in the Cairngorms. On the water garden's nature trail along the banks of the River Teviot (almost a kilometre long and buggy-friendly apart from the first few steps) children are asked to spot wildlife, gaining points depending on the rarity (otter 10 points, blackbird 1, etc.). Meanwhile, if you're feeling lazy, just use the telescope at the back of the shop and make it up ('that's another otter for me').

Open *daily 9am–5pm.* ***Main courses*** *around £7.95.* ***Credit*** *MC, V.* ***Amenities*** *children's menu (99p), highchairs.*

The Sunflower

*4 Bridgegate, Peebles, 01721 722420, **www.thesunflower.net**.*

A homely three-roomed restaurant with a toybox for children. Food is light Mediterranean bistro-style lunches and dinners, and although there's no children's menu staff serve smaller adult portions or mix-and-match from the menu (our daughter had cheese on toast, a banana and home-made chips for under £5). For adults warm Forsyth rolls are the main-stay (grilled chicken breast with chilli and mint, £7.50) along with bruschetta (£6.95, £10.95 for a large one). In the evening it's more pricey, and mains bulk up to fillet steak or duck for between £9 and £15. If you really like what you ate, buy the restaurant's own cookbook for £7.95.

INSIDER TIP

If you have a buggy don't leave it outside on the street. We did and it blew down the hill, almost killing a family of four. You can deposit buggies safely down the restaurant's side-alley.

***Open** Mon–Sat 10–11.30am (for tea and cakes), noon–3pm and Thurs–Sat also 6pm–1am (last orders 9pm). **Main courses** £6.95–15. **Credit** AmEx, MC, V. **Amenities** baby-changing, highchairs.*

INEXPENSIVE

Cream O'Galloway ★★

*Rainton, Gatehouse of Fleet, Castle Douglas, ☎ 01557 814040, **www.creamogalloway.co.uk**. Signposted off A75.*

Children can work off their burgers here on an adventure playground with a crow's nest from which you can see the sea. The farm also has an ice-cream factory and 32 hectares of nature trails, plus the Smugglers' Warren where adults can watch children playing over a coffee and a sit down. The playground costs £6 and comes with either a guided farm tour (daily 2.45pm) where youngsters watch the dairy heard come in for milking, or a visit to the ice-cream factory (daily 11.30am), both of which it's best to book in advance. The nature trails include a short, 1½ km buggy-friendly walk taking in a scenic pond and wildlife hides where it's possible (if unlikely) to see red squirrels. Their Burger Barn has tasty soup starters and children's beef burgers made from the organic farm's own herd for £2.70 (adult burgers £3–6). There are also 30 flavours of ice-cream (£1.30 a scoop).

***Open** 15th Mar–31st Aug 10am–6pm, Sep–Oct 10am–5pm. **Main courses** from £3. **Credit** MC, V. **Amenities** playground, highchairs.*

Globe Inn

*56 High Street, Dumfries, ☎ 01387 252 335, **www.globeinn.dumfries.co.uk**.*

This is where Burns came for a pint of beer after a long day collecting excise duty, and also where he had an affair with the 'gowden locked' Anna Parks, the niece of the landlord, with whom he fathered an illegitimate child in the bedroom upstairs. Burns' favourite chair by the fire is still in the back dining room, but if you're thinking of having your photo taken in it, be warned: anyone who parks themselves there is expected to recite Burns poetry or buy everyone else in the pub a drink. Luckily for the unwary (my wife), there are some examples of his work on the napkins. The pub has a children's menu (chicken nuggets, etc.) or will serve half-portions of adult choices such as haddock, chicken curry and steak pie. If you're lucky 'Grumpy Jack' will show you the upstairs bedroom on whose window Burns inscribed two verses of poetry.

***Open** noon–3pm. **Main courses** from £5.95. **Credit** MC, V. **Amenities** highchairs, children's menu (£3.50).*

Rabbie Burns Café

7 Bank Street, Dumfries, ☎ 01387 261075.

When we visited, this central café was full of tourists, Burns fans and tired shoppers with shopping bags discussing hummus with great animation. Burns worked in the excise office that used to stand here, and lived upstairs in a small flat you can see sketched on the café wall. It serves everything from bacon roll breakfasts to sirloin steak lunches (£8.95). Not fantastically geared towards families (no highchairs or baby-changing), it is nevertheless a friendly place, and will serve half-portions (at half-price) for your children. You can learn a little about Burns' life from the menu and the owner doesn't mind if you take up large areas of his limited floor space with a monstrous buggy.

Open *9am–5.30pm Mon–Sat.* ***Main courses*** *around £8.95.*

Solway Tide

16 St Cuthbert Street, Kirkcudbright, 01557 330735.

A relaxed café with harbour view and board-games for children, close to the town centre and serving light panini and wrap-style lunches. The restaurant, with Jack Johnson at muted volume, large windows and local artists' work on the walls, would have lulled me to sleep over my tuna mayonnaise *panino* (£4) if my wife hadn't been trying to teach our daughter draughts (No use. She hoarded the disks in her hand shouting, when my wife tried to prize them off her, 'No, thank you. No, thank you.'). The restaurant is popular with seniors who know a good scone when they see one, locals, families and summer tourists. Buggy drivers can avoid steps by entering through an alleyway at the side. Children are served half-priced, smaller portions.

Open *10.30am–4.30pm.*
Amenities *highchairs.*

Waggon Inn

10 Coal Market, Kelso, 01573 224568, ***www.thewaggoninn.com****.*

A friendly, busy pub with a children's menu and a playroom where you can watch your youngsters drawing on chalkboards or fighting each other for crayons, while you enjoy a post-meal pint. Under-2s eat free, 2–5-year-olds for £2.50 and over-5s £3.50. The fish goujons and chicken fingers are home-made. Adult mains include steak pie, pasta and fish and chips.

Open *Mon–Fri 12–2.30pm and 5–9.30pm, Sat and Sun 12–9.30pm.* ***Main courses*** *from £7.95.* ***Credit*** *AmEx, MC, V.* ***Amenities*** *children's menu.*

Index

C

D

E

F

G

H

I

J

K

L

M

N

O

P

Q

R

S

T

U

V

W

Notes

Notes